T0330008

Entrepreneurship and the Shadow Economy

Entrepreneurship and the Shadow Economy

Edited by

Arnis Sauka

Stockholm School of Economics in Riga, Latvia

Friedrich Schneider

Professor of Economics, Johannes Kepler University of Linz, Austria

Colin C. Williams

Professor of Public Policy, Management School, University of Sheffield, UK

Cheltenham, UK • Northampton, MA, USA

Published by
Edward Elgar Publishing Limited
The Lypiatts
15 Lansdown Road
Cheltenham
Glos GL50 2JA
UK

Edward Elgar Publishing, Inc.
William Pratt House
9 Dewey Court
Northampton
Massachusetts 01060
USA

A catalogue record for this book
is available from the British Library

Library of Congress Control Number: 2016931501

This book is available electronically in the **Elgar**online
Business subject collection
DOI 10.4337/9781784719883

ISBN 978 1 78471 987 6 (cased)
ISBN 978 1 78471 988 3 (eBook)

Typeset by Servis Filmsetting Ltd, Stockport, Cheshire
Printed and bound in Great Britain by TJ International Ltd, Padstow

Contents

Contributors

Yasser Abdih, is a Senior Economist working on Jordan at the IMF's Middle East and Central Asia Department. Prior to joining the Jordan team, Yasser covered regional policy issues in the Middle East and Central Asia and was an author of the *Regional Economic Outlook*. Before that, he was involved in capacity building and training of government officials at the IMF Institute. Prior to joining the IMF, Yasser was as Assistant Professor of Economics at Bowling Green State University and Washington and Lee University. He holds a doctorate in Economics from The George Washington University.

José Ernesto Amorós is Professor at EGADE Business School, Tecnológico de Monterrey, Mexico. He is also a visiting researcher at Universidad del Desarrollo's School of Business and Economics in Santiago, Chile. He is a member of the Board of Directors of the Global Entrepreneurship Monitor (GEM) project. He is also a visiting researcher at EGADE Business School, Mexico. Amorós holds a PhD in Management Sciences from ESADE Business School, and a Bachelor's degree in Business Administration and MSc in Marketing from Tecnológico de Monterrey, Mexico. He is a member of several academic organizations and VP of the Iberoamerican Academy of Management. Professor Amorós's research interests are in entrepreneurship and competitiveness, high growth new businesses, entrepreneurship and gender, and corporate entrepreneurship. His work has been published in several international journals as well as books and research monographs.

Alexander Chepurenko is Professor and Head of the Department of Sociology of the Higher School of Economics, Moscow, Russia. He is also a Head of the Laboratory of Entrepreneurship research of the HSE and co-head of the European summer school 'Exploring entrepreneurship'. Alexander has over twenty years' experience in entrepreneurship and small business research as well as in SME policy advice and expertise in Russia and other transition economies.

Juan Pablo Couyoumdjian is an Associate Professor at the School of Government and the School of Economics and Business at the Universidad del Desarrollo in Santiago, Chile. His research areas include economics and entrepreneurship, political economy and economic and business history. He has published in journals in economics, politics and economic history. He holds a BA in Economics from the University of Chile, and a PhD in Economics from George Mason University.

Oscar Cristi is University Professor at the School of Economics and Business of Universidad San Sebastián, Chile. Dr Cristi is an academic lecturer with teaching experience in natural resource economics, applied econometrics and microeconomics at the top five Chilean universities. He holds a PhD in Agricultural and Resource Economics from University of Maryland, College Park. He has an MS in International Economics and a Bachelor's degree in Economics from Universidad de Chile. Dr Cristi's research interests are in resource economics, water economics and entrepreneurship dynamics. He is also founder of the Chilean Public Policy Association.

Elena Denisova-Schmidt, PhD, MBA, is a Lecturer at the University of St Gallen (HSG) in Switzerland. She has taught and conducted research at the Humboldt University in Berlin, the Kennan Institute of the Woodrow Wilson International Center for Scholars in Washington, DC, the German Institute for International and Security Affairs, the UCL School of Slavonic and East European Studies, the Edmond J. Safra Center for Ethics at Harvard University and the Aleksanteri Institute (University of Helsinki). Before moving into academia, Denisova-Schmidt worked for the VSMPO-AVISMA Corporation in Russia. Her current research interests cover corruption and informal practices in various settings in Russia and Ukraine.

Ioana A. Horodnic is a Lecturer in the Faculty of Economics and Business Administration at the Alexandru Ioan Cuza University of Iasi in Romania and a post-doctoral researcher at the Romanian Academy. Her current research interests are in the informal sector and academic performance.

Leandro Medina is an Economist working on Mozambique at the IMF's African Department. Prior to joining the Mozambican team, Leandro focused on macro fiscal issues in South-East Asia at the Fiscal Affairs Department and he covered regional policy issues in the Middle East and Central Asia. He was also an author of the *Regional Economic Outlook*. Before joining the IMF, Leandro worked as an international consultant at the Inter-American Development Bank, participating in Portfolio Review and Policy Dialogue missions to Argentina, Bolivia and Uruguay. His research covers a variety of topics in macroeconomics and international finance. He holds a doctorate in Economics from The George Washington University.

Maria Minniti is Professor and L. Bantle Chair of Entrepreneurship and Public Policy at Syracuse University, USA and Visiting Distinguished Professor at Aalto University, Finland. Dr Minniti holds a PhD in Economics from New York University. She has been a visiting professor at the London Business School, Humboldt University, Copenhagen Business School and the Max Planck Institute of Economics. Dr Minniti is field editor for the *Journal of Business Venturing* and associate editor for the *Small Business Economics Journal.* Her work has been published in the *Journal of Management, Economics Letters, Journal of Economic Behavior and Organization, Journal of Business Venturing, Journal of Economic Psychology, Strategic Entrepreneurship Journal, IEEE Transactions on Engineering Management, Entrepreneurship Theory and Practice, Small Business Economics Journal,* and the *Oxford Bulletin of Economics and Statistics,* among others. Minniti's recent work focuses on the political economy of entrepreneurship and innovation, and on the relationship between aging and employment choice at both the microeconomic and macroeconomic levels.

Yaroslav Prytula is a Professor at the Lviv Business School of the Ukrainian Catholic University and an Associate Professor in the Department of International Economic Analysis and Finance at Lviv Ivan Franko National University (LIFNU) in Lviv, Ukraine. Previously, he served as an Academic Secretary at LIFNU. Prytula has taught and conducted research at George Mason University and the Institute for Higher Education Policy (Washington, DC), and in 2013–14 he was a Fulbright Scholar at George Washington University. His current research focuses on socio-economic regional development in Ukraine, including the shadow economy and corruption issues.

Tālis J. Putniņš is Professor at UTS Business School, Sydney, Australia, Stockholm School of Economics in Riga and Research Associate at the Baltic International Centre for Economic Policy Studies, Latvia. His research interests include financial economics, market microstructure, market manipulation, tax evasion and partial detection modelling. Tālis has a PhD from the University of Sydney and has been a Visiting Scholar at Columbia University and New York University.

Arnis Sauka is an Associate Professor and Director of the Centre for Sustainable Business at the Stockholm School of Economics in Riga, Latvia. Prior to joining the doctoral programme at the University of Siegen (Germany), Arnis was a visiting PhD candidate at Jönköping International Business School (Sweden) and University College London (UK). Arnis has served as an advisor to the Minister of Health of the Republic of Latvia on economic and financial matters (2011–14), has consulted for the Ministry of Finance of the Republic of Latvia on entrepreneurship and shadow economy issues (since 2013), has worked as an Academic Vice Rector at Ventspils University College, Latvia (2011–14), has been a consultant for PricewaterhouseCoopers (2008) as well as taking a number of management positions in various business organizations (2000–2004). His main research interests are related to the shadow economy, internationalization of SMEs, entrepreneurship policies, business strategies, competitiveness and social contribution of entrepreneurs.

Friedrich Schneider is Professor of Economics at the Johannes Kepler University of Linz, Austria. He obtained his PhD in Economics from the University of Konstanz and has held numerous visiting and honorary positions. He was the European editor of *Public Choice* and he has published extensively in leading economics journals including *The Quarterly Journal of Economics*, *The American Economic Review*, *The Economic Journal*, and *Kyklos*. He has published 70 books, 206 articles in scientific journals and 178 articles in edited volumes.

Markku Virtanen is an independent researcher and CEO at Emind Oy and up to December 2015 was Research Director in Aalto University School of Business Small Business Center, Finland. He obtained his doctorate in Entrepreneurship in 1996 from Helsinki School of Economics where he acted as a Professor of Entrepreneurship in the Department of Management and International Business from October 2004 to August 2012. The main emphasis of his research includes entrepreneurship theories, growth and success of SMEs, entrepreneurial finance and venture capital, development of opportunities, ethnic entrepreneurship and social capital, incubators and post-incubation gazelles, and regional development and SME policy. He acts as a Country Vice President of the European Council for Small Business and Entrepreneurship (ECSB). He is a member of the board in several SMEs.

Colin C. Williams is Professor of Public Policy in the Management School at the University of Sheffield in the UK. His current research interests include work organization, the informal economy and the future of work, and his recent books include *Confronting the Shadow Economy* (2014, Edward Elgar), *The Shadow Economy* (2013, Institute of Economic Affairs) and *The Hidden Enterprise Culture* (2006, Edward Elgar).

Jan Windebank is Professor of French and European Societies in the School of Languages and Cultures at the University of Sheffield in the UK. Her research interests are in the gender division of work, the informal economy and social exclusion in European societies.

Acknowledgements

We acknowledge support from the TeliaSonera, TSI at SSE Riga, including organization of the TeliaSonera Business Day 2014 where this book was initiated.

Introduction

Arnis Sauka, Friedrich Schneider and Colin C. Williams

The shadow economy is important to address because of its negative consequences. One major problem is that it hampers economic growth by pushing the allocation of resources from productive to unproductive use, causing countries to spiral into 'bad equilibrium' where tax evasion generally leads to increasing tax rates, resulting in further increases in the shadow economy (Estrin and Mickiewicz, 2012; Putniņš and Sauka, 2015). Given such consequences, tackling the shadow economy has become a focus – and in some cases even a priority – of policy makers around the world, both in relatively more and less developed countries.

Yet, despite the increasing number of attempts to measure both the size and determinants of the shadow economy, research in this area is still very much at the preliminary stage. Arguably, the main reason for this is that the shadow economy is very difficult to measure and currently there is no consensus on a commonly accepted method for measuring the size of the phenomenon. This is further hampered by the lack of a broadly accepted definition of the shadow economy in the literature.

The multidimensional nature of the research area makes exploring the shadow economy even more difficult. Specifically, since the prevalence of the shadow economy can be socially or culturally embedded, understanding the ethics, morality and social justification of practices leading to the shadow economy output are crucial perspectives that should be captured in such studies. Even more importantly, the shadow economy has a contextual dimension and it is not a static phenomenon but an evolutionary process. Moreover, the size and determinants of shadow economies can also vary across industries, company sizes and the economic cycle. For these reasons, both research and policy recommendations to decrease the shadow economy need to be seen as complex problems that should be constantly reassessed.

In the context of this discussion, this book aims to collect evidence that could shed some more light onto the existing discussion regarding the size and determinants of the shadow economy, linking the phenomenon with the entrepreneurship process. More specifically, this volume includes nine chapters – contributions by leading scholars in shadow economy research – that can be further divided into three main parts. The first part of the book deals with introducing the importance of exploring the shadow economy in particular in relation to entrepreneurship research and reviews the main existing methods that measure its size as well as the determinants of the shadow economy. In the second part, contributors then explore informal entrepreneurship and the shadow economy in various contexts, such as Russia, Ukraine and Finland as well as the Caucasus and Central Asia. The third and final part summarizes the policy perspectives and strategies on decreasing shadow economies in various contexts.

More specifically, the book starts with a chapter entitled 'The bottom-up power of informal entrepreneurship', written by José Ernesto Amorós, Juan Pablo Couyoumdjian, Oscar Cristi and Maria Minniti. The main contribution of this chapter is to review the nature of the informal sector, addressing the phenomenon taking into consideration contextual differences across the countries, thus shaping the background for further contributions within this book. The authors argue that even though it is generally perceived as having negative consequences, the involvement of entrepreneurs in the shadow economy can also be beneficial, especially in environments where institutions are weak. According to Amorós et al., in countries with weak institutions, such benefits can appear both at the individual level as well as the aggregate level, in that they can both improve the living standard of the population as well as actually increasing economic growth.

This chapter indeed raises issues that are not only interesting from a research perspective but also from a policy perspective. Namely, questions such as 'How much shadow economy is acceptable?', 'What would be the impact of rapidly reducing the shadow economy?', 'Shall we fight the shadow economy or simply let it be?', 'In what proportions should "stick" and "carrot" policies be used to reduce the shadow economy?' are of crucial importance, especially in countries with weaker institutions where the size of the shadow economy tends to be higher compared with more developed economies. Both in the light of the aforementioned questions as well as the findings of Amorós et al., who indeed find a positive relationship between informal entrepreneurship and contributions to the individual and economy, we would also encourage researchers and policy makers to consider the time dimension. Specifically, once formal institutions become stronger with time, informal institutions (attitudes and beliefs on what is acceptable and what is not) might not change (for example, Sauka, 2008). Thus, in the longer term, a policy of 'letting the shadow economy be', enjoying short-term benefits, might be very difficult to deal with.

The persistence of a large shadow economy over time within countries with comparably weak formal institutions, as indicated by the findings of the next chapter within this volume, can at least partly be explained by the acceptance of such behaviour; a potential indirect outcome of the aforementioned policies. Or lack of appropriate policies, perhaps? More specifically, in his contribution 'Estimating the size of the shadow economies of 162 countries using the MIMIC method', Friedrich Schneider applies this specific method to measure the size of the shadow economy across the globe. Even though, as discussed by the author of this contribution himself, the 'multiple indicator multiple cause' (MIMIC) method has a number of drawbacks, so far it is the only method that, applied by Schneider, has been used to measure the size of the shadow economy in so many countries across time. For this reason, many policy makers are using these indicators both to refer to the size of the shadow economies within particular countries as well as a measure for the success of their policy initiatives to decrease the shadow economy.

The first part of the book then proceeds by introducing another method to measure the size of the shadow economy. This is the contribution by Tālis Putniņš and Arnis Sauka, entitled 'The components and determinants of the shadow economy: evidence from the Baltic countries'. In contrast to the method applied by Schneider, which is of an indirect nature, Putniņš and Sauka develop a direct method that is based on an annual survey of entrepreneurs. This method draws on the notion that those likely to know how much production/income goes unreported are the entrepreneurs that themselves engage in misreporting and shadow production. Given the sensitive nature of the shadow economy, Putniņš and Sauka use various tools to elicit more truthful answers from the respondents which results in estimates of the size of the shadow economy as a proportion of GDP (see Putniņš and Sauka, 2015 for more information).

Highlighting the benefits of their method, Putniņš and Sauka argue that it requires fewer assumptions than most existing methods, in particular compared with methods based on macro indicators, and is relatively precise about what parts of the economy are captured. Even more importantly, the method by Putniņš and Sauka allows one to directly link the amount with the key determinants of the shadow economy, thus providing some valuable evidence on why the shadow economy exists and what can be done to reduce its size within specific environments. Putniņš and Sauka apply this method to measure the size and analyse determinants of the shadow economy in the Baltic countries, namely Estonia, Latvia and Lithuania.

The first part of the book concludes with the contribution of Colin Williams, Ioana Horodnic and Jan Windebank, who present and apply yet another method to measure some important aspects of the shadow economy. Their contribution 'The participation of the self-employed in the shadow economy in the European Union' draws on a Eurobarometer survey conducted in 28 countries involving 1969 face-to-face interviews with the self-employed about their participation in the shadow economy. This contribution focuses on the self-employed, aiming to evaluate which groups of self-employed engage in the shadow economy. The authors argue that until now, the self-employed people participating in the shadow economy have been predominantly viewed as marginalized populations such as those on a lower income and living in deprived regions (that is, the 'marginalization thesis'). However, an alternative emergent 'reinforcement thesis' conversely views these marginalized self-employed as less likely to do so. Their key contribution is thus evaluating these competing perspectives.

The contribution of Williams et al. has a number of policy implications. First, the authors demonstrate the need for specific policy instruments that need to be applied to target specific populations in specific contexts. In this light, Williams et al. highlight the need for more in-depth thinking when allocating resources, such as European structural funds, for fighting the shadow economy. The authors emphasize that, so far, East-Central and Southern Europe have received most of the support, yet, as exemplified by their study, the self-employed in relatively developed EU regions have significantly higher participation rates in the shadow economy. Williams et al. also complement their contribution by providing some valuable policy suggestions which can be used by policy makers to decrease the participation of the self-employed in the shadow economy.

The second part of the book starts with two chapters that aim to explore the specifics of the shadow economy in rather particular contexts, certainly very interesting for shadow economy research, namely Russia and Ukraine. In his contribution 'Informal entrepreneurship and informal entrepreneurial activity in Russia', Alexander Chepurenko aims to explore the motives and forms of informal entrepreneurship in Russia, drawing on a survey of start-ups located in Moscow. The key argument of this study is that, similar to more advanced market economies, in countries with a Soviet past, most informal entrepreneurship happens within formally registered companies, not companies or units that work entirely illegally. Given that involvement in informal entrepreneurship within registered companies is high or at least existent, depending on the context, one of the implications of such a conclusion is that entrepreneurship research simply cannot neglect both the individual- and aggregate-level impact of the part that is operated informally.

Yet, in this contribution, Chepurenko also finds and discusses the characteristics that shape informal entrepreneurship in the specific context of Russia. This in turn results in targeted and context-specific policy suggestions to decrease informal entrepreneurship activity and thus also the size of the shadow economy in Russia. Context-specific policy suggestions are also provided by Elena Denisova-Schmidt and Yaroslav Prytula who explore the nature of the shadow economy in Ukraine. This chapter, entitled 'The shadow economy and entrepreneurship in Ukraine', once again highlights the role of the context, weak institutions in particular, which shapes entrepreneurs' strategies.

In particular, Denisova-Schmidt and Prytula argue that entrepreneurs in Ukraine react to market discrepancies by involving themselves in certain corruption activities and other informal entrepreneurship practices, often seeing this as a solution to save their business and retain their employees. Yet also gaining competitive advantage is mentioned as one of the reasons for involvement in informal entrepreneurship which in turn implies that part of the reason entrepreneurs involve themselves in the shadow economy is a result of rational choice. Obviously, the likelihood of being caught and the severity of punishment is not an obstacle for these businesses. Another explanation could be that entrepreneurs simply see that other businesses in their industry are involved in the shadow economy and thus working entirely formally could mean losing competitive advantage. We have referred to this process as 'bad equilibrium' at the beginning of the introduction and already discussed the potential drawbacks of such processes, especially in the longer run. To avoid this, Denisova-Schmidt and Prytula call for more targeted and evidence-based policy measures to fight the shadow economy in Ukraine, pointing to the lack of political will to implement such reforms.

The second part of the book then proceeds with exploring the shadow economy in contexts other than Russia and Ukraine. The contribution of Markku Virtanen, 'A normative analysis of the measures to prevent the shadow economy in Finland', aims to explore the share of various informal entrepreneurship activities and forms of shadow economy as well as to suggest some policy measures for reducing the shadow economy in Finland. The author also reviews previous key efforts of policy makers in Finland to reduce the shadow economy in the country. To do that, Virtanen mainly draws on the information available in various reports available from the Ministry of Finance and the Ministry of Employment and Economy of Finland.

The second part of this volume concludes with the contribution of Yasser Abdih and Leandro Medina entitled 'The informal economy in the Caucasus and Central Asia: size and determinants'. As the title suggests, the authors concentrate on exploring the amount of shadow economy and the reasons behind it in this particular region. By using the MIMIC method, Abdih and Medina find that the inappropriate tax system and excessive regulation of financial and product markets, as well as the rigid labour market, are the main contributors to the shadow economy in the region. Overall, this study is one of the few available that aims to link the size of the shadow economy with its determinants, thus potentially being useful for policy makers to design context-specific policies for fighting the shadow economy.

This volume concludes with the third part, which consists of one chapter: 'What is to be done about entrepreneurship in the shadow economy?', written by Colin Williams. In his contribution, Williams provides an extensive review and evaluation of policy options, approaches and measures available to policy makers to address the shadow economy. In particular, Williams offers to choose amongst 'taking no action', 'eradicating shadow entrepreneurship', 'moving legitimate entrepreneurship into the shadow economy' or 'transforming shadow entrepreneurship into legitimate entrepreneurship'. The author then examines which of these policy approaches, which, as stated by himself, are not mutually exclusive, are most efficient, taking into consideration influential factors both on the micro and macro levels.

By collecting contributions that analyse the nature of the shadow economy and key available policy measures, which explore the shadow economy in particular contexts and provide an overview of available policy measures to decrease the shadow economy, we aim to encourage further research on this often challenging research topic. In this regard, apart from uncovering new ways to measure the shadow economy, we would call for research on the shadow economy exploring regional variations and differences across the sectors. Furthermore, little is still known about the relationship between the motives of entrepreneurs or the general population and the size of the shadow economy, which is another relevant area for further in-depth research. Altogether, apart from facilitating an interesting academic discussion, this will provide policy makers in particular countries with more evidence-based and targeted tools to decrease the shadow economy and thus, in the longer term, foster economic development and growth.

REFERENCES

Estrin, S. and T. Mickiewicz (2012), 'Shadow economy and entrepreneurial entry', *Review of Development Economics*, **16** (4), 559–78.

Putniņš, T.J. and A. Sauka (2015), 'Measuring the shadow economy using company managers', *Journal of Comparative Economics*, **43** (2), 471–90.

Sauka, A. (2008), *Productive, Unproductive and Destructive Entrepreneurship: A Theoretical and Empirical Exploration*, Frankfurt am Main: Peter Lang.

PART I

Methods to Measure the Amount and
Determinants of the Shadow Economy

1. The bottom-up power of informal entrepreneurship

José Ernesto Amorós, Juan Pablo Couyoumdjian, Oscar Cristi and Maria Minniti

INTRODUCTION

Interest in the informal sector has a long history in economics (see Gerxhani, 2004 and Schneider and Enste, 2000 for a review of the literature), and is now receiving increasing attention in management (Bruton et al., 2008; Bowen and De Clercq, 2008; and Godfrey, 2012) and in entrepreneurship research (see the special issue of *Strategic Entrepreneurship Journal*, 2014).

Traditionally, the informal sector is perceived as an inefficient and potentially negative side of the economy since its operations tend to be characterized by low productivity. Informal activities are also viewed as having negative social dimensions. For example, since workers in the informal sector usually lack the protection of safety nets existing in the formal labor market, they are considered to be exposed to the risk of exploitation. In addition, informality is perceived as producing unfair competition for formal companies, as well as imposing a burden on national finances since it allows for the avoidance of taxes (Schneider and Enste, 2000). Considerations about the opportunity costs of the informal sector are particularly significant when taking into account that, while an informal sector exists in virtually every country, in some of them it accounts for more than half of total GDP (Schneider et al., 2010; ILO, 2011).

Yet De Soto (1989) suggested that the informal sector plays an important role in economic development and that such a role goes beyond its contribution to GDP per capita (Sen, 1999; Misturelli and Heffernan, 2008) and that, in fact, GDP alone does not capture the real contribution potentially provided by informal activity. Within this context, Gries and Naudé (2011), Gollin (2008), Maloney (2004) and Shane (2009) all have noted the relationship between informal activities and entrepreneurial activities and pointed out that much of the legal activity in the informal sector takes the form of small ventures. Although there is no denying the efficiency price associated with informal economic activity in an environment characterized by efficient institutions, we argue that, in an environment with weak institutions and, therefore, high costs of doing business, participation in the informal sector may be linked to measurable positive outcomes as suggested by De Soto.

Specifically, we claim that informal economic activity is inherently entrepreneurial. As a result, contrary to standard arguments stating that development is negatively correlated to the size of the informal sector, we suggest that, under certain conditions, the informal sector allows for the exploitation of otherwise idled opportunities. In addition, we argue that the informal sector is an important vehicle for economic activity with a positive and important effect on human development even though such an effect may not be reflected in changes in per capita GDP. For example, a significant portion of female employment in developing countries consists of micro-entrepreneurial activity in the informal sector. While at the aggregate level this activity does not have a measurable impact on per capita GDP, it does generate improvements in living standards and allows women to circumvent cultural and institutional barriers.

We use country-level data to support our argument. Specifically, using data from the Global Entrepreneurship Monitor (GEM) project, the International Labour Organization (ILO), the Shadow Economic Index, and the United Nations Human Development Index (HDI), we investigate the existence of a positive relationship between the size of the informal economy and human development. Our results provide evidence that the informal sector has in fact a positive effect on development and that, in countries with weak institutions, it provides a viable substitute for activity in the formal sector and is associated with positive changes in human development. In other words, our results show that, in the presence of incongruent institutions, a certain amount of informal activity is desirable not only at the individual level, but at the aggregate level as well. Our results are robust across several model specifications.

We contribute to the literature investigating the role that informality plays in the economy in three important ways. First, we highlight the entrepreneurial dimensions of legal informal activity. Second, we re-evaluate the role of the informal sector in the process of development, a relationship that had been previously addressed only indirectly, and show that the effect may be positive and desirable, especially in developing countries. Thus, our work complements De Soto (1989), who argues in favor of living with informality. Second, our results provide some preliminary evidence on the size of the positive effect that the informal sector has on economic development. Within this context, we show that much of the impact of informal entrepreneurship is mediated by the effectiveness of a country's institutional context. Thus, our work complements Baumol's (1990) seminal work on the role institutions play on the distribution of entrepreneurial activity across alternative types, and Webb et al.'s (2009) analysis of the relationship between informal activity and the existence of incongruent institutions.

The next section presents our theoretical framework. The second section describes the data and variables used in the chapter. We then show our estimation strategies and results. Finally, the last section concludes and briefly discusses the limitations and implications of our work.

LITERATURE REVIEW AND THEORY DEVELOPMENT

Webb et al. (2009) define the informal economy as the set of illegal yet legitimate activities through which individuals exploit opportunities. Consistently, a generally agreed upon definition for the informal sector (or shadow economy) is that it describes the use of illegal means to pursue legal activities that have a positive economic value (Schneider and Enste, 2000). The extant literature has also shown convincingly that a significant portion of entrepreneurial activity takes place in the informal sector which is, in fact, constituted primarily by smaller subsistence-oriented ventures (Webb et al., 2013).

Recent studies have examined empirically the determinants of informality and found that the size of the informal sector in an economy depends on the extent of tax-burdens, labor market regulations, the quality of government institutions, and financial credit constraints (Loayza, 1996; Loayza et al., 2005; Schneider and Enste, 2000). Importantly, the effects of a higher tax burden on informality have been shown to depend not only on the tax rates, but also on how the tax system is administered (Johnson et al., 1998). Similarly, regulatory burden and uncertainty, and their impact on corruption and weak respect for the rule of law, have been linked to the size of the informal sector (Johnson et al., 1998; Anokhin and Schulze, 2009). These effects are also consistent with evidence on the regulation of entry (Djankov et al., 2002).

Clearly, institutions play a crucial role in determining individuals' choices regarding whether to operate in the formal or informal sector (Dell'Anno, 2010), a role that has been shown to be quite robust across countries and alternative political systems (De Soto, 1989; Friedman et al., 2000). These findings are consistent with and complement our extant understanding that institutions influence the distribution of entrepreneurial activity across alternative types of entrepreneurship (Baumol, 1990; Boettke and Coyne, 2007). Good institutions lead to an efficient allocation of resources and generate the correct incentives for innovation and productive entrepreneurship (Baumol et al., 2007; Baumol, 1990). Furthermore, in a recent fine-grained qualitative study, De Castro et al. (2014) have highlighted the mediating role institutions play between entrepreneurs and their environment.

As Webb et al. (2009) put it, informal activity emerges when individual and public incentives are misaligned. That is, a gap exists between activity sanctioned as being legal and activity perceived as being legitimate by sufficiently large groups.[1] Thus, doing business in the informal sector may be considered as the individual's legitimate response to the relative incentives created by an environment where weak institutions limit, whether by imposing constraints or by increasing costs, one's ability to start a business in the formal sector of the economy. Since economic decision-making always takes place in the context of scarce resources, the desirability of informal activity stems from the fact that it constitutes an individual's best response to the specific environment she or he is facing (Yamada, 1996).

Taken together, the evidence provided by this literature shows that institutions matter for the emergence of informal activity because they guide the allocation of resources in the economy (Easterly, 2002; North, 1990). Thus, in a world with good institutions the advantages for engaging in the informal sector are limited and informality will primarily have the negative effect predicted by much of the literature. For example, informal firms would not be able to realize the advantages of well-defined property rights or expand their activities to the extent allowed by a free market (De Soto, 2000). On the other hand, in countries characterized by incongruent institutions, undertaking activities informally may be a rational and well-being enhancing choice.

Of course, individuals' best responses do not necessarily produce desirable results at the aggregate level. Research focusing on the macroeconomic role played by the informal economy has focused primarily on three groups of issues related to this point. First, issues related to the size and scope of the regulations that influence the distribution of activity between the formal and the informal sectors (Yamada, 1996). Second, micro-level issues associated with social concerns and with the impact the informal sector has on poverty and lack of opportunities (Tokman, 2007; Banerjee and Duflo, 2007). Third, issues related to the contribution, if any, to productivity and the value generated by activities in the informal sector (Maloney, 2004). We are interested in the aggregate effects of the informal economy on human development. Thus, our chapter fits primarily in the third group.

The amount of research aimed at assessing the aggregate impact of the informal sector on development is relatively limited. More importantly, the empirical literature provides conflicting results. Loayza (1996) found the effect of informality on economic growth to be negative. Easterly (2002) showed growth to be negatively related to informal production. Similarly, LaPorta and Shleifer (2008) found evidence that the size of the informal economy has a strong negative correlation with per capita income and that firms established in the formal sector are the main sources of productivity in the economy. These findings are consistent with the view that informality is primarily a transitory and involuntary alternative to formal activity. As Tokman (2007) points out, this survivalist view of informality implies an overall fragility and vulnerability of the informal sector and underlies its undesirable character.

In contrast, Maloney (2004) found evidence that most economic agents decide to work in the informal sector voluntarily and, as a result, argued that informality has an important voluntary component. Similarly, in a comprehensive study of Latin America undertaken by the IBRD and the World Bank, Perry et al. (2007) argued that the majority of informal activity is voluntary and that most workers attach significant value to non-pecuniary benefits and choose deliberately to exit formal social protection systems. Amorós and Cristi (2011) also found similar results, even in the context of necessity-motivated entrepreneurship in Latin America.

Overall, the heterogeneity of motives for engaging in informal activities cautions against simple generalizations. While exclusion from formal employment explains the undertaking of activities in the informal sector for some individuals, the documented voluntary nature of much informality suggests that the latter satisfies needs that may not necessarily be reflected in income changes. For example, owning a business, albeit a small and informal one, may signal leadership ability and status in a community, or increase empowerment and self-reliance. Also, for people with low educational attainments, self-employment may provide more upward mobility than the formal sector, or supplemental sources of income. These are just a few of the many economic and non-economic factors that may motivate individuals to choose informality voluntarily.

If one embraces the entrepreneurial and voluntary nature of much informal activity, informality does not emerge necessarily as a weak and negative aspect of business life but, rather, as an effective coping strategy to external constraints, even though its positive effects may not be measurable in changes in per capita GDP. According to this view, informality is the manifestation of a dynamic entrepreneurial spirit in an economy. This is consistent with the observation that some level of informal activity emerges even in economies characterized by well-functioning institutions. Similarly, the bottom-up nature of informal entrepreneurship is at the core of De Soto's 1989 seminal work. For example, De Soto described the state of affairs in the public transport industry in Lima, Peru, where, at the time he was writing, more than half of the industry was part of the shadow economy. These transportation services emerged as small entrepreneurial ventures and operated informally in response to the excessive burden of regulations imposed on the industry. These informal entrepreneurial activities, De Soto contends, provided a significant contribution to Lima's development.

To summarize, in a world with efficient institutions we would expect to see only a limited informal sector. On the other hand, in a world with inefficient institutions, activity in the informal sector is the entrepreneurial response to institutional constraints and allows for the mobilization of resources that, otherwise, these constraints would leave unused or under-used. Given the entrepreneurial nature characterizing the activities taking place in it, we hypothesize that the informal sector, and its entrepreneurial component in particular, have a positive aggregate effect on human development and that, as a result, a certain amount of informal activity may be desirable. We also hypothesize the strength of this effect to be associated to the quality of formal institutions.

DATA AND VARIABLES

To measure a country's level of economic development we use two alternative variables. First, we use the Human Development Index (HDI) calculated by the United Nations Development Program and published in the Human Development Reports.[2] The HDI is a composite index that measures average achievement in a country by considering three dimensions of human development: life expectancy at birth (long and healthy life); adult literacy rate (education and knowledge); and GDP per capita in purchasing power parities. Since its three dimensions reflect the major themes and topics associated with poverty (Misturelli and Heffernan, 2008), the HDI is broadly accepted as a proxy for economic development. The HDI is calculated as the geometric mean of normalized indices for life expectancy, education and income per capita, and takes values between 0 and 1, with 1 representing the highest attainable standards.

Second, as an alternative proxy for human development we calculate the Non-Income Human Development Index (NIHDI) by subtracting the income effect from the HDI. A country's per capita GDP is correlated with the HDI directly but also indirectly through the impact of income on life expectancy and education. In fact, the correlation coefficient between HDI and per capita GDP for our sample is 0.85. However, the fact that the correlation between these variables is not perfect suggests that factors other than achieved GDP also contribute to human development. Furthermore, some countries are better than others at translating income into human development. Thus, the purpose of the NIHDI is to capture more effectively the fraction of HDI that is not due to GDP. To compute the NIHDI we estimate the equation:

$$HDI_{it} = \chi_0 + \chi_1 g(GDP_{it}) + \varepsilon_{it} \tag{1.1}$$

Where, χ_0 is an intercept term, χ_1 is a slope coefficient, $g(GDP)$ is some transformation of per capita income and ε is an error term. The NIHDI for any given country is simply the absolute value of the estimated value of ε_{it} obtained from estimating equation (1.1). In other words, $NIHDI_{it} = |\hat{\varepsilon}_{it}|$. The transformation of income in equation (1.1) accounts for the possibility that the relationship between HDI and per capita income may be non-linear and we use the Box–Cox transformation to allow the data to determine which functional form is more appropriate. This Box–Cox transformation is:

$$g(GDP_{it}) = \frac{GDP_{it}^{\lambda} - 1}{\lambda} \tag{1.2}$$

where λ is an unknown parameter. We then substitute equation (1.2) into equation (1.1) and obtain the pooled Maximum Likelihood estimates $\hat{\chi}_0, \hat{\chi}_1, \hat{\lambda}$ and $\hat{\varepsilon}$ for χ_0, χ_1, λ and ε respectively. Results for these estimates are presented in Table 1.1 and indicate that λ is statistically significant at the

Table 1.1   *Estimates of the parameters of the Box–Cox transformation in equation (1.1) with data for period 2000–2010*

Variable	Pooled Maximum Likelihood Estimates
Lambda	−0.07**
	(0.03)
Transformed GDP	0.2***
Chi-squared value for test H0: $\chi_1 = 0$	1354
Constant	−0.7
Sigma	0.04
LR Chi-squared	1354***
Number of observations	704

Notes: Standard error between brackets. ***, **, * indicate significance level at 1%, 5% and 10% respectively.

5 percent level and its point estimation is −0.07. Moreover, transformed GDP is statistically significant.

To proxy the size of the informal economy, as others before us, we face the challenge of obtaining accurate measurements of the scope of these activities. Current efforts to develop such measurements include indirect estimation (Schneider et al., 2010), labor force statistical profiles (ILO, 2011), and direct estimation measures such as labor force and household surveys (Tickamyer and Wood, 2003).[3] In this chapter, we use three alternative proxies: necessity-driven entrepreneurship as measured by Global Entrepreneurship Monitor (GEM) data; the proportion of self-employment in the labor force from the LABORSTA database of the International Labor Organization (ILO); and the Shadow Economic Index built by Schneider et al. (2010). While each of these proxies suffers from some shortcomings, they are routinely used to estimate informal activity. More importantly, we believe that the comparative use of all three may have the twofold merit of highlighting different though complementary aspects of informal activity as well as serving as a robustness check.

Our first proxy for the informal sector consists of the percentage of the adult population involved in necessity entrepreneurship (NEC), that is, the percentage of the adult population actively involved in starting a business because of the lack of alternative employment opportunities. NEC data are obtained from the adult population surveys conducted annually by the Global Entrepreneurship Monitor (GEM) project.[4] Started in 1999, GEM is the largest ongoing data collection effort focusing on entrepreneurs, their motivations, and the characteristics of their businesses.[5] NEC entrepreneurship consists primarily of self-employed individuals, is significantly higher in low and middle-income countries (Acs and Amorós, 2008; Bosma et al., 2008), and captures most of the informal activities accomplished by survivalist entrepreneurs (Shane, 2009). Ample evidence exists that the majority of necessity based self-employed individuals operate in the informal sector (Banerjee and Duflo, 2007; De Soto, 1989), especially in Latin America and Africa (Parker, 2004; Shane, 2009). For these reasons, NEC entrepreneurship is a reasonable proxy for the informal sector or, at least, that part of the informal economy that is involved in the creation of micro-enterprises (Naudé et al., 2008).

As a second proxy for the informal sector we use the ratio of self-employed to total workers from the LABORSTA database of the ILO. Gollin (2008), Maloney (2004), Naudé et al. (2008), and Nichter and Goldmark (2009) all have shown that the vast majority of self-employed individuals are active within micro-enterprises that operate in the informal sector. While suffering from clear shortcomings, self-employment is none-theless a 'popular measure' of informality (Perry et al., 2007, pp. 1–2). In order to make our analysis of self-employment comparable with analysis on GEM data, we only consider data for countries that participated in the GEM project.

Finally, our third proxy for the informal sector is the Shadow Economic Index (SEI) built by Schneider et al. (2010). The index estimates the size of the informal economy in 162 countries for the 1999–2007 period. The SEI uses data on a set of institutional variables that may cause a shadow economy to develop; namely, share of direct taxation, size of govern-ment, fiscal freedom, business freedom index, government effectiveness, unemployment rate and Gross Domestic Product (GDP) per capita. In this case, the size of the informal sector is expressed as a percentage of GDP. The strength of SEI data is that, to our knowledge, they are the only available measure built using the same estimation and sampling techniques with the specific purpose of assessing the size of the informal sector in a large number of countries. The main weakness of the SEI data is that they provide only an indirect measure of the size of the informal sector.

In the previous section we argued that changes in a country's develop-ment over time depend, at least in part, on informal activity which, in turn, is a function of the country's institutional context. In the short run, institutions can be considered exogenous to the relationship between development and informal activity, that is as an unobserved effect in the panel data analysis. Thus, we use Regulation Quality (RQ) and Economic Freedom (EF) to proxy the institutional environment in each country and as instruments in our models.

The variable RQ comes from the World Bank's Worldwide Governance Indicators which include aggregate and individual governance indicators at the country level (Kaufmann et al., 2009). This variable is related to the capability of the government to formulate and implement programs, poli-cies and regulations that permit and promote private sector development. Within this context, regulation of better quality implies increased incen-tives to abandon the informal economy. The EF variable, instead, comes from the annual Index of Economic Freedom produced by *The Wall Street Journal* and The Heritage Foundation. The Index covers 10 freedoms – from property rights to entrepreneurship – and tracks economic freedom around the world. In this chapter we use the overall score of the total Economic Freedom Index (EF).

Finally, we include dummy variables for each country in order to capture other country-specific heterogeneity.[6] Table 1.2 shows the sample size for each variable.

Table 1.2 Sample size

Variable	Number of countries (n)	Average length of the data (average Ti)*	n × Ti
HDI	64	11	704
SE	60	6.9	413
NEC	85	4.8	406
SEI	78	7.9	622
EF	82	8.4	686
RQ	84	9.2	777

Note: * Ti = average number of years for which we observe that variable for country i.

ESTIMATION PROCEDURES AND RESULTS

Empirical Model and Estimation Strategy

We test the hypothesis that, given the entrepreneurial nature of the informal sector, a positive relationship exists between the size of the informal sector and a country's economic development. Empirically, we are thus interested in modeling a country's development trend, that is, the changes in its HDI, as a function of the size of that country's informal economy over time. By doing so, we capture the idea that changes in a country's development do not depend on the size of the informal economy in any specific year but on the persistency of that variable over time. In addition, doing so allows us to correct for possible misleading effects of the business cycle. To incorporate trends, we calculate moving averages for all specifications of our model. In general, our model takes the form:

$$Development\ index_{it} - Development\ index_{it-s} = \alpha_0 + \alpha_1\ Average\ size$$
$$informal\ sector_{it} + \alpha_i + \varepsilon_{it}$$

where α_0 and α_1 are unknown parameters; parameters α_i are country-specific effects that capture unobserved countries' institutional settings; and ε_{it} are random disturbances distributed with 0 mean ($E[\varepsilon_{it}] = 0$).

We use two alternative measures of changes in development. First, we consider the change in HDI over a five-year period for each country. We choose a five-year period to be consistent with the Human Development Index report that calculates the short-term progress of human development as the change in the HDI over that same time period. Second, we consider the change in the Non-Income Human Development Index (NIHDI) over a four-year period for each country. The four-year period is chosen instead of a five-year period to avoid losing too many observations.

As discussed earlier, measures for the average size of the informal sector are: (a) each country's five-year moving average of NEC; (b) each country's five-year moving average of SE; and (c) each country's four-year moving average of SEI. For empirical purposes we relate the moving averages for NEC entrepreneurship and SE to that of the HDI, and the moving average of SEI to that of NIHDI. We do not test for the relationship between changes in HDI and changes in SEI due to collinearity issues since both indexes are a function of GDP per capita. Table 1.3 summarizes the descriptive statistics, whereas Table 1.4a and Table 1.4b provide the full correlation matrices for the five-year HDI trend and moving averages, and for the four-year NIHDI trend and moving averages respectively.

Importantly, the relationship between a country's development and its informal sector may be characterized by two-way causality with resulting endogeneity problems. Although we are not aware of any study that addresses this point explicitly, Van Stel et al. (2005) and Thurik et al. (2008) have provided evidence of two-way causality between entrepreneurial activity and GDP (which is included in the HDI). Thus, the appropriate estimation methods for the parameters of the proposed model depend on whether the average measures of the size of the informal economy are endogenous, as well as on whether there is a correlation between them and the random variable that captures the unobserved institutional context of a country (α_i). If proxies for the informal economy are endogenous we need an estimation approach based on instrumental variables.

An instrument is a variable that does not itself belong in the explanatory equation and is correlated with the endogenous explanatory variables, conditional on the other covariates. More specifically, the instrumental variables must be correlated with the endogenous explanatory variables, informal activity in our case, but cannot be correlated with the error term in the explanatory equation. To address this potential problem, we use the generalized method of moments (GMM) distance statistics 'C' test.[7] GMM estimators are consistent, asymptotically normal and efficient. We performed tests for the endogeneity of the variables used to proxy the informal sector assuming a fixed effect model. This ensured that we test also for the correlation between these variables and the random disturbance.

We implemented that 'C' test using country dummies together with moving averages for *EF* and *RQ* as instruments. Results indicate that we cannot reject the null hypothesis that the moving average of *NEC*, *SE* and *SEI* are exogenous. Thus, we can be reasonably confident of the consistency of our estimates.

Table 1.3 *Descriptive statistics*

Variable	Obs.	Mean	Std. Dev.	Min.	Max.
$HDI_{it} - HDI_{it-5}$	384	0.0200379	0.0122133	−0.0189963	0.0545191
5 year AverageNEC	94	1.506548	1.412785	0.2395	5.966667
5 year AverageEF	346	64.29455	9.637039	42.7	89.68333
5 year AverageRQ	308	37.19258	71.9506	−156.9125	183.33
5 year AverageSE	149	3597.923	7093.553	14.48333	44539.83
$NIHDI_{it} - NIHDI_{it-4}$	448	0.022591	0.0297748	0.0003369	0.315751
4 year AverageSEI	310	27.94516	12.5787	8.46	67.4
4 year AverageEF	404	64.26499	9.889334	40.88	89.72

Table 1.4a   Correlation matrix of the full set of variables used in the estimation process (five-year HDI trend and moving averages)

Variable	$HDI_{it} - HDI_{it-5}$	5 year AverageNec	5 year Average Economic Freedom	5 year Average Regulation Quality	5 year AverageSE
$HDI_{it} - HDI_{it-5}$	1				
5 year AverageNEC	0.0321	1			
5 year AverageEF	-0.199	-0.3086	1		
5 year AverageRQ	-0.2162	-0.386	0.9006	1	
5 year AverageSE	-0.4673	0.7866	-0.1429	-0.2626	1

Entrepreneurship and the shadow economy

Table 1.4b   *Correlation matrix of the full set of variables used in the estimation process (four-year NIHDI trend and moving averages)*

	$NIHDI_{it} - NIHDI_{it-4}$	4 year Average SEI	4 year Average Economic Freedom
$NIHDI_{it} - NIHDI_{it-4}$	1		
4 year AverageSEI	0.2573	1	
4 year AverageEF	0.0182	−0.3702	1

In addition, we use a Hausman test to assess whether the unobserved institutional context of a country is correlated with the size of its informal sector. The Hausman test indicated that it is not possible to reject the hypothesis that the correlations between them are, in fact, 0. Thus, it is possible to get consistent and efficient estimates for the parameters of our models using a random effect model or a pooled OLS model. If OLS is used, a panel-corrected standard error and t-statistics must be used for statistical inference. This leads to a panel-robust estimate of the asymptotic variance matrix of the pooled OLS estimator which controls for both serial correlation and heteroskedasticity.

Results

Given the result of the Hausman test, we chose the estimation procedure providing the most efficient estimates. To measure the effect of the five-year moving average of NEC on the five-year moving average of HDI, estimation efficiency is reached with pooled OLS and by allowing for intragroup correlation and variance heterogeneity for the residuals. Efficiency is also reached in this case with a random effect model allowing for variance heterogeneity in the residuals. Columns 1 and 2 in Table 1.5 show the results of these two estimation procedures. The two methods provide very similar results, suggesting that the latter are robust. Specifically, the results show that increases in the moving average value of NEC are associated with increases in HDI. This provides some support for our hypothesis that the size of the informal sector has a positive effect on countries' development.

In order to gain a better understanding of the impact value of our estimates, we use the estimated coefficients to calculate the elasticity between the two variables. That is, we measure the percentage change in the moving average of HDI resulting from a 1 percent change in the moving average of NEC. Our calculations indicate that such elasticities vary across countries ranging in absolute values from 0.08 (Slovenia) to 1.16 (Brazil) in the

Table 1.5 *Estimates of the models for HDI and NIHDI trend as a function of different measures of the informal economy*

Variable		5 year HDI trend		4 year NIHDI trend
	OLS estimates with intragroup correlation and heterogeneity of variance of the residuals.	Random effects estimates with heterogeneity of variance of the residuals.	OLS estimates with intragroup correlation and heterogeneity of variance of the residuals.	Random effects estimates
Constant	0.01***	0.007***	0.02***	0.007
	(0.002)	(0.003)	(0.002)	(0.01)
5 year moving average of NEC	0.003**	0.002**		
	(0.001)	(0.001)		
5 year moving average of SE			2.67E-07**	
			(1.26E-07)	
4 year moving average of SEI				0.0006*
				(0.0003)
Number of countries	24	24	35	63
Number of observations	91	91	124	250
R-sq overall	0.15	0.15	0.04	0.03
F-test	6.11**		4.49**	
Wald chi^2		4.85**		3.41*

Notes: Standard deviations are between brackets. ***, ** and * indicate 1%, 5% and 10% significance level respectively.

OLS model and from 0.05 (Slovenia) up to 0.78 (Brazil) in the random effects model.[8]

To measure the effect of the five-year moving average of SE on the five-year moving average of HDI, estimation efficiency is reached with pooled OLS and allowing for intragroup correlation and variance heterogeneity for the residuals. Column 3 in Table 1.5 shows that increases in the moving average value of *SE* are associated to increases in HDI. Our calculations also indicate that the elasticity between the HDI's trend and the moving average for *SE* varies across countries and range in absolute value from 0.0003 (Iceland) to 0.38 (Brazil).[9] Finally, to measure the effect of the four-year moving average of SEI on the four-year moving average of NIHDI, estimation efficiency is reached with a random effect model. Column 4 in Table 1.5 shows that as *SEI* increases, a country's NIHDI also increases. Our calculations indicate that the elasticity between the NIHDI's trend and the moving average of *SEI* varies across countries and range in absolute value from 0.14 (Uganda) to 8.4 (Croatia).

We noted that the R^2 values for the last models are low (4 percent and 3 percent respectively). This implies that, although both models provide further support for our hypothesis that the informal sector has a positive effect on countries' development, their predictive power is limited. In the context of our argument, however, this is not a problem, especially since the F-tests are significant for all models. In fact, our goal is not to predict changes in human development but, rather, to show that informal activity contributes to explaining human development granted, of course, that the latter depends on a number of additional factors.

CONCLUSION

Our results support our hypothesis that the size of the informal sector has a positive effect on economic development. The rationale for our argument is that most activities in the informal sector are entrepreneurial and that their unintended macroeconomic consequence leads to the mobilization of otherwise unused resources and, as a result, to improvements in economic development, albeit their effect may not be measurable in immediate changes in per capita GDP. In their famous essay on the economic lives of the poor, for example, Banerjee and Duflo (2007) described the relationship between low levels of economic development and entrepreneurship in the following way: 'All over the world, a substantial fraction of the poor act as entrepreneurs in the sense of raising capital, carrying out investment, and being the full residual claimants for the resulting earnings' (p. 151).

Our results hold true for all three proxies we use to measure informality. Furthermore, differences in country-specific elasticities between measures of informality and economic development suggest that the magnitude of this relationship is significantly mediated by observed and unobserved institutional factors. This is consistent with extant research suggesting that institutions have a strong influence on both entrepreneurial activity (whether necessity or opportunity driven) and economic development (Boettke and Coyne, 2007).

In spite of commendable recent efforts (Schneider et al., 2010), the availability of reliable data on the informal sector remains a major challenge for research in this area and, of course, for this chapter. While stemming from the difficulty to obtain accurate measurements of the size of the informal sector, the use of different measures of informality in our analysis provides robustness checks for our results. Our suggestive evidence supports the idea that the informal sector should not be viewed as a negative element in the economy (De Soto, 1989) and that, given the bottom-up nature of the entrepreneurial activities undertaken in the informal sector, informality has a positive effect on economic development (Asea, 1996) by allowing individuals to circumvent the costs of compliance imposed by regulatory constraints (Stigler, 1971). In an environment with sub-optimal institutions and, therefore, high costs of doing business, participating in the informal sector is a rational choice at the individual level and may yield efficient outcomes at the aggregate level.

Entrepreneurial activities may be formal or informal and the decision of an individual to operate in one of these sectors or, sometimes, in both, depends on the opportunity costs of each option which, in turn, depend on the quality of institutions (Baumol, 1990; Boettke and Coyne, 2007). On the one hand, the lack of institutions or the existence of a weak institutional environment increases the costs of operating in the formal sector relative to the informal sector (Djankov et al., 2002). On the other hand, doing business in an informal environment exposes entrepreneurs to possible sanctions and fines, involves non-secure property rights, and makes access to credit and the potential realization of productivity-enhancing investments unlikely (De Soto, 2000).

Efficient institutions are those that minimize transaction costs (North, 1990). In a country with efficient institutions, resources flow to those activities where returns are higher and nascent entrepreneurs are able to allocate their efforts with no resources wasted in deciding whether to operate their business in the formal or informal sector. In other words, in a world with efficient institutions, we should not expect a significant informal sector. In practice, however, many institutional arrangements do not minimize transaction costs. Sometimes they reduce them; in many cases, they simply change the nature of these costs or redistribute them among transaction participants (Baumol, 1990; North, 1990). In this case, the informal sector provides a form of competition for the formal sector and, as a result, allows for the mobilization of otherwise unused resources. The size of the informal sector is also shown to matter and the calculated elasticities shed light as to the sizes of the effects involved.

Our results also have clear implications for policy decisions with respect to the necessity to eliminate the informal sector and the cost associated with such an endeavor. In fact, the resources spent in attempts to eradicate informal activities may be better spent correcting institutional inefficiency. Our results suggest that in countries where an informal sector already exists, its elimination is not necessarily welfare enhancing since formality may come at a significant cost. In general, a useful way to think about the trade-offs between formal and informal activities is to view them as complementary. Thus, governments may opt for a posture of benevolent indifference where each entrepreneur can choose whether to operate in the formal or informal sector based on relative returns and transaction costs. In turn, the distribution of entrepreneurs between the formal and informal sectors will influence growth and economic development.

Finally, our work lends itself to an immediate and, we believe, important extension: as suggested by Frey (1989), if a certain amount of informal activity is desirable, it would be interesting to investigate whether an optimal size for the informal sector may be identified. An empirical answer to such a question may be impossible to find but analytical models of the economy may prove fruitful in assessing the optimal trade-off between formal and informal activity in the presence of incongruent institutions.

NOTES

1. Consistently with existing literature and our operationalization of the variables, our study does not include renegade (Webb et al., 2009) or destructive (Baumol, 1990) activity.
2. For more information see the Human Development Report (UNDP, 2013) and, in particular, its statistical annex.
3. For an interesting survey on approaches used to measure the informal economy see Alderslade et al. (2006).
4. Detailed information on the GEM project can be found at www.gemconsortium.org.
5. See Bosma et al. (2012) for sampling and collection procedures, as well as a detailed description of the data and their statistical properties.
6. Countries included in our study are Algeria, Argentina, Australia, Austria, Belgium, Bolivia, Brazil, Canada, Chile, China, Colombia, Croatia, Czech Republic, Denmark, Dominican Republic, Ecuador, Egypt, Finland, France, Greece, Guatemala, Hong Kong, Hungary, Iceland, India, Indonesia, Iran, Ireland, Israel, Italy, Jamaica, Japan, Jordan, Kazakhstan, Korea, Latvia, Lebanon, Malaysia, Mexico, Morocco, Netherlands, New Zealand, Norway, Panama, Peru, Philippines, Poland, Portugal, Romania, Russia, Saudi Arabia, Slovenia, Spain, Sweden, Switzerland, Tunisia, Turkey, Uganda, United Arab Emirates, United Kingdom, United States, Uruguay, Venezuela.
7. More details about this test can be found in Wooldridge (2002, Section 8.5) and in Baum et al. (2003).
8. Following standard economics, elasticities were calculated as $d(y)/d(x)* (y/x)$ using countries' mean values for the trend of HDI and the moving average value of *NEC*.
9. Elasticities were calculated as described in note 8 using estimates for *SE* instead of *NEC*.

REFERENCES

Acs, Z.J. and J.E. Amorós (2008), 'Entrepreneurship and competitiveness dynamics in Latin America', *Small Business Economics*, **31** (3), 305–22.

Alderslade, J., J. Talmage and Y. Freeman (2006), 'Measuring the informal economy: one neighborhood at a time', Discussion Paper, The Brookings Institution Metropolitan Policy Program, Washington, DC.

Amorós, J.E. and O. Cristi (2011), 'Poverty and entrepreneurship in developing countries', in M. Minniti (ed.), *The Dynamics of Entrepreneurship: Evidence from Global Entrepreneurship Monitor Data*, Oxford: Oxford University Press, pp. 209–30.

Anokhin, S. and W. Schulze (2009), 'Entrepreneurship, innovation and corruption', *Journal of Business Venturing*, **24** (5), 465–76.

Asea, P. (1996), 'The informal sector: baby or bath water?', *Carnegie-Rochester Conference Series on Public Policy*, **45**, 163–71.

Banerjee, A.V. and E. Duflo (2007), 'The economic lives of the poor', *The Journal of Economic Perspectives*, **21** (1), 141–67.

Baum, C.F., M.E. Schaffer and S. Stillman (2003), 'Instrumental variables and GMM: estimation and testing', *Stata Journal*, **3** (1), 1–31.

Baumol, W.J. (1990), 'Entrepreneurship: productive, unproductive and destructive', *The Journal of Political Economy*, **98** (5), 893–921.

Baumol, W.J., R.E. Litan and C.J. Schramm (2007), *Good Capitalism, Bad Capitalism and the Economics of Growth and Prosperity*, New Haven, CT: Yale University Press.

Boettke, P. and C. Coyne (2007), 'Entrepreneurial behavior and institutions', in M. Minniti (ed.), *Entrepreneurship: The Engine of Growth, Vol. 1 Perspective Series*, Westport, CT: Praeger Press-Greenwood Publishing Group, pp. 119–34.

Bosma, N., K. Jones, E. Autio and J. Levie (2008), *Global Entrepreneurship Monitor, 2007 Executive Report*, Wellesley, MA and London, UK: Babson College and London Business School.

Bosma, N., A. Coduras, Y. Litovsky and J. Seaman (2012), *GEM Manual: Design, Data and Quality Control*, Wellesley, MA and London, UK: Babson College and London Business School.

Bowen, H.P. and D. de Clercq (2008), 'Institutional context and the allocation of entrepreneurial effort', *Journal of International Business Studies*, **39** (1), 747–67.

Bruton, G.D., D. Ahlstrom and K. Obloj (2008), 'Entrepreneurship in emerging economies: where are we today and where should the research go in the future', *Entrepreneurship Theory and Practice*, **32** (1), 1–14.

De Castro, J., S. Khavul and G. Bruton (2014), 'Shades of grey: how do informal firms navigate between macro and meso institutional environments?', *Strategic Entrepreneurship Journal*, **8** (1), 75–94.

De Soto, H. (1989), *The Other Path: The Invisible Revolution in the Third World*, New York: Harper & Row.

De Soto, H. (2000), *The Mystery of Capital*, New York: Basic Books.

Dell'Anno, R. (2010), 'Institutions and human development in the Latin American informal economy', *Constitutional Political Economy*, **21** (3), 207–30.

Djankov, S., R. La Porta, F. Lopez-de-Silanes and A. Shleifer (2002), 'The regulation of entry', *Quarterly Journal of Economics*, **117** (1), 1–37.

Easterly, W. (2002), *The Elusive Quest for Growth: Economists' Adventures and Misadventures in the Tropics*, Cambridge, MA: MIT Press.

Frey, B.S. (1989), 'How large (or small) should the underground economy be?', in E.L. Feige (ed.), *The Underground Economy: Tax Evasion and Information Distortion*, Cambridge: Cambridge University Press, pp. 111–29.

Friedman, E., S. Johnson, D. Kaufmann and P. Zoido-Lobatón (2000), 'Dodging the grabbing hand: the determinants of unofficial activity in 69 countries', *Journal of Public Economics*, **76** (3), 459–93.

Gerxhani, K. (2004), 'Informal sector in developed and less developed countries: a literature survey', *Public Choice*, **120** (3–4), 267–300.

Godfrey, P. (2012), 'Toward a theory of the informal economy', *The Academy of Management Annals*, **5** (1), 231–77.

Gollin, D. (2008), 'Nobody's business but my own: self-employment and small enterprise in economic development', *Journal of Monetary Economics*, **55** (2), 219–33.

Gries, T. and W. Naudé (2011), 'Entrepreneurship and human development: a capability approach', *Journal of Public Economics*, **95** (3–4), 216–24.

International Labor Organization, ILO (2011), 'Statistical update on employment in the informal economy', Geneva: Department of Statistics, ILO, available at: http://laborsta.ilo.org/sti/DATA_FILES/20110610_Informal_Economy.pdf.

Johnson, S., D. Kaufmann and P. Zoido-Lobatón (1998), 'Regulatory discretion and the informal economy', *The American Economic Review*, **88** (2), 387–92.

Kaufmann, D., A. Kraay and M. Mastruzzi (2009), 'Governance matters VIII: aggregate and individual governance indicators for 1996–2008', World Bank Policy Research Working Paper No. 4978, World Bank, Washington, DC.

LaPorta, R. and A. Shleifer (2008), 'The unofficial economy and economic development', *Brookings Papers on Economic Activity*, **2**, 275–364.

Loayza, N. (1996), 'The economics of the informal sector: a simple model and some evidence from Latin America', *Carnegie-Rochester Conference Series on Public Policy*, **45**, 129–62.

Loayza, N., L. Servén and A.M. Oviedo (2005), 'The impact of regulation on growth and informality: cross-country evidence', World Bank Policy Research Working Paper No. 3623, World Bank, Washington, DC.

Maloney, W. (2004), 'Informality revisited', *World Development*, **32** (7), 1159–78.

Misturelli, F. and C. Heffernan (2008), 'What is poverty? A diachronic exploration of the discourse on poverty from the 1970s to the 2000s', *The European Journal of Development Research*, **20** (4), 666–84.

Naudé, W., T. Gries, E. Wood and A. Meintjies (2008), 'Regional determinants of entrepreneurial start-ups in a developing country', *Entrepreneurship Regional Development*, **20** (2), 111–24.

Nichter, S. and L. Goldmark (2009), 'Small firm growth in developing countries', *World Development*, **37** (9), 1453–64.

North, D.C. (1990), *Institutions, Institutional Change and Economic Performance*, Cambridge: Cambridge University Press.

Parker, S.C. (2004), *The Economics of Self-employment and Entrepreneurship*, New York: Cambridge University Press.

Perry, G. et al. (2007), *Informality: Exit and Exclusion*, Washington, DC: The International Bank for Reconstruction and Development/The World Bank.

Schneider, F. and D.H. Enste (2000), 'Shadow economies: size, causes, and consequences', *Journal of Economic Literature*, **38** (1), 77–114.

Schneider, F., A. Buehn and C.E. Montenegro (2010), 'Shadow economies all over the world: new estimates for 162 countries from 1999 to 2007', The World Bank Policy Research Working Papers, WPS5356.

Sen, A. (1999), *Development as Freedom*, New York: Alfred A. Knopf.

Shane, S. (2009), 'Why encouraging more people to become entrepreneurs is bad public policy', *Small Business Economics*, **33** (2), 141–9.

Stigler, G.J. (1971), 'The theory of economic regulation', *The Bell Journal of Economics and Management Science*, **2** (1), 3–21.

Strategic Entrepreneurship Journal (2014), Special Issue: 'Entrepreneurship and Strategy in the Informal Economy', **8** (1), 1–100.

Thurik, R., M.A. Carree, A. van Stel and D.B. Audretsch (2008), 'Does self-employment reduce unemployment?', *Journal of Business Venturing*, **23** (6), 673–86.

Tickamyer, A.R. and T. Wood (2003), 'The social and economic context of informal work', in W.W. Falk, M.D. Schulman and A.R. Tickamyer (eds), *Communities of Work: Rural Restructuring in Local and Global Contexts*, Athens, OH: Ohio University Press, pp. 394–418.

Tokman, V. (2007), 'Modernizing the informal sector', UN/DESA Working Paper No. 42.

United Nations Development Program (UNDP) (2013), *Human Development Report*, New York: United Nations.

Van Stel, A., M. Carree and R. Thurik (2005), 'The effect of entrepreneurial activity on national economic growth', *Small Business Economics*, **24** (3), 311–21.

Webb, J., G.D. Bruton, L. Tihanyi and D. Ireland (2013), 'Research on entrepreneurship in the informal economy: framing a research agenda', *Journal of Business Venturing*, **28** (5), 598–614.

Webb, J., L. Tihanyi, D. Ireland and D. Sirmon (2009), 'You say illegal, I say legitimate: entrepreneurship in the informal economy', *Academy of Management Review*, **34** (3), 492–510.

Wooldridge, J. (2002), *Econometric Analysis of Cross Section and Panel Data*, Cambridge, MA: The MIT Press.

Yamada, G. (1996), 'Urban informal employment and self-employment in developing countries: theory and evidence', *Economic Development and Cultural Change*, **44** (2), 289–314.

2. Estimating the size of the shadow economies of 162 countries using the MIMIC method[1]

Friedrich Schneider

1 INTRODUCTION

Information about the size of the shadow economy is crucial for making effective and efficient decisions regarding the allocation of a country's resources. Unfortunately, it is very difficult to get accurate information about shadow economy activities on the goods and labor market, because not all individuals engaged in these activities wish to be identified. Hence, the goal of this chapter is twofold: (1) to undertake the difficult task of estimating the shadow economy for 162 countries all over the world as well as to provide some insights into the main causes of the shadow economy; and (2) to explain the MIMIC estimation procedure as well as to discuss its advantages and disadvantages.

This chapter is organized as follows: in section 2 some theoretical considerations about the shadow economy are made, in section 3 the estimation procedure, here the MIMIC method, is explained in detail and in section 4 the size of the shadow economy of 162 countries is shown. Finally, in section 5 a summary is given and some conclusions are drawn.

2 SOME THEORETICAL CONSIDERATIONS ABOUT THE SHADOW ECONOMY

One commonly used working definition of the shadow economy is all currently unregistered economic activities that contribute to the officially calculated (or observed) Gross National Product.[2] Smith (1994, p. 18) defines it as 'market-based production of goods and services, whether legal or illegal, that escapes detection in the official estimates of GDP.' In this chapter the following more narrow definition of the shadow economy is used: the shadow economy includes all market-based legal production of goods and services that is deliberately concealed from public authorities to avoid (1) payment of income, value-added or other taxes, (2) payment of social security contributions, (3) having to meet certain legal labor market standards, such as minimum wages, maximum working hours, safety standards and so on, and (4) having to comply with certain administrative procedures.

Given this definition, important determinants of the shadow economy are outlined below.

Tax and Social Security Contribution Burdens

A number of studies show that the overall tax and social security contribution burdens are among the main causes for the existence of the shadow economy.[3] The bigger the difference between the total cost of labor in the official economy and the after-tax earnings (from work), the greater is the incentive to avoid this difference and to work in the shadow economy. Since this difference depends broadly on the social security burden/payments and the overall tax burden, the latter are key features of the existence and the increase of the shadow economy.

The concrete measurement of the tax and social security contribution burdens is not easy to define, because the tax and social security systems are vastly different among the countries. In order to have some general comparable proxies, the following variables are used:

1. Indirect taxes as a proportion of total overall taxation (positive sign expected).
2. Share of direct taxes: direct taxes as proportion of overall taxation (positive sign expected).
3. Size of government: general government final consumption expenditures (in percentage of GDP, which includes all government current expenditures for purchases of goods and services; positive sign expected).
4. Fiscal freedom as subcomponent of the Heritage Foundation's economic freedom index measures the fiscal burden in an economy; that is, top tax rates on individual and corporate income. The index ranges from 0 to 100, where 0 is least fiscal freedom and 100 maximum degree of fiscal freedom (negative sign expected).

Intensity of Regulations

Increased intensity of regulations is another important factor which reduces the freedom (of choice) for individuals engaged in the official economy. One can think of labor market regulations such as minimum wages or dismissal protections, trade barriers such as import quotas, and labor market restrictions for foreigners such as restrictions regarding the free movement of foreign workers. Johnson et al. (1997, 1998b) find significant overall empirical evidence of the influence of (labor) regulations on the shadow economy. Regulations lead to a substantial increase in labor costs in the official economy. But since most of these costs can be shifted to the employees, these costs provide another incentive to work in the shadow economy, where they can be avoided. This empirical evidence is supported by the model of Johnson et al. (1997).

To measure the intensity of regulation or the impact of regulation on the decision of whether to work in the official or unofficial economy is a difficult task, and the following variables are used:

1. Business freedom: this is a subcomponent of the Heritage Foundation's economic freedom index; it measures the time and efforts of business activity. It ranges from 0 to 100, where 0 is least business freedom and 100 maximum business freedom (negative sign expected).
2. Economic freedom: Heritage Foundation economic freedom index which ranges from 0 to 100, where 0 is least economic freedom and 100 maximum economic freedom (negative sign expected).
3. Regulatory quality: World Bank's regulatory quality index including measures of the incidents of market-unfriendly policies, such as price controls or inadequate bank supervision, as well as perceptions of the burdens imposed by excessive regulation in areas, such as foreign trade and business development. It scores between -2.5 and $+2.5$ with higher scores corresponding to better outcomes (negative sign expected).

Public Sector Services

An increase of the shadow economy can lead to reduced state revenues, which in turn reduce the quality and quantity of publicly provided goods and services. Ultimately, this can lead to an increase in the tax rates for firms and individuals in the official sector, quite often combined with a deterioration in the quality of the public goods (such as the public infrastructure) and of the administration, with the consequence of even stronger incentives to participate in the shadow economy. To capture this effect, the following variable is used: Government Effectiveness from the World Bank's Worldwide Governance Indicators. This captures perceptions of the quality of public services, the quality of the civil service and the degree of its independence from political pressures, the quality of policy formulation and implementation, and the credibility of government's commitment to such policies. The scores of this index lie between −2.5 and +2.5, with higher scores corresponding to better outcomes (negative sign expected).

Official Economy

As has been shown in a number of studies (Schneider, 2010, 2011, 2015; Feld and Schneider, 2010) the situation of the official economy also plays a crucial role in people's decision to work or not to work in the shadow economy. In a booming official economy, people have many opportunities to earn a good salary and 'extra money' in the official economy. This is not the case in an economy facing a recession and more people try to compensate their losses of income from the official economy through additional shadow economy activities. In order to capture this, the following variables are used:

1. GPD per capita based on Purchasing Power Parity (PPP), measured in constant 2005 US$ (negative sign expected).
2. Unemployment rate defined as total unemployment in percentage of total labor force (positive sign expected).
3. Inflation rate: GDP deflator (annual rate in percent); inflation is measured by the annual growth rate of the GDP implicit deflator, it shows the rate of price changes in the economy as a whole (positive sign expected).
4. Openness: openness corresponds to trade (in percentage of GDP). Trade is the sum of exports and imports of goods and services, measured as a share of gross domestic product (negative sign expected).

Because the shadow economy cannot be directly measured, indicators are used in which shadow economy activities are reflected.

Monetary Indicators

Given that people who engage in shadow economy transactions do not want to leave traces, they conduct these activities in cash. Hence, most shadow economy activities are reflected in an additional use of cash (or currency). To take this into account, two indicators are used:

1. M0/M1: M0 corresponds to the currency outside the banks; the usual definition for M1 is M0 plus deposits.
2. Currency/M2: this corresponds to the currency outside the banks as a proportion of M2.

Labor Market Indicators

Shadow economy activities are also reflected in labor market indicators. Two indicators are used:

1. Labor force participation rate: labor force participation rate is the proportion of the population that is economically active.
2. Growth rate of the total labor force: total labor force comprises people aged 15 and older who meet the International Labor Organisation's (ILO) definition of the economically active population.[4]

State of the Official Economy

Also, shadow economy activities are reflected in the state of the official economy. For this reason, two indicators are included:

1. GDP per capita: GDP per capita is gross domestic product converted to international dollars using Purchasing Power Parity rates, divided by the population.
2. Growth rate of GDP per capita: as (1), but the annual growth rate of the GDP per capita.

3   THE MODEL OR MIMIC APPROACH – STRENGTH AND WEAKNESSES[5]

General Remarks

Most estimation methods consider just one indicator with which they try to capture all effects of the shadow economy. However, shadow economy effects show up simultaneously in the production, labor and money markets. An even more important point of criticism is that the causes that determine the size of the shadow economy are taken into account only in some of the monetary approach studies that usually consider one cause, the burden of taxation. The model approach explicitly considers multiple causes of the existence and growth of the shadow economy,[6] as well as the multiple effects of the shadow economy over time. The empirical method used is quite different from those used so far. It is based on the statistical theory of unobserved variables, which considers multiple causes and multiple indicators of the phenomenon to be measured.

As the size of the shadow economy is an unknown (hidden) figure, a latent estimator approach using the MIMIC (multiple indicators, multiple causes) estimation procedure is applied. This method is based on the statistical theory of unobserved variables. The statistical idea behind such a model is to compare a sample covariance matrix, that is, a covariance matrix of observable variables, with the parametric structure imposed on this matrix by a hypothesized model.[7] Using covariance information among the observable variables, the unobservable variable is in the first step linked to observable variables in a factor analytical model, also called a measurement model. Second, the relationships between the unobservable variable and observable variables are specified through a structural model. Therefore, a MIMIC model is the simultaneous specification of a factor and a structural model. In this sense, the MIMIC model tests the consistency of a 'structural' theory through data and is thus a confirmatory, rather than an exploratory, technique. An economic theory is thus tested examining the consistency of actual data with the hypothesized relationships between the unobservable (latent) variable or factor and the observable (measurable) variables.[8] In general, a confirmatory factor analysis has two goals: (1) to estimate parameters such as coefficients and variances; and (2) to assess the fit of the model. For the analysis of shadow economy activities these two goals are (1) to estimate the relationships between a set of observable variables, divided into causes and indicators, and the shadow economy activity (unobservable variable); and (2) to test if the researcher's theory or the derived hypotheses as a whole fit the data. MIMIC models are, compared to regression models, a method rarely used by economists, which might be due to an under-evaluation of their capabilities with respect to their potential contribution to economic research.

A Detailed Description of the MIMIC Model

The idea of the MIMIC model application is to examine the relationships between the latent variable size of shadow economy activities and observable variables in terms of the relationships among a set of observable variables by using their covariance information. The observable variables are divided into causes and indicators of the latent variable (see Figure 2.1). The key benefits of the MIMIC model are that it allows modeling shadow economy activities as an unobservable (latent) variable and that it takes into account its multiple determinants (causes) and multiple effects (indicators). A factor-analytic approach is used to measure the size of shadow economy activities as an unobserved variable over time. The unknown coefficients are estimated in a set of structural equations, as the 'unobserved' variable, that is, the size of the shadow economy, cannot be measured directly. Formally, the MIMIC model consists of two parts: the structural equation model and the measurement model.

CAUSES   INDICATORS

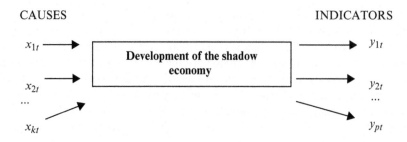

Figure 2.1   The MIMIC model

In the measurement model, the unobservable variable η_t determines a p vector $y'_t = (y_{1t}, y_{2t}, \ldots, y_{pt})'$ of indicators, that is, observable variables that reflect the shadow economy activities, subject to a p vector of random error terms $\varepsilon'_t = (\varepsilon_{1t}, \varepsilon_{2t}, \ldots, \varepsilon_{pt})'$. The unobservable variable η_t is a scalar and λ is a p column vector of parameters that relates y_t to η_t. The measurement equation is given by:

$$y_t = \lambda\eta_t + \varepsilon_t \qquad (2.1)$$

The structural model determines the unobservable variable η_t by a set of exogenous causes $x'_t = (x_{1t}, x_{2t}, \ldots, x_{qt})'$ that may be useful in predicting its movement and size, subject to a structural disturbance error term ς_t. The structural equation is given by:

$$\eta_t = \gamma'x_t + \varsigma_t \qquad (2.2)$$

where γ' is a q row vector of structural parameters.[9] In equations (2.1) and (2.2) it is assumed that ς_t and the elements of ε_t are normally, independently and identically distributed, the variance of the structural disturbance term ς_t is denoted by ψ, and $\Theta_\varepsilon = E(\varepsilon_t\varepsilon_t')$ is the $(p \times p)$ covariance matrix of the measurement errors.[10] Figure 2.1 shows the path diagram of the MIMIC model.

The MIMIC model of shadow economy activities estimated in this chapter uses three indicators and nine causes. Hence, within this model, equations (2.1) and (2.2) are specified as follows:

$$\begin{bmatrix} y_{1t} \\ y_{2t} \\ y_{3t} \end{bmatrix} = \begin{bmatrix} \lambda_1 \\ \lambda_2 \\ \lambda_3 \end{bmatrix} \cdot \eta_t + \begin{bmatrix} \varepsilon_{1t} \\ \varepsilon_{2t} \\ \varepsilon_{3t} \end{bmatrix} \qquad (2.3)$$

$$\eta_t = [\gamma_1\gamma_2\gamma_3\gamma_4\gamma_5\gamma_6\gamma_7\gamma_8\gamma_9] \cdot \begin{bmatrix} x_{1t} \\ x_{2t} \\ x_{3t} \\ x_{4t} \\ x_{5t} \\ x_{6t} \\ x_{7t} \\ x_{8t} \\ x_{9t} \end{bmatrix} + \varsigma_t \qquad (2.4)$$

Substituting (2.1) into (2.2) yields a reduced form equation which expresses the relationships between the observed causes and indicators, that is, between x_t and y_t. This is shown in equation (2.5):

$$y_t = \Pi x_t + z_t \qquad (2.5)$$

where: $\Pi = \lambda\gamma'$ is a (3×9) reduced form coefficient matrix and $z_t = \lambda\varsigma_t + \varepsilon_t$ is a reduced form vector of a linear transformation of disturbances that has a (3×3) reduced form covariance matrix Ω given as:

$$\Omega = \text{Cov}(z_t) = E[(\lambda\varsigma_t + \varepsilon_t)(\lambda\varsigma_t + \varepsilon_t)'] = \lambda\psi\lambda' + \Theta_\varepsilon \qquad (2.6)$$

In equation (2.6), $\psi = \text{Var}(\varsigma_t)$ and $\Theta_\varepsilon = E(\varepsilon_t \varepsilon_t')$ is the measurement error's covariance matrix.

In general, estimation of a MIMIC model uses covariance information of sample data to derive estimates of population parameters. Instead of minimizing the distance between observed and predicted individual values, as in standard econometrics, the MIMIC model minimizes the distance between an observed (sample) covariance matrix and the covariance matrix predicted by the model the researcher imposes on the data. The idea behind that approach is that the covariance matrix of the observed variables is a function of a set of model parameters:

$$\Sigma = \Sigma(\theta) \qquad (2.7)$$

where Σ is the population covariance matrix of the observed variables, θ is a vector that contains the parameters of the model and $\Sigma(\theta)$ is the covariance matrix as a function of θ, implying that each element of the covariance matrix is a function of one or more model parameters. If the hypothesized model is correct and the parameters are known, the population covariance matrix would be reproduced exactly, that is, Σ will equal $\Sigma(\theta)$. In practice, however, one does not know either the population variances and covariances or the parameters, but instead uses the sample covariance matrix and sample estimates of the unknown parameters for estimation (Bollen, 1989, p. 256).

Estimation is thus performed by finding values for $\hat{\theta} = f(\hat{\lambda}, \hat{\gamma}, \hat{\psi}, \hat{\Phi}, \hat{\Theta}_\varepsilon)$ producing an estimate of the model's covariance matrix $\hat{\Sigma}$ that most closely corresponds to the sample covariance matrix S. During this estimation procedure, all possible matrices that meet the imposed restrictions are considered. If an estimate Σ^* of $\hat{\Sigma}$ is close to S, one might conclude that θ^* is a reasonable estimate of the model's parameters. Hence, estimation of a MIMIC model is reduced to the problem of measuring how close Σ^* is to S and if this estimate is the most accurate, that is, if it is the best estimate given the set of all possible estimates that meet the imposed restrictions (Long, 1983b, pp. 42–5). The covariance equation of the MIMIC model can be derived and has the following functional form:

$$\hat{\Sigma} = \left[\begin{array}{c|c} \hat{\lambda}(\hat{\gamma}'\hat{\Phi}\hat{\gamma} + \hat{\psi})\hat{\lambda}' + \hat{\Theta}_\varepsilon & \hat{\lambda}\hat{\gamma}'\hat{\Phi} \\ \hline \hat{\Phi}\hat{\gamma}\hat{\lambda}' & \hat{\Phi} \end{array} \right] \quad (2.8)$$

The function measuring how close a given Σ^* is to the sample covariance matrix S is called the fitting function $F(S; \Sigma^*)$. The θ^* of all possible θ^* that meets the imposed constraints on λ, γ, Φ, ψ and Θ_ε and minimizes the fitting function, given the sample covariance matrix S, is the sample estimate $\hat{\theta}$ of the population parameters. This means that if one set of estimates θ_1^* produces the matrix Σ_1^* and a second set θ_2^* produces the matrix Σ_2^* and if $F(S;\Sigma_1^*) < F(S;\Sigma_2^*)$, Σ_1^* is then considered to be closer to S than Σ_2^* (Long, 1983a, p. 56).

The most widely used fitting function is the Maximum Likelihood (ML) function.[11] Under the assumption that $\Sigma(\theta)$ and S are positive definite, that is, non-singular, and S has a Wishart distribution, the following fitting function is minimized:

$$F_{ML} = \log|\Sigma(\theta)| + tr[S\Sigma^{-1}(\theta)] - \log|S| - (p+q) \quad (2.9)$$

where $\log||$ is the log of the determinant of the respective matrix and $(p + q)$ is the number of observed variables. In general, no closed form or explicit solution for the structural parameters that minimize F_{ML} exists. Hence, the values of λ, γ, Φ, ψ and Θ_ε that minimize the fitting function are estimated applying iterative numerical procedures.[12] The ML estimator is widely used because of its desirable properties:[13]

- *First*, the ML estimator is asymptotically unbiased.
- *Second*, the ML estimator is consistent, that is plim $\hat{\theta} = \theta$ ($\hat{\theta}$ is the ML estimator and θ is the population parameter).
- *Third*, the ML estimator is asymptotically efficient, that is, among all consistent estimators no other has a smaller asymptotic variance.
- *Fourth*, the ML estimator is asymptotically normally distributed, meaning that the ratio of the estimated parameter and its standard error approximate a z-distribution in large samples.
- *Fifth*, a final important characteristic of the ML estimator is scale invariance (Swaminathan and Algina, 1978). The scale invariance property implies that changes in the measurement unit of one or more of the observed variables do not change the value of the fitting function. This means that $\hat{\lambda}$, $\hat{\gamma}$, $\hat{\Phi}$, $\hat{\psi}$ and $\hat{\Theta}_\varepsilon$ are the same for any change of scale.

It is widely accepted by most scholars who estimate the size and development of shadow economic activities using the MIMIC model or more general Structural Equation Models (SEMs) with more than one unobservable variable that such an empirical exercise is a 'minefield', regardless of which method is used. For example, in evaluating the currently available shadow economy estimates of different scholars, one should keep in mind that there is no best or commonly accepted method. Each approach has its strengths and weaknesses and can provide specific insights and results. Although SEM/MIMIC model applications in economics are 'accompanied' by criticisms, they are increasingly used for estimating the shadow economy and other informal economic activities.

In comparison with other statistical methods, SEMs or MIMIC models offer several advantages for the estimation of shadow economic activities. According to Giles and Tedds (2002), the MIMIC approach is a wider approach than most other competing methods, since it allows one to take multiple indicator and causal variables into consideration at the same time. Moreover, it is quite flexible, allowing one to vary the choice of causal and indicator variables according to the particular features of the shadow economic activity studied, the period in question, and the availability of data. SEMs and MIMIC models lead to a formal estimation and to testing procedures, such as those based on the method of maximum likelihood. These procedures are well known and are generally 'optimal' if the sample is sufficiently large (Giles and Tedds, 2002). Schneider and Enste (2000) emphasize that these models lead to some progress in estimation techniques for the size and development of the shadow economy, because this methodology allows a wide flexibility in its application. Therefore, they consider it potentially superior to other estimation methods. Cassar (2001) argues that, when compared to other methods, SEMs or MIMIC models do not need restrictive assumptions to operate. Analogously, Thomas (1992, p. 168) argues that the only real constraint of this approach is not in its conceptual structure, but the choice of variables. These positive aspects of the SEM approach in general and the MIMIC model in particular apply not only in its application to the shadow economy, but to all informal economic activities. This means, again, that the MIMIC procedure relies on a broad definition of the shadow economy.

Of course this method has its disadvantages or limitations, too, which are identified in the literature. The three most important points of criticism focus on the model's implementations, the sample used and the reliability of the estimates:

1. The most common objection to estimating shadow economic activities using SEMs concerns the meaning of the latent variable (for example, Helberger and Knepel, 1988; Dell'Anno, 2003). The confirmatory rather than exploratory nature of this approach means that one is more likely to determine whether a certain model is valid than to 'find' a suitable model. Therefore, it is possible that the specified model includes potential definitions or informal economic activities other than the one studied. For example, it is difficult for a researcher to ensure that traditional crime activities such as drug dealing are completely excluded from the analysis of the shadow economy. This criticism, which is probably the most common in the literature, remains difficult to overcome as it goes back to the theoretical assumptions behind the choice of variables and empirical limitations on data availability.

2. Helberger and Knepel (1988) argue that SEMs or MIMIC model estimations lead to unstable coefficients with respect to changes of the sample size and alternative model specifications. Dell'Anno (2003) shows, however, that instability disappears asymptotically as the sample size increases. Another issue is the application of SEMs to time series data because only simple analytical tools such as q- and stemleaf plots are available to analyze the properties of the residuals (Dell'Anno, 2003).[14]

3. Criticism is also related to the benchmarking procedure used to derive 'real world' figures of shadow economic activities (Breusch, 2005a, 2005b). As the latent variable and its unit of measurement are not observed, SEMs just provide a set of estimated coefficients from which one can calculate an index that shows the dynamics of the unobservable variable. Application of the so-called calibration or benchmarking procedure, regardless of which one is used, requires experimentation

and a comparison of the calibrated values in a wide academic debate. Unfortunately, at this stage of research on the application of the SEM/ MIMIC approach in economics it is not clear which benchmarking method is the best or the most reliable.[15]

The economic literature using SEMs is well aware of these limitations. Consequently, it acknowledges that it is not an easy task to apply this methodology to an economic dataset, but also argues that this does not mean one should abandon the SEM approach. On the contrary, following an interdisciplinary approach to economics, SEMs are valuable tools for economic analysis, particularly when studying the shadow economy. However, the mentioned objections should be considered as an incentive for further (economic) research in this field rather than as a suggestion to abandon this method. Again, going back to the definition of the shadow economy, the MIMIC estimation provides upper bound macro value added figures, including mostly legally bought material.

4 THE SIZE OF THE SHADOW ECONOMY FOR 162 COUNTRIES[16]

Econometric Results

Table 2.1 presents seven different specifications in order to investigate which variables turn out to be significant, especially if one uses subsamples of countries, where more and different causal variables are available. The ideal situation of course would be that a large data set would be available for all countries over the total period of 1996 up to 2007, but this is unfortunately not the case.

For the total sample two estimations are shown, one for the 151 countries from 1996 to 2007 and, with more causal variables, one sample for 120 countries from 1996 to 2006. In addition to the total sample estimations, econometric estimations using the MIMIC approach are presented for 98 (88) developing countries, 21 Eastern European and Central Asian (mostly former transition) countries and 25 high income OECD countries. For the developing countries, two estimations with and without the direct tax burden rate as causal variable are presented; without direct tax burden rate the number of developing countries increases from 88 to 98. For the high income OECD countries again two estimations are shown, one over the period 1996 to 2006 and one over the period 1996 to 2007. For the 98 (88) developing countries and the 21 Eastern European and Central Asian countries, the estimation was done over the period 1994 to 2006 and for

Table 2.1 *MIMIC model estimation results*

Independent variables	Specification 1 98 developing countries (1994–2006)	Specification 2 88 developing countries (1994–2006)	Specification 3 21 transition countries (1994–2006)	Specification 4 25 high income OECD countries (1996–2006)	Specification 5 25 high income OECD countries (1996–2007)	Specification 6 151 countries (1996–2007)	Specification 7 120 countries (1996–2006)
Causal variables							
Size of government	0.14 (5.97)***	0.15 (5.57)***	0.18 (3.49)***			0.05 (2.64)***	0.10 (3.77)***
Share of direct taxation		0.06 (2.57)**					0.05 (2.39)**
Total tax burden				0.05 (2.05)**	0.06 (1.78)*		
Fiscal freedom	−0.06 (2.90)***	−0.03 (1.69)*	−0.08 (1.68)*	−0.07 (2.84)***			−0.04 (2.08)**
Business freedom	−0.05 (2.18)**	−0.05 (2.33)**		−0.23 (5.93)***			−0.04 (1.84)*
Economic freedom			−0.09 (1.91)*				
Unemployment rate	0.01 (0.67)	−0.00 (0.06)	0.08 (1.84)*	0.05 (1.89)*	0.11 (3.16)***	0.04 (2.08)**	0.02 (0.89)
GDP per capita	−0.27 (8.79)***	−0.26 (6.87)***				−0.38 (15.89)***	−0.33 (9.15)***
Regulatory quality				−0.21 (5.45)***	−0.31 (6.50)***	−0.05 (2.64)***	−0.04 (2.11)**
Government effectiveness							
Openness			−0.15 (2.47)**				
Inflation rate			0.22 (2.83)***				

	(1)	(2)	(3)	(4)	(5)	(6)	(7)
Indicator variables							
Growth rate of GDP per capita	−1.01 (7.88)***	−1.39 (6.70)***	−0.76 (4.41)***			−0.79 (10.93)***	−0.99 (8.42)***
GDP per capita	0.05 (0.59)	0.02 (0.14)		−1.52 (6.71)***	−1.25 (8.36)***		
Labor force participation rate				−1.11 (5.45)***	−1.03 (7.70)***	−0.19 (3.15)***	
Currency	1	1	1	1	1	1	1
Statistical tests							
RMSEA (*p*-value)	0.03 (0.99)	0.03 (0.99)	0.00 (1.00)	0.00 (0.88)	0.00 (0.99)	0.03 (1.00)	0.02 (1.00)
Chi-square (*p*-value)	38.70 (0.00)	44.43 (0.02)	17.75 (0.91)	17.74 (0.60)	3.55 (0.94)	29.95 (0.00)	51.82 (0.03)
AGFI	0.98	0.98	0.97	0.95	0.99	0.99	0.98
Degrees of freedom	20	27	27	20	9	13	35
Number of observations	1045	741	213	145	243	1563	942

Notes: Absolute *z*-statistics in parentheses. ***, **, * denote significance at the 1, 5 and 10% significance level. All variables are used as their standardized deviations from mean. According to the MIMIC models identification rule (see also section 3.1), one indicator has to be fixed to a prior value. We have consistently chosen the currency variable. The degrees of freedom are determined by $0.5(p + q)(p + q + 1) - t$; with p = number of indicators; q = number of causes; t = the number for free parameters.

Source: Schneider et al. (2010, Table 1, p. 449).

the 25 OECD countries over the period 1996 to 2007. For the total sample of 151 (120) countries, data for the period from 1996 up to 2007 (2006) is used.

For the developing countries, the following six variables are used as cause variables: (1) share of direct taxation (direct taxes in percent of overall taxation); (2) size of government (general government final consumption expenditure, as a percentage of GDP) as proxy for indirect taxation and a variable; (3) fiscal freedom (an index consisting of top individual income tax rate, top individual corporal tax rate, and total tax revenues as a percentage of GDP) as three tax burden variables in a wide sense; (4) regulatory intensity for state regulation; (5) the business freedom index (which is composed of the following components: time to open a business, financial costs to start a business, minimum capital stock to start a business, and costs for obtaining a license); and (6) the state of economy with the two variables: the unemployment rate and GDP per capita. As indicator variables, we us growth rate of GDP per capita, the labor force participation rate (people over 15 economically active as a percentage of total population), and as currency we use M0 divided by M1. For the Eastern European and Central Asian (mostly former transition) countries, we apply as cause variables the size of government, the fiscal freedom index, for state regulation the business freedom index, and for the state of the economy the unemployment rate, inflation rate and openness (sum of export and imports of goods and services, as percentage of GDP). As indicators, the growth rate of GDP per capita, the growth rate of total labor force, and the ratio M0 over M1 are used. For the 25 OECD countries, the total tax burden (total tax revenues as percentage of GDP) is used together with the fiscal and business freedom indices, a regulatory quality index, and the unemployment rate. As indicator variables, GDP per capita, the labor force participation rate and a measure for currency (M0 over M2) are applied. For the total sample of 151 countries, the cause variables are the size of the government, the unemployment rate, government effectiveness and the GDP per capita. As indicators, currency (M0 over M1), the growth rate of GDP per capita, and the labor force participation rate are used. For the 120 countries, there are additional causal variables. The size of the government, the fiscal freedom index, the share of direct taxation, the business freedom index, the unemployment rate, government effectiveness, and the GDP per capita are considered. As indicator variables, currency (M0 over M1), the growth rate of GDP per capita, and the growth rate of total labor force are used.

The estimation results for the 98 developing countries over the period 1994 to 2006 are shown in specification 1, and the estimation results for the 88 developing countries (including direct taxation) over the same period are shown in specification 2. In both estimations, all estimated coefficients of the cause variables have the theoretically expected signs. Except for the unemployment rate, all other cause variables are statistically significant, at least at the 90 percent confidence level. The share of direct taxation and the size of government are highly statistically significant, as well as the fiscal freedom and the business freedom variable. Also, the GDP per capita is in both equations highly statistically significant with the expected negative sign. If one turns to the indicator variables, the labor force participation rate and the growth rate of GDP per capita are in both equations highly statistically significant. The test statistics are also quite satisfactory.

In specification 3, the MIMIC estimation result for the 21 Eastern European and Central Asian (mostly former transition) countries over the period 1994 to 2006 is shown. The variables of the size of government and the fiscal freedom variable (both capturing the overall state burden) are highly statistically significant and have the expected signs. Turning to regulation, the economic freedom variable has the expected negative significant sign. As these countries experienced periods of high inflation, the inflation rate, which has the expected positive, highly significant sign, is included. The variable openness, modeling in a certain way the transition process, is also statistically significant. Considering the indicator variables, the growth rate of the total labor force is statistically significant, as well as the growth rate of GDP per capita. Also, here the test statistics are quite satisfactory.

In specifications 4 and 5, the estimation results for the 25 high income OECD countries are shown over the period 1996 to 2006 and 1996 to 2007.[17] In specification 4, the two variables capturing government burden (total tax burden and fiscal freedom) are highly statistically significant and have the expected sign. The unemployment rate has the expected sign and is at 95 percent confidence level statistically significant. The two variables capturing the regulatory burden, which are business freedom and regulatory quality, have the expected signs and are highly statistically significant. Turning to the indicator variables, the labor force participation rate and currency (ratio of M0 over M2) are both highly statistically significant. Also, the test statistics for this equation are quite satisfactory. Specification 5 excludes fiscal and business freedom, which allows us to estimate the model up to the year 2007. All causal variables are highly statistically significant and have the expected signs and the same is true for the indicators.

Specifications 6 and 7 present two estimations of 151 and 120 countries. In specification 6 the results of 151 countries estimated over the period 1996 to 2007 are presented. Turning first to the causal variables, one realizes that the size of government has the expected positive sign and is highly statistically significant. The same holds for the two variables which describe the state of the economy, the unemployment variable, statistically significant with a positive sign, and GDP per capita, which is highly statistically significant with the expected negative sign. Turning to the indicator variables, the growth rate of GDP per capita and the labor force participation rate have the expected signs and are highly statistically significant. If one reduces this sample to 120 countries, one can include more causal variables and the results are presented in specification 7. Here we see that we have three variables capturing the burden of taxation (in a wide sense): the size of government, fiscal freedom and share of direct taxation. All three have the expected signs and are statistically significant. As regulatory variables, business freedom and government effectiveness, which, again, have the expected negative signs, are statistically significant. For the state of the economy, we have the unemployment rate, which is not statistically significant, and GDP per capita, which is statistically significant with the expected negative sign. For the indicators, the currency (M0 over M1), the labor force participation rate and GDP per capita, are statistically significant and show the expected signs.

The Size of the Shadow Economies for 162 Countries from 1999 to 2007

The estimated MIMIC coefficients allow me to determine only relatively estimated sizes of the shadow economy, which describe the pattern of the shadow economy in a particular country over time. In order to calculate the size and trend of the shadow economy, I must convert the MIMIC index into 'real world' figures measured as a percentage of official GDP. This final step requires an additional procedure, the so-called benchmarking or calibration procedure. Unfortunately, no consensus exists in the literature as to which benchmarking procedure to use. The methodology used was promoted by Dell'Anno (2007) and Dell'Anno and Solomon (2008). In the first step, the MIMIC model index of the shadow economies is calculated using the structural equation (2.10), that is, by multiplying the coefficients of the significant causal variables with the respective time series. For the numerical example of specification 1, the structural equation is given as:

$$\tilde{\eta}_t = 0.14 \cdot x_{1t} - 0.06 \cdot x_{2t} - 0.05 \cdot x_{3t} - 0.27 \cdot x_{4t}.[18] \qquad (2.10)$$

Second, this index is converted into absolute values of the shadow economies taking base values in a particular base year. The base values necessary for this final step of the calibration procedure are from the year 2000 and taken from Schneider (2007), who estimated the shadow economies in 145 countries around the world using the currency demand approach. Thus, the size of the shadow economy $\hat{\eta}_t$ at time t is given as:

$$\hat{\eta}_t = \frac{\tilde{\eta}_t}{\tilde{\eta}_{2000}} \eta^*_{2000},\qquad(2.11)$$

where $\tilde{\eta}_t$ denotes the value of the MIMIC index at t according to equation (2.10), $\tilde{\eta}_{2000}$ is the value of this index in the base year 2000, and η^*_{2000} is the exogenous estimate (base value) of the shadow economies in 2000. Applying this benchmarking procedure, the final estimates of the shadow economies can be calculated.[19]

Of course, when showing the size of the shadow economies for countries that are quite different in location and developing stage, one should be aware that such country comparisons give only a rough picture of the ranking of the size of the shadow economy in these countries and over time, because the MIMIC and the currency demand methods have shortcomings (see, for example, Breusch, 2005a, 2005b and Ahumada et al., 2007). Table 2.2 shows (in alphabetical order of country) the development of the shadow economy in 162 countries between 1999 and 2007.

5 SUMMARY AND CONCLUSIONS

There are many obstacles to overcome when measuring the size of the shadow economy and when analyzing its consequences on the official economy. But, as this chapter shows, some progress can be made. I provide estimates of the size of the shadow economies for 162 countries over the period 1999 to 2007 using the MIMIC procedure for the econometric estimation, and a benchmarking procedure for calibrating the estimated MIMIC into absolute values of the size of the shadow economy. The new knowledge/insights gained with respect to the size and trend of the shadow economy of 162 countries lead to three conclusions.

The first conclusion from these results is that for all countries investigated, the shadow economy has reached a large size of a weighted (unweighted) average value of 17.1 (33.0) percent of official GDP over 162 countries over 1999 to 2007. However, equally important is the clear negative trend of the size of the shadow economy over time. The unweighted average size of the shadow economies of all of these 162 countries (developing, Eastern European and Central Asian and high income OECD countries) decreased from 34.0 percent of official GDP in 1999 to 31.2 percent of official GDP in 2007.

The second conclusion is that shadow economies are a complex phenomenon present to an important extent in all types of economy (developing, transition and highly developed). People engage in shadow economic

Table 2.2 Ranking of 162 countries in alphabetical order

No.	Country	Years									Country average
		1999	2000	2001	2002	2003	2004	2005	2006	2007	
1	Albania	35.7	35.3	34.9	34.7	34.4	33.9	33.7	33.3	32.9	34.3
2	Algeria	34.2	34.1	33.8	33.3	32.5	31.7	31.1	31.0	31.2	32.5
3	Angola	48.8	48.8	48.4	47.4	47.3	47.1	45.0	44.0	42.1	46.5
4	Argentina	25.2	25.4	26.1	27.6	26.4	25.5	24.7	23.8	23.0	25.3
5	Armenia	46.6	46.3	45.4	44.5	43.9	43.6	42.7	42.1	41.1	44.0
6	Australia	14.4	14.3	14.3	14.1	13.9	13.7	13.7	13.7	13.5	14.0
7	Austria	10.0	9.8	9.7	9.8	9.8	9.8	9.8	9.6	9.5	9.8
8	Azerbaijan	61.0	60.6	60.3	60.0	59.1	58.6	56.7	54.0	52.0	58.0
9	Bahamas, The	26.3	26.2	26.4	26.5	27.0	27.4	26.7	26.2	26.2	26.5
10	Bahrain	18.6	18.4	18.2	18.0	17.8	17.4	17.1	–	–	17.9
11	Bangladesh	36.0	35.6	35.5	35.7	35.6	35.5	35.1	34.5	34.1	35.3
12	Belarus	48.3	48.1	47.9	47.6	47.0	46.1	45.2	44.2	43.3	46.4
13	Belgium	22.7	22.2	22.1	22.0	22.0	21.8	21.8	21.4	21.3	21.9
14	Belize	45.2	43.8	43.3	43.4	42.3	42.0	42.1	41.7	42.0	42.9
15	Benin	51.2	50.2	49.8	49.6	49.3	49.5	49.8	49.6	49.1	49.8
16	Bhutan	29.6	29.4	29.2	29.1	28.7	28.7	28.3	28.2	27.7	28.8
17	Bolivia	67.0	67.1	67.6	67.7	67.7	66.9	64.3	62.8	63.5	66.1
18	Bosnia & Herzegovina	34.3	34.1	34.0	33.9	33.5	33.6	33.2	32.9	32.8	33.6
19	Botswana	33.9	33.4	33.2	33.3	33.0	32.8	32.7	32.3	31.9	32.9
20	Brazil	40.8	39.8	39.9	39.9	39.6	38.6	38.4	37.8	36.6	39.0
21	Brunei Darussalam	31.3	31.1	31.0	30.2	29.9	31.2	31.8	30.8	31.2	30.9
22	Bulgaria	37.3	36.9	36.6	36.1	35.6	34.9	34.1	33.5	32.7	35.3
23	Burkina Faso	41.3	41.4	41.3	41.4	40.3	40.1	39.7	39.7	39.6	40.5

#	Country										
24	Burundi	39.1	39.5	39.6	39.4	39.6	39.6	39.7	39.6	39.6	39.5
25	Cambodia	50.4	50.1	49.6	50.0	49.2	48.8	47.8	46.8	46.0	48.7
26	Cameroon	33.3	32.8	32.4	32.1	31.7	31.6	31.6	31.4	31.4	32.0
27	Canada	16.3	16.0	15.9	15.8	15.7	15.6	15.5	15.3	15.3	15.7
28	Cape Verde	36.5	36.1	35.9	35.9	35.7	35.8	35.4	34.1	33.4	35.4
29	Central African Republic	42.8	42.6	43.1	44.0	46.9	47.3	46.9	45.9	45.1	45.0
30	Chad	45.8	46.2	45.5	45.1	44.2	41.5	41.1	41.7	42.2	43.7
31	Chile	19.9	19.8	19.6	19.6	19.4	19.1	18.9	18.7	18.5	19.3
32	China	13.2	13.1	13.0	12.9	12.8	12.6	12.5	12.2	11.9	12.7
33	Colombia	39.4	39.1	38.9	38.9	37.9	37.1	36.1	35.1	33.5	37.3
34	Comoros	39.3	39.6	39.0	37.7	37.6	39.0	38.0	38.4	39.4	38.7
35	Congo, Dem. Rep.	47.2	48.0	48.2	48.1	47.1	46.9	46.8	46.8	46.7	47.3
36	Congo, Rep.	49.5	48.2	47.2	46.8	46.8	46.2	44.7	43.3	44.6	46.4
37	Costa Rica	26.1	26.2	26.4	26.4	26.1	25.9	25.6	25.0	24.0	25.7
38	Côte d'Ivoire	41.4	43.2	44.3	45.5	46.0	46.1	46.3	46.8	47.0	45.2
39	Croatia	33.8	33.4	33.2	32.6	32.1	31.7	31.3	30.8	30.4	32.1
40	Cyprus	29.2	28.7	28.2	27.8	28.2	28.1	27.7	27.3	26.5	28.0
41	Czech Republic	19.3	19.1	18.9	18.8	18.7	18.4	17.8	17.3	17.0	18.4
42	Denmark	18.4	18.0	18.0	18.0	18.0	17.8	17.6	17.0	16.9	17.7
43	Dominican Republic	32.4	32.1	32.4	32.1	32.1	32.4	31.7	31.0	30.5	31.9
44	Ecuador	34.2	34.4	33.7	33.3	32.8	31.6	30.8	30.4	30.4	32.4
45	Egypt, Arab Rep.	35.5	35.1	35.2	35.7	35.4	35.0	34.8	34.1	33.1	34.9
46	El Salvador	46.5	46.3	46.2	45.6	45.2	44.9	44.5	43.8	43.0	45.1
47	Equatorial Guinea	32.7	32.8	32.0	31.5	31.2	30.8	30.5	30.6	30.1	31.4
48	Eritrea	38.1	40.3	39.4	39.4	40.3	40.6	40.5	41.2	41.4	40.1
49	Estonia	–	32.7	32.4	32.0	31.4	31.1	30.5	29.8	29.5	31.2
50	Ethiopia	40.6	40.3	39.5	39.6	40.1	38.6	37.7	36.3	35.1	38.6
51	Fiji	32.9	33.6	33.3	32.6	32.5	31.9	31.4	31.0	32.6	32.4

Table 2.2 (continued)

No.	Country	Years									Country average
		1999	2000	2001	2002	2003	2004	2005	2006	2007	
52	Finland	18.4	18.1	17.9	17.8	17.7	17.6	17.4	17.1	17.0	17.7
53	France	15.7	15.2	15.0	15.1	15.0	14.9	14.8	14.8	14.7	15.0
54	Gabon	46.2	48.0	47.4	47.6	47.5	48.0	47.7	48.0	47.3	47.5
55	Gambia, The	46.1	45.1	44.7	47.1	45.4	43.8	43.6	42.4	40.9	44.3
56	Georgia	68.3	67.3	67.2	67.2	65.9	65.5	65.1	63.6	62.1	65.8
57	Germany	16.4	16.0	15.9	16.1	16.3	16.1	16.0	15.6	15.3	16.0
58	Ghana	42.0	41.9	41.8	41.6	41.3	40.9	39.5	38.6	38.3	40.7
59	Greece	28.5	28.7	28.2	28.0	27.4	27.1	26.9	26.4	26.5	27.5
60	Guatemala	51.6	51.5	51.6	51.2	50.7	50.5	50.2	49.0	47.9	50.5
61	Guinea	39.7	39.6	39.3	38.7	38.8	38.5	38.4	38.9	39.2	39.0
62	Guinea-Bissau	40.4	39.6	39.6	40.7	41.5	41.9	41.7	41.5	41.6	40.9
63	Guyana	33.4	33.6	33.3	33.7	33.9	33.4	34.3	33.8	34.0	33.7
64	Haiti	54.8	55.4	56.1	56.5	56.4	57.4	57.1	57.0	57.1	56.4
65	Honduras	50.3	49.6	49.7	49.6	48.9	48.3	47.3	46.1	45.1	48.3
66	Hong Kong, China	17.0	16.6	16.6	16.6	16.4	15.9	15.5	15.0	14.7	16.0
67	Hungary	25.4	25.1	24.8	24.5	24.4	24.1	24.0	23.7	23.7	24.4
68	Iceland	16.0	15.9	15.8	16.0	15.9	15.5	15.1	15.0	15.0	15.6
69	India	23.2	23.1	22.8	22.6	22.3	22.0	21.7	21.2	20.7	22.2
70	Indonesia	19.7	19.4	19.4	19.3	19.1	18.8	18.6	18.3	17.9	18.9
71	Iran, Islamic Rep.	19.1	18.9	19.0	18.7	18.2	17.9	18.1	17.7	17.3	18.3
72	Ireland	16.1	15.9	15.9	15.9	16.0	15.8	15.6	15.5	15.4	15.8
73	Israel	22.7	21.9	22.3	22.7	22.7	22.1	21.8	21.2	20.7	22.0
74	Italy	27.8	27.1	26.7	26.8	27.0	27.0	27.1	26.9	26.8	27.0

No.	Country										
75	Jamaica	36.4	36.4	36.2	36.2	34.4	33.9	34.0	32.9	32.5	34.8
76	Japan	11.4	11.2	11.2	11.3	11.2	10.9	10.7	10.4	10.3	11.0
77	Jordan	19.4	19.4	19.2	18.9	18.7	18.3	18.0	17.5	17.2	18.5
78	Kazakhstan	43.8	43.2	42.5	42.0	41.1	40.6	39.8	38.9	38.4	41.1
79	Kenya	33.7	34.3	34.0	34.8	34.6	33.7	32.7	31.1	29.5	33.2
80	Korea, Rep.	28.3	27.5	27.3	26.9	26.8	26.5	26.3	25.9	25.6	26.8
81	Kuwait	20.1	20.1	20.2	20.3	19.3	18.8	18.1	17.9	–	19.4
82	Kyrgyz Republic	41.4	41.2	40.8	41.4	40.5	39.8	40.1	39.8	38.8	40.4
83	Lao PDR	30.9	30.6	30.2	30.0	29.8	29.4	28.9	28.4	28.0	29.6
84	Latvia	30.8	30.5	30.1	29.8	29.4	29.0	28.4	27.7	27.2	29.2
85	Lebanon	34.1	34.1	33.7	33.5	33.2	32.4	32.4	32.8	32.0	33.1
86	Lesotho	31.7	31.3	31.1	31.0	30.7	30.1	30.2	29.3	28.8	30.5
87	Liberia	44.2	43.2	43.2	43.1	45.0	45.4	44.9	44.5	44.2	44.2
88	Libya	34.7	35.1	34.5	33.8	34.9	33.9	33.1	32.0	30.9	33.7
89	Lithuania	33.8	33.7	33.3	32.8	32.0	31.7	31.0	30.4	29.7	32.0
90	Luxembourg	10.0	9.8	9.8	9.8	9.8	9.8	9.7	9.6	9.4	9.7
91	Macao, China	13.3	13.1	13.0	12.9	12.5	12.1	11.9	11.7	11.1	12.4
92	Macedonia	39.0	38.2	39.1	38.9	38.4	37.4	36.9	36.0	34.9	37.6
93	Madagascar	40.1	39.6	38.7	44.8	43.4	41.6	40.8	39.8	38.5	40.8
94	Malawi	39.9	40.3	42.5	44.4	43.4	42.5	42.6	41.3	39.4	41.8
95	Malaysia	32.2	31.1	31.6	31.5	31.2	30.7	30.4	30.0	29.6	30.9
96	Maldives	30.3	30.3	30.0	29.4	29.2	28.9	29.6	29.3	28.6	29.5
97	Mali	42.5	42.3	40.8	40.2	39.9	40.6	40.1	39.9	39.9	40.7
98	Malta	27.4	27.1	27.3	27.3	27.5	27.6	27.3	27.0	26.5	27.2
99	Mauritania	35.5	36.1	36.0	35.8	35.8	35.1	34.4	31.7	–	35.1
100	Mauritius	23.3	23.1	22.9	23.0	22.7	22.4	22.4	22.2	21.9	22.7
101	Mexico	30.8	30.1	30.3	30.4	30.5	30.1	29.9	29.2	28.8	30.0
102	Moldova	45.6	45.1	44.1	44.5	44.6	44.0	43.4	44.3	–	44.5

Table 2.2 (continued)

No.	Country	Years									Country average
		1999	2000	2001	2002	2003	2004	2005	2006	2007	
103	Mongolia	18.4	18.4	18.3	18.0	17.7	17.4	17.1	16.7	16.4	17.6
104	Morocco	36.5	36.4	35.7	35.5	35.0	34.2	34.9	33.1	33.1	34.9
105	Mozambique	41.1	40.3	40.4	39.8	39.8	39.7	38.9	38.6	–	39.8
106	Myanmar	51.6	52.6	51.5	50.7	49.0	49.1	47.8	–	–	50.3
107	Namibia	31.4	31.4	31.2	31.3	30.7	29.7	29.6	28.8	28.5	30.3
108	Nepal	37.2	36.8	36.7	37.1	36.9	36.8	36.7	36.3	36.0	36.7
109	Netherlands	13.3	13.1	13.1	13.2	13.3	13.2	13.2	13.2	13.0	13.2
110	New Zealand	13.0	12.8	12.6	12.4	12.2	12.0	12.1	12.1	12.0	12.4
111	Nicaragua	45.7	45.2	45.3	45.5	45.0	44.2	43.8	43.5	43.1	44.6
112	Niger	41.7	41.9	40.9	40.3	39.7	40.7	39.7	38.6	–	40.4
113	Nigeria	58.0	57.9	57.8	57.6	56.3	55.1	53.8	53.0	–	56.2
114	Norway	19.2	19.1	19.0	19.0	19.0	18.5	18.5	18.2	18.0	18.7
115	Oman	19.1	18.9	18.5	18.5	18.4	18.3	18.0	17.6	–	18.4
116	Pakistan	37.0	36.8	37.0	36.8	36.2	35.3	34.9	33.8	33.6	35.7
117	Panama	64.8	64.1	64.7	65.1	64.4	63.5	61.7	60.0	–	63.5
118	Papua New Guinea	35.5	36.1	36.8	37.1	37.1	37.0	37.2	37.1	36.5	36.7
119	Paraguay	38.0	39.8	39.7	40.1	39.1	38.3	38.2	37.4	–	38.8
120	Peru	60.1	59.9	60.2	59.1	58.6	57.9	57.2	55.7	53.7	58.0
121	Philippines	43.8	43.3	43.0	42.5	42.0	41.6	40.1	39.5	38.3	41.6
122	Poland	27.7	27.6	27.7	27.7	27.5	27.3	26.9	26.4	26.0	27.2
123	Portugal	23.0	22.7	22.6	22.7	23.0	23.1	23.3	23.2	23.0	23.0
124	Quatar	–	19.0	19.3	19.0	19.6	17.4	18.4	–	–	14.1
125	Romania	34.3	34.4	33.7	33.5	32.8	32.0	31.7	30.7	30.2	32.6

#	Country										
126	Russian Federation	47.0	46.1	45.3	44.5	43.6	43.0	42.4	41.7	40.6	43.8
127	Rwanda	40.5	40.3	40.6	39.9	40.7	40.2	39.3	39.1	–	40.1
128	Saudi Arabia	18.7	18.4	18.7	19.2	18.3	17.7	17.4	17.4	16.8	18.1
129	Senegal	45.0	45.1	44.5	45.1	44.4	43.2	42.3	42.4	41.7	43.7
130	Sierra Leone	48.6	48.6	47.6	45.4	44.8	44.4	44.3	43.6	42.9	45.6
131	Singapore	13.3	13.1	13.3	13.3	13.1	12.8	12.7	12.4	12.2	12.9
132	Slovak Republic	18.9	18.9	18.8	18.6	18.3	18.1	17.6	17.2	16.8	18.1
133	Slovenia	27.3	27.1	26.7	26.6	26.4	26.2	25.8	25.3	24.7	26.2
134	Solomon Islands	31.7	33.4	34.5	34.8	34.7	33.8	33.4	33.2	32.7	33.6
135	South Africa	28.4	28.4	28.4	28.0	27.8	27.1	26.5	26.0	25.2	27.3
136	Spain	23.0	22.7	22.4	22.4	22.4	22.5	22.4	22.4	22.2	22.5
137	Sri Lanka	45.2	44.6	44.6	44.1	43.8	43.9	43.4	42.9	42.2	43.9
138	Sudan	34.1	–	–	–	–	–	–	–	–	34.1
139	Suriname	39.7	39.8	39.3	38.9	38.1	36.9	36.5	35.9	35.1	37.8
140	Swaziland	43.5	41.4	41.3	40.9	40.2	40.1	39.3	38.9	–	40.7
141	Sweden	19.6	19.2	19.1	19.0	18.7	18.5	18.6	18.2	17.9	18.8
142	Switzerland	8.8	8.6	8.6	8.6	8.8	8.6	8.5	8.3	8.1	8.5
143	Syrian Arab Republic	19.3	19.3	19.2	19.1	19.3	19.1	19.0	18.7	18.5	19.1
144	Taiwan	25.7	25.4	25.7	25.4	25.2	24.7	24.5	24.2	23.9	25.0
145	Tajikistan	43.5	43.2	42.9	42.7	42.1	41.7	41.5	41.2	41.0	42.2
146	Tanzania	58.6	58.3	57.7	56.9	56.6	56.0	55.4	54.7	53.7	56.4
147	Thailand	53.4	52.6	52.4	51.5	50.2	49.6	49.0	48.5	48.2	50.6
148	Togo	34.4	35.1	35.4	34.5	34.9	35.0	35.0	34.6	–	34.9
149	Trinidad and Tobago	34.7	34.4	34.3	34.4	33.4	33.1	32.9	31.9	31.5	33.4
150	Tunisia	38.7	38.4	37.8	37.8	37.4	36.9	36.7	35.9	35.4	37.2
151	Turkey	32.7	32.1	32.8	32.4	31.8	31.0	30.0	29.5	29.1	31.3

Table 2.2 (continued)

No.	Country	Years									Country average
		1999	2000	2001	2002	2003	2004	2005	2006	2007	
152	Uganda	43.5	43.1	42.9	42.9	42.5	42.4	42.2	41.0	40.3	42.3
153	Ukraine	52.7	52.2	51.4	50.8	49.7	48.8	47.8	47.3	46.8	49.7
154	United Arab Emirates	26.3	26.4	27.0	27.4	26.3	25.4	24.8	23.5	–	25.9
155	United Kingdom	12.8	12.7	12.6	12.6	12.5	12.4	12.4	12.3	12.2	12.5
156	United States	8.8	8.7	8.8	8.8	8.7	8.6	8.5	8.4	8.4	8.6
157	Uruguay	50.5	51.1	51.7	54.0	53.6	51.1	49.2	48.5	46.1	50.6
158	Venezuela, RB	33.8	33.6	33.5	35.5	36.9	34.9	33.5	32.0	30.9	33.8
159	Vietnam	15.8	15.6	15.5	15.3	15.2	15.1	14.7	14.6	14.4	15.1
160	Yemen, Rep.	27.7	27.4	27.3	27.2	27.0	27.0	26.6	26.8	26.8	27.1
161	Zambia	49.3	48.9	48.3	48.1	47.5	46.8	46.3	45.0	43.9	47.1
162	Zimbabwe	59.6	59.4	61.5	62.8	63.7	62.3	62.0	62.3	62.7	61.8
	Time Average	34.0	33.7	33.6	33.6	33.3	32.9	32.5	32.1	31.2	

Source: Schneider et al. (2010, Table 2, pp.454–8).

activities for a variety of reasons. Among the most important are government actions, most notably, taxation and regulation.

The third conclusion is that there are regional disparities in the level of informality, but obvious regional clusters. At the top level of informality we find sub-Saharan Africa, and at the lowest level of informality we find the OECD countries.

Considering these three conclusions, it is obvious that one of the big challenges for every government is to undertake efficient incentive orientated policy measures in order to make work less attractive in the shadow economy and, hence, to make the work in the official economy more attractive. Successful implementation of such policies may lead to a stabilization, or even reduction, of the size of the shadow economy. Of course, even after 20 years of intensive research the size, causes and consequences of the shadow economy are still controversially debated in the literature and further research is necessary to improve our understanding about the shadow economy.

NOTES

1. This chapter is a summarized version of articles that have previously been published in various outlets. I acknowledge that sections 2 and 4, on theoretical considerations, are taken from Schneider et al. (2010). Section 3 is taken from Schneider and Buehn (2015). Versions of this section have also appeared in: Schneider (2007; 2008, pp. 92–4), Buehn and Schneider (2009), Schneider (2009), Feld and Schneider (2010), Schneider (2010), Buehn and Schneider (2012), Schneider and Williams (2013) and Schneider (2014, Table 1, p. 233).
2. This definition is used, for example, by Feige (1989, 1994), Schneider (2005, 2007, 2010), Feld and Schneider (2010) and Frey and Pommerehne (1984). Do-it-yourself activities are not included. For estimates of the shadow economy and the do-it-yourself activities for Germany see Buehn et al. (2009).
3. See Schneider (1986, 2005, 2007, 2010); Johnson et al. (1998a, 1998b); Tanzi (1999); Giles (1999a); Giles and Tedds (2002); Feld and Schneider (2010); and Schneider and Williams (2013).
4. See also Williams (2013) and Williams and Lansky (2013).
5. This chapter closely follows Schneider and Buehn (2015, pp. 19–28).
6. Thomas (1992); Schneider (2003, 2005, 2011); Pozo (1996); Johnson et al. (1998a, 1998b); Giles (1997a, 1997b, 1999a, 1999b, 1999c); Giles and Tedds (2002); Giles et al. (2002); Del'Anno (2003) and Del'Anno and Schneider (2004).
7. Estimation of a MIMIC model with a latent variable can be done by means of a computer program for the analysis of covariance structures, such as LISREL (Linear Structural Relations). A useful overview of the LISREL software package in an economics journal is Cziraky (2004).
8. On the other hand, in an exploratory factor analysis a model is not specified in advance, which means that beyond the specification of the number of latent variables (factors) and observed variables the researcher does not specify any structure of the model. This means that one assumes that all factors are correlated, all observable variables are directly influenced by all factors, and all measurement errors are uncorrelated with each other. In practice, however, the distinction between a confirmatory and an exploratory

factor analysis is less strong. Facing poorly fitting models, researchers using the MIMIC model often modify their models in an exploratory way in order to improve the fit. Thus, most applications fall between the two extreme cases of exploratory (non-specified model structure) and confirmatory (*ex-ante* specified model structure) factor analysis (Long, 1983a, pp. 11–17).

9. Without loss of generality, all variables are taken as standardized deviations from their means.
10. In the standard MIMIC model the measurement errors are assumed to be independent of each other, but this restriction could be relaxed (Stapleton, 1978, p. 53).
11. Other estimation procedures such as Unweighted Least Squares (ULS) and Generalized Least Squares (GLS) are also available. ULS has the advantage that it is easier to compute and leads to a consistent estimator without the assumption that the observed variables have a particular distribution. Important disadvantages of ULS are, however, that ULS does not lead to the asymptotically most efficient estimator of θ and that F_{ULS} is not scale invariant. The GLS estimator has similar statistical properties to the ML estimator but the significance tests are no longer accurate if the distribution of the observed variables has very 'fat' or 'thin' tails. Moreover, F_{GLS} accepts the wrong model more often than ML and parameter estimates tend to suffer when using F_{GLS}. Thus, ML seems to be superior (see, for example, Bollen, 1989, pp. 111–15; Olsson et al., 1999, 2000; Jöreskog and Sörbom, 2001, pp. 20–24).
12. See Appendix 4C in Bollen (1989) for details.
13. The properties are only briefly reviewed. For a detailed discussion see Bollen (1989, pp. 107–23).
14. Particularly critical are the assumptions $E(\varsigma_{ik}^2) = Var(\varsigma_i)$ for all k (homoskedasticity assumption) and $Cov(\varsigma_{ik}, \varsigma_{il}) = 0$ for all $k \neq l$ (no autocorrelation in the error terms). Unfortunately, corrections for autocorrelated and heteroskedastic error terms have not yet received sufficient attention in models with unobservable variables (Bollen, 1989, p. 58). An interesting exception is Folmer and Karmann (1992).
15. See Dell'Anno and Schneider (2009) for a detailed discussion on different benchmarking procedures.
16. This chapter closely follows Schneider et al. (2010, pp. 448–59).
17. A number of variables are not available for 2007, hence we have two different sets of cause variables.
18. x_{1t} is size of government, x_{2t} and x_{3t} are the fiscal and business freedom index, and x_{4t} represents GDP per capita. According to the MIMIC approach, all series are standardized deviations from mean.
19. The base values originate from the year 2000 except for some developing countries, for which we sometimes used base values from the year 2005 because of data availability. The MIMIC index has been adjusted to the positive range by adding a positive constant.

REFERENCES

Ahumada, H., F. Alvaredo and A. Canavese (2007), 'The monetary method and the size of the shadow economy: a critical assessment', *Review of Income and Wealth*, **53** (2), 363–71.

Bollen, K.A. (1989), *Structural Equations with Latent Variables*, New York: Wiley.

Breusch, T. (2005a), 'The Canadian underground economy: an examination of Giles and Tedds', *Canadian Tax Journal*, **53**, 367–91.

Breusch, T. (2005b), 'Estimating the underground economy using MIMIC models', Working Paper, available at: http://econwpa.wustl.edu/eps/em/papers/0507/0507003.pdf.

Buehn, A. and F. Schneider (2009), 'Shadow economies and corruption all over the world: revised estimates for 120 countries', *Economics: The Open-Access, Open-Assessment E-Journal*, **1** (2007-9), 1–53 (Version 2), available at http://dx.doi.org/10.5018/economics-ejournal.ja.2007-9.

Buehn, A. and F. Schneider (2012), 'Shadow economies around the world: novel insights, accepted knowledge, and new estimates', *International Tax and Public Finance*, **19** (1), 139–71.

Buehn, A., A. Karmann and F. Schneider (2009), 'Shadow economy and do-it-yourself activities: the German case', *Journal of Institutional and Theoretical Economics*, **164** (4), 701–22.

Cassar, A. (2001), 'An index of the underground economy in Malta', *Bank of Valletta Review*, **23**, 44–62.

Cziraky, D. (2004), 'LISREL 8.54: a program for structural equation modelling with latent variables', *Journal of Applied Econometrics*, **19**, 135–41.

Dell'Anno, R. (2003), 'Estimating the shadow economy in Italy: a structural equation approach', Working Paper 2003-7, Department of Economics, University of Aarhus, Denmark.

Dell'Anno, R. (2007), 'The shadow economy in Portugal: an analysis with the MIMIC approach', *Journal of Applied Economics*, **10**, 253–77.

Dell'Anno, R. and F. Schneider (2004), 'The shadow economy of Italy and other OECD countries: what do we know?', Discussion Paper, Department of Economics, University of Linz, Austria.

Dell'Anno, R. and F. Schneider (2009), 'A complex approach to estimate shadow economy: the structural equation modelling', in M. Faggnini and T. Looks (eds), *Coping with the Complexity of Economics*, Berlin: Springer, pp. 110–30.

Dell'Anno, R. and O.H. Solomon (2008), 'Shadow economy and unemployment rate in USA: is there a structural relationship? An empirical analysis', *Applied Economics*, **40**, 2537–55.

Feige, E.L. (1989), *The Underground Economies: Tax Evasion and Information Distortion*, Cambridge: Cambridge University Press.

Feige, E.L. (1994), 'The underground economy and the currency enigma', *Supplement to Public Finance/Finances Publiques*, **49**, 119–36.

Feld, L. and F. Schneider (2010), 'Survey on the shadow economy and undeclared earnings in OECD countries', *German Economic Review*, **11** (2), 109–49.

Folmer, H. and A. Karmann (1992), 'The permanent income hypothesis revisited – a dynamic LISREL approach', *Methods of Operations Research*, **64** (3), 355–9.

Frey, B.S. and W. Pommerehne (1984), 'The hidden economy: state and prospect for measurement', *Review of Income and Wealth*, **30** (1), 1–23.

Giles, D.E.A. (1997a), 'Causality between the measured and underground economies in New Zealand', *Applied Economics Letters*, **4**, 63–67.

Giles, D.E.A. (1997b), 'Testing the asymmetry in the measured and underground business cycles in New Zealand', *Economic Record*, **71**, 225–32.

Giles, D.E.A. (1999a), 'Measuring the hidden economy: implications for econometric modelling', *The Economic Journal*, **109** (456), 370–80.

Giles, D.E.A. (1999b), 'Modelling the hidden economy in the tax-gap in New Zealand', *Empirical Economics*, **24** (4), 621–40.

Giles, D.E.A. (1999c), 'The rise and fall of the New Zealand underground economy: are the reasons symmetric?', *Applied Economics Letters*, **6**, 185–9.

Giles, D.E.A. and L.M. Tedds (2002), *Taxes and the Canadian Underground Economy*, Toronto: Canadian Tax Foundation.

Giles, D.E.A., L.M. Tedds and W. Gugsa (2002), 'The Canadian underground and measured economies', *Applied Economics*, **34**, 2347–52.

Helberger, C. and H. Knepel (1988), 'How big is the shadow economy? A re-analysis of the unobserved-variable approach of B.S. Frey and H. Weck-Hannemann', *European Economic Review*, **32** (4), 965–76.

Jöreskog, K.G. and D. Sörbom (2001), *LISREL 8: User's Reference Guide*, Lincolnwood: Scientific Software International.

Johnson, S., D. Kaufmann and A. Shleifer (1997), 'The unofficial economy in transition', *Brookings Papers on Economic Activity*, **2**, 159–221.

Johnson, S., D. Kaufmann and P. Zoido-Lobatón (1998a), 'Regulatory discretion and the unofficial economy', *The American Economic Review*, **88** (2), 387–92.

Johnson, S., D. Kaufmann and P. Zoido-Lobatón (1998b), *Corruption, Public Finances and the Unofficial Economy*, Washington, DC: The World Bank.

Long, J.S. (1983a), *Confirmatory Factor Analysis*, Beverly Hills, CA: Sage Publishing Company.

Long, J.S. (1983b), *Covariance Structure Models: An Introduction to LISREL*, Beverly Hills: Sage Publishing Company.

Olssen, U.H., S.V. Troye and R.D. Howell (1999), 'Theoretic fit and empirical fit: the performance of maximum likelihood versus generalized least squares estimation in structural equations models', *Multivariate Behavioral Research*, **34** (1), 31–58.

Olssen, U.H., T. Foss, S.V. Troye and R.D. Howell (2000), 'The performance of ML, GLS, and WLS estimation in structural equation modeling under conditions of misspecification and nonnormality', *Structural Equation Modeling*, **7**, 557–95.

Pozo, S. (ed.) (1996), *Exploring the Underground Economy: Studies of Illegal and Unreported Activity*, Michigan: W.E. Upjohn, Institute for Employment Research.

Schneider, F. (1986), 'Estimating the size of the Danish shadow economy using the currency demand approach: an attempt', *The Scandinavian Journal of Economics*, **88** (4), 643–68.

Schneider, F. (1997), 'The shadow economies of Western Europe', *Journal of the Institute of Economic Affairs*, **17** (3), 42–48.

Schneider, F. (2003), 'The shadow economy', in C.K. Rowley and F. Schneider (eds), *Encyclopedia of Public Choice*, Dordrecht: Kluwer Academic Publishers, pp. 286–96.

Schneider, F. (2005), 'Shadow economies around the world: what do we really know?', *European Journal of Political Economy*, **21** (3), 598–642.

Schneider, F. (2007), 'Shadow economies and corruption all over the world: new estimates for 145 countries', *Economics*, 2007–9, July.

Schneider, F. (2009), 'Size and development of the shadow economy in Germany, Austria and other OECD countries: some preliminary findings', *Revue économique*, **60** (5), 1079–116.

Schneider, F. (2010), 'The influence of public institutions on the shadow economy: an empirical investigation for OECD countries', *Review of Law and Economics*, **6** (3), 441–68.

Schneider, F. (ed.) (2011), *Handbook on the Shadow Economy*, Cheltenham, UK and Northampton, MA, USA: Edward Elgar Publishing.

Schneider, F. (2014), 'In the shadow of the state: the informal economy and informal economy labour force', *Law and Economics Review*, **5** (4), 227–48.

Schneider, F. (2015), 'Schwarzarbeit, Steuerhinterziehung und Korruption: Was ökonomische und nicht-ökonomische Faktoren zur Erklärung beitragen', *Perspektiven der Wirtschaftspolitik*, **16** (4), 412–25.

Schneider, F. and A. Buehn (2015), 'Estimating the size of the shadow economy: methods, problems and open questions', forthcoming in *Review of Behavioural Economics*.

Schneider, F. and D. Enste (2000), 'Shadow economies: size, causes, and consequences', *The Journal of Economic Literature*, **38** (1), 77–114.

Schneider, F. and C.C. Williams (2013), *The Shadow Economy*, London: IEA Institute for Economic Affairs.

Schneider, F., A. Buehn and C.E. Montenegro (2010), 'New estimates for the shadow economies all over the world', *International Economic Journal*, **24** (4), 443–61.

Smith, P. (1994), 'Assessing the size of the underground economy: the Statistics Canada perspectives', *Canadian Economic Observer*, **7**, 3.16–3.33.

Stapleton, D.C. (1978), 'Analyzing political participation data with a MIMIC model', *Sociological Methodology*, **15** (1), 52–74.

Swaminathan, H. and J. Algina (1978), 'Scale freeness in factor analysis', *Psychometrika*, **43**, 581–3.

Tanzi, V. (1999), 'Uses and abuses of estimates of the underground economy', *The Economic Journal*, **109** (456), 338–40.

Thomas, J.J. (1992), *Informal Economic Activity*, Handbooks in Economics, London: Harvester Wheatsheaf.

Williams, C.C. (2013), 'Evaluating cross-national variations in the extent and nature of informal employment in the European Union', *Industrial Relations Journal*, **44** (5–6), 479–94.

Williams, C.C. and M.A. Lansky (2013), 'Informal employment in developed and developing economies: perspectives and policy responses', *International Labor Review*, **152** (3–4), 355–80.

3. The components and determinants of the shadow economy: evidence from the Baltic countries

Tālis J. Putniņš and Arnis Sauka

1 INTRODUCTION

The aim of this chapter is to provide evidence on the size and composition of the shadow economies in Estonia, Latvia and Lithuania, as well as to explore the main factors that influence participation in the shadow economy. We use the term 'shadow economy' to refer to all legal production of goods and services that is deliberately concealed from public authorities.[1] By applying the novel, direct method of measuring the shadow economy developed in Putniņš and Sauka (2015), this chapter aims (1) to further the discussion of how the shadow economy can be measured, illustrating the advantages and disadvantages of direct methods, and (2) to provide policymakers with detailed information about the structure and determinants of the shadow economy to help them make informed policy decisions about the shadow economy in Central/Eastern Europe and beyond.

The method of measuring the shadow economy in this chapter is based on annual surveys of entrepreneurs. This approach is based on the notion that those most likely to know how much production/income goes unreported are the entrepreneurs who themselves engage in the misreporting and shadow production. Our estimates of the size of the shadow economy as a proportion of GDP (the 'Shadow Economy Index') combine misreported business income, unregistered or hidden employees, as well as unreported 'envelope' wages. The method used in this chapter requires fewer assumptions than most existing methods, in particular compared to methods based on macro indicators, and is relatively precise about what parts of the economy are captured. The Shadow Economy Index can be used through time or across sectors and countries and thus is a useful tool for evaluating the effectiveness of policy designed to minimize the shadow economy. We illustrate one of the main advantages of our method by analyzing the individual components that make up the shadow economy and thereby providing insights into the structure of the shadow economy.

Survey-based approaches face the risk of underestimating the total size of the shadow economy due to non-response and untruthful response given the sensitive nature of the topic. The Shadow Economy Index minimizes this risk by employing a number of survey and data collection techniques shown in previous studies to be effective in eliciting more truthful responses.[2] These include confidentiality with respect to the identities of respondents, framing the survey as a study of satisfaction with government policy, gradually introducing the most sensitive questions after less sensitive questions, phrasing misreporting questions indirectly and, in the analysis, controlling for factors that correlate with potential untruthful response such as tolerance towards misreporting. Further advantages and disadvantages compared to other methods are discussed in Putniņš and Sauka (2015).

The next section describes how the Index is constructed, starting with the survey and then the calculations. The third section of this chapter presents estimates of the Index and analyzes the various forms of shadow activity – the structure of the shadow economy. Sections 4 and 5 analyze the determinants of entrepreneurs' involvement in the shadow sector and their attitudes towards shadow activities. Finally, section 6 draws conclusions and discusses policy implications.

2 METHODS USED IN CONSTRUCTING THE INDEX

2.1 The Survey of Entrepreneurs

The Shadow Economy Index is based on an annual survey of company owners/managers in Estonia, Latvia and Lithuania, following the method of Putniņš and Sauka (2015). For ease of reference, we repeat the main steps in this method below and add some examples of how the method works, but refer the interested reader to Putniņš and Sauka (2015) for full details. The surveys are conducted between February and March of each year since 2010, and contain questions about shadow activity during the previous two years. For example, the survey conducted in February–March 2015 collects information about shadow activity during 2013 and 2014. The overlap of one year in consecutive survey rounds (for example, collecting information about 2013 shadow activity in both the 2014 and 2015 survey rounds) is used to validate the consistency of responses.

We use random stratified sampling to construct samples that are representative of the population of firms in each country. Starting with all active firms in each of the three Baltic countries (obtained from the Orbis database maintained by Bureau Van Dijk), for each country we form size quintiles (using book value of assets) and take equal sized random samples from each size quintile. In total a minimum of 500 phone interviews are conducted in each of the three Baltic countries in each survey round.

To increase the response rate and truthfulness of responses the questionnaire begins with non-sensitive questions about satisfaction with the government and tax policy, before moving to more sensitive questions about shadow activity and deliberate misreporting. This 'gradual' approach is recommended by methodological studies of survey design in the context of tax evasion and the shadow economy (for example, Gerxhani, 2007 and Kazemier and van Eck, 1992). Further, the survey is framed as a study of satisfaction with government policy, rather than a study of tax evasion and misreporting (similar to Hanousek and Palda, 2004). We also guarantee respondents 100 per cent confidentiality with respect to their identities.

Details of the questionnaire and the questionnaire form itself are available in Putniņš and Sauka (2015). For conciseness, here we only describe the second section of the questionnaire, which deals with shadow activity. We assess the amount of shadow activity by asking entrepreneurs to estimate the degree of underreporting of business income (net profits), underreporting of the number of employees, underreporting of salaries paid to employees and the percentage of revenues that firms pay in bribes. We use the 'indirect' approach for these questions, asking entrepreneurs about 'firms in their industry' rather than 'their firm'. This approach is discussed by Gerxhani (2007) as a method of obtaining more truthful answers, and is used by Hanousek and Palda (2004), for example. The study conducted by Sauka (2008) shows that even if asked indirectly, entrepreneurs' answers can be attributed to the particular respondent or company that the respondent represents. The second section of the questionnaire also elicits entrepreneurs' perceptions of the probability of being caught for various forms of shadow activity and the severity of penalties if caught deliberately misreporting.

In the 2015 survey, the questionnaire section on shadow activity also includes a question about the amount of unregistered business in all three Baltic countries. We ask owners/managers of registered businesses the following question: 'In some industries, in addition to registered companies such as yours, unregistered enterprises also operate but do not report any of their activity to authorities. In your opinion, what percentage of your industry's total production of goods/services is carried out by unregistered enterprises in 2014? In 2013?' Even though we ask this question to owners/managers of registered businesses, we believe that being experts in their industry they are likely to know approximately how many unregistered businesses operate in their industry. Registered companies compete with unregistered ones and therefore should be aware of such companies.

2.2   Calculation of the Index

Appendix 3A.1 illustrates the key parts of the unobserved economy and helps understand which components we measure:

- Unreported income of registered producers. This is what we refer to as the 'shadow economy' and have measured with our annual Index since 2010. It includes misreported business income, misreported 'envelope' wages, and unregistered employees, in registered companies.
- Unreported income of unregistered producers. This is an additional component of the broader unobserved economy that we have measured since 2015 and report in this chapter.
- Income from production of illegal goods/services. We still do not measure this component of the unobserved economy since it requires different methods.

The details of the Index calculation are provided in Putniņš and Sauka (2015). Here, we outline the procedure for reference, and then provide an illustrative example to convey the general idea.

The Index measures the size of the shadow economy as a percentage of GDP.[3] There are three common methods of measuring GDP: the output, expenditure and income approaches. The income approach calculates GDP as the sum of gross remuneration of employees (gross personal income) and gross operating income of firms (gross corporate income). Given our questionnaire provides company-level estimates of misreported wages and misreported income of firms, the income approach to GDP measurement provides a natural basis for aggregating company-level components of the shadow economy into estimates of the size of the aggregate shadow economy.

There are three steps in aggregating company-level components of the shadow economy into estimates of the size of the aggregate shadow economy: (1) estimate the degree of underreporting of employee remuneration and underreporting of firms' operating income using the survey responses; (2) estimate each firm's shadow production as a weighted average of its underreported employee remuneration and underreported operating income, with the weights reflecting the proportions of employee remuneration and firms' operating income in the composition of GDP; and (3) calculate a production-weighted average of shadow production across firms.

Step 1

In the first step we translate questionnaire responses into company-level estimates of (1) misreported operating income and (2) misreported employee remuneration. Underreporting of firm i's operating income, $UR_i^{Operating\ Income}$, is estimated directly from the corresponding survey question (question 7).[4] Underreporting of employee remuneration consists of two components: (1) underreporting of salaries, or 'envelope wages' (question 11); and (2) unreported employees (question 9).[5] Combining the two components, firm i's total unreported proportion of employee remuneration is:

$$UR_i^{Employee\ Remuneration} = 1 - (1 - UR_i^{Salaries})(1 - UR_i^{Employees})$$

Step 2

In the second step we combine each firm's underreported operating income and underreported employee remuneration to arrive at an estimate of that firm's unreported (shadow) production as a proportion of the firm's total production. This step follows the logic of the income approach to GDP measurement. Recognizing that the sum of wages is not necessarily equal to the sum of firms' operating income, estimating each firm's shadow production proportion requires taking a weighted average as follows:

$$Shadow\ Proportion_i = \alpha_c UR_i^{Employee\ Remuneration} + (1 - \alpha_c) UR_i^{Operating\ Income}$$

where α_c is country c's ratio of employees' remuneration (*Eurostat* item D.1) to the sum of employees' remuneration and gross operating income of firms (*Eurostat* items B.2g and B.3g). We calculate α_c for each country, c, in each year using data from *Eurostat*. Taking a weighted average of the underreporting measures rather than a simple average is important to allow the Shadow Economy Index to be interpreted as a proportion of GDP, as we illustrate in an example calculation below.

Step 3

The third step aggregates company-level estimates into country-wide estimates. Two aspects of this step are important to produce a valid country-wide estimate of the size of the shadow economy: (1) using a representative sample of companies (which we ensure with stratified random sampling), and (2) weighting companies according to their contribution to the country's GDP. We take a weighted average of underreported production, *Shadow Proportion$_i$*, across firms in country c to arrive at the Shadow Economy Index for that country:

$$INDEX_c^{Shadow\ Economy} = \sum_{i=1}^{N_c} w_i\,Shadow\ Proportion_i$$

The weights, w_i, are the relative contribution of each firm to the country's GDP, which we approximate by the relative amount of wages paid by the firm.

In reporting the Shadow Economy Index, we follow the methodology of the *World Economic Forum* in their *Global Competitiveness Report* and apply a weighted moving average of $INDEX_c^{Shadow\ Economy}$ calculated from the most recent two survey rounds.[6]

2.3 Example of Index Calculation

To illustrate how the three-step procedure outlined above works and how the aggregation of company-level shadow economy components via a series of weighted averages produces a valid estimate of the aggregate shadow economy, consider the following simplified example. Suppose in an economy there are 100 large companies, 100 medium companies and 100 small companies. They each produce $100, $50 and $10 of true GDP per company. They participate in the shadow economy to different extents, with large companies underreporting their production by 20 per cent, medium companies by 40 per cent and small companies by 50 per cent. (These numbers correspond to the *Shadow Proportion$_i$* variable that is computed in Step 2.) This example is illustrated in Table 3.1 and shows that total reported production in the economy is $11 500, total shadow economy is $4500, giving true hypothetical GDP of $16 000 and a shadow economy that is 28.125 per cent of GDP ($4500/$16 000).

If we could observe all firms in the economy, then a weighted average of their individual shadow proportions would give an identical estimate of the shadow economy as a percentage of GDP, that is,

$$INDEX_c^{Shadow\ Economy} = 0.625 \times 20\% + 0.3125 \times 40\% + 0.0625 \times 50\%$$

$$= 28.125\%\ of\ GDP$$

But we cannot survey *all* companies, so we survey a sample that is stratified by size and randomly selected within size quintiles. In our example above, suppose we were to sample 10 of the 100 large companies, 10 of the 100 medium companies and 10 of the 100 small companies. Then our sample is as shown in Table 3.2.

Because our sample is a size-stratified random sample, although we are only measuring one tenth of the total economy, the shadow economy

Table 3.1 The full economy

Company size	Production	Weight	Shadow Proportion (%)	Number of such companies in economy	Total reported production	Total shadow production
Large	Each produces $100 of GDP of which $80 is reported and $20 is unreported (in the shadow)	$100/$160 = 0.625	$20/$100 = 20%	100	100 × $80 = $8000	100 × $20 = $2000
Medium	Each produces $50 of GDP of which $30 is reported and $20 is unreported (in the shadow)	$50/$160 = 0.3125	$20/$50 = 40%	100	100 × $30 = $3000	100 × $20 = $2000
Small	Each produces $10 of GDP of which $5 is reported and $5 is unreported (in the shadow)	$10/$160 = 0.0625	$5/$10 = 50%	100	100 × $5 = $500	100 × $5 = $500
TOTALS				300	$11 500	$4500

Table 3.2   *The sample*

Company size	Production	Weight	Shadow Proportion (%)	Number of companies in sample	Total reported production	Total shadow production
Large	Each produces $100 of **GDP** of which $80 is reported and $20 is unreported (in the shadow)	$100/$160 = 0.625	$20/$100 = 20%	10	10 × $80 = $800	10 × $20 = $200
Medium	Each produces $50 of GDP of which $30 is reported and $20 is unreported (in the shadow)	$50/$160 = 0.3125	$20/$50 = 40%	10	10 × $30 = $300	10 × $20 = $200
Small	Each produces $10 of **GDP** of which $5 is reported and $5 is unreported (in the shadow)	$10/$160 = 0.0625	$5/$10 = 50%	10	10 × $5 = $50	10 × $5 = $50
TOTALS				30	$1150	$450

proportion in our sample is the same 28.125 per cent of GDP ($450/$1600). However, we do not directly observe these amounts of reported and unreported production. Instead, we estimate each company's *Shadow Proportion$_i$* from questionnaire responses (as detailed in Steps 1 and 2) and estimate each company's weight in the composition of GDP by comparing it to the size of other companies in the sample (proxied by total wages), and then compute the weighted average (as detailed in Step 3), which gives:

$$INDEX_c^{Shadow Economy} = 0.625 \times 20\% + 0.3125 \times 40\% + 0.0625 \times 50\%$$

$$= 28.125\% \text{ of GDP}$$

What this illustrates is that it does not matter that we have only a sample of companies; the method of taking a weighted average will (in expectation) produce the same estimate of the size of the shadow economy as a percentage of GDP. This of course relies on having a representative sample, which we achieve through stratified random sampling.

3   SHADOW ECONOMY INDEX FOR THE BALTIC COUNTRIES, 2009–14

This section reports the Shadow Economy Index in the Baltic countries during the past six years. We also separately examine each of the types of shadow activity that make up the Index, as well as bribery/corruption and the prevalence of unregistered enterprises.

Table 3.3 and Figure 3.1 report the size of the shadow economies as a percentage of GDP in the years 2009–14. The size of the shadow economy in 2009–11 is considerably higher in Latvia than in Estonia and Lithuania (for example, in 2011 the shadow economy is estimated as 30.2 per cent, 18.9 per cent and 17.1 per cent in the three countries respectively). Latvia also stands out from the neighboring countries in that it has experienced the largest reductions in the size of its shadow economy from 2009 to 2012, in both absolute and relative terms (from 36.6 per cent in 2009 to 21.1 per cent in 2012).

In the most recent year (2014) the estimated size of the shadow economy has decreased in all three Baltic countries and reached 13.2 per cent of GDP in Estonia, 12.5 per cent of GDP in Lithuania and 23.5 per cent of GDP in Latvia. The decrease in 2014, however, is statistically significant only in Lithuania and Estonia (decreases of 2.5 and 2.8 percentage points, respectively), that is, the size of the Latvian shadow economy has remained approximately unchanged from 2013 to 2014. Consequently, the

Table 3.3   Shadow Economy Index for the Baltic countries, 2009–14

	Estonia	Latvia	Lithuania
2009	20.2%	36.6%	17.7%
	(18.7%, 21.7%)	(34.3%, 38.9%)	(15.8%, 19.7%)
2010	19.4%	38.1%	18.8%
	(18.0%, 20.8%)	(35.9%, 40.3%)	(16.9%, 20.6%)
2011	18.9%	30.2%	17.1%
	(16.8%, 20.9%)	(27.6%, 32.7%)	(15.2%, 19.0%)
2012	19.2%	21.1%	18.2%
	(16.6%, 21.9%)	(18.5%, 23.6%)	(16.4%, 20.1%)
2013	15.7%	23.8%	15.3%
	(13.5%, 17.9%)	(20.7%, 26.9%)	(13.6%, 17.1%)
2014	13.2%	23.5%	12.5%
	(11.3%, 15.1%)	(20.5%, 26.6%)	(11.0%, 13.9%)
2013–14	−2.5%	−0.5%	−2.8%
	(−4.6%, −0.5%)	(−3.4%, 2.8%)	(−4.4%, −1.2%)

Note: This table reports point estimates and 95% confidence intervals for the size of the shadow economies as a proportion of GDP. The last row reports the change in the relative size of the shadow economy from 2013 to 2014.

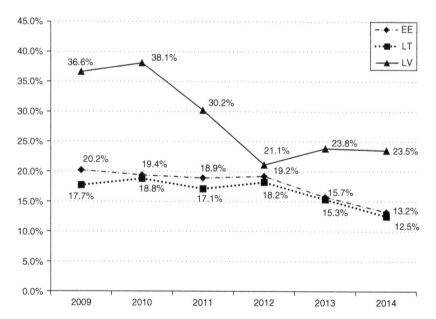

Figure 3.1   SSE Riga Shadow Economy Index for the Baltic countries, 2009–14

gap between Latvia and neighboring Baltic countries in the size of their shadow economies has further increased.

Figure 3.2 illustrates the relative size of the components of the shadow economy in each of the three countries. Similarly to results from 2013, the

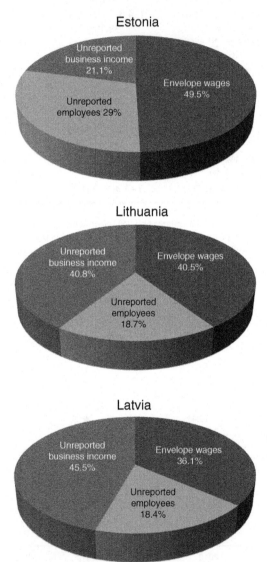

Figure 3.2   Components of the shadow economies in each of the Baltic countries, 2014

largest component of the shadow economies in Latvia and Lithuania in 2014 is unreported business income. According to our data, the proportion of the shadow economy made up by unreported business income has increased in Latvia, which is an important signal for policy makers (increase from 42.0 per cent in 2013 to 45.5 per cent in 2014). In Estonia, however, envelope wages continue to be the main component of the shadow economy (49.5 per cent in 2014). Envelope wages are the second largest component of the shadow economy in Latvia and Lithuania (36.1 per cent and 40.5 per cent accordingly).

Figures 3.3 and 3.4 illustrate the degree of underreporting of business income (profits). Figure 3.3 shows the dynamics of underreporting profits from 2009 to 2014, whereas Figure 3.4 shows the distribution of firms that underreport profits within a given range. According to Figure 3.3, Latvia is the only Baltic country where underreporting of business income has increased compared to 2013, which is also reflected in the components of the shadow economy in Figure 3.2. In Estonia underreporting of profits in 2014 is estimated as 6.7 per cent, whereas in Lithuania it is 9.4 per cent, and in contrast, in Latvia it is 21.7 per cent. Similar to 2013, approximately 40 per cent of respondents from Estonia state that underreporting 'in the industry' in 2014 is 0 per cent, that is, that companies report 100 per cent of their actual profits (see Figure 3.4). In Latvia and Lithuania, however, 100

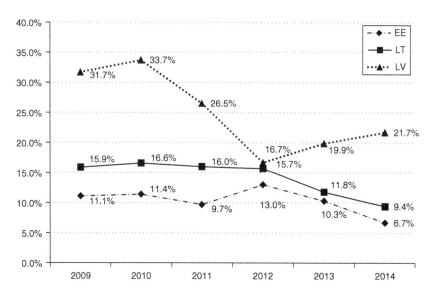

Figure 3.3   Underreporting of business income (percentage of actual profits), 2009–14

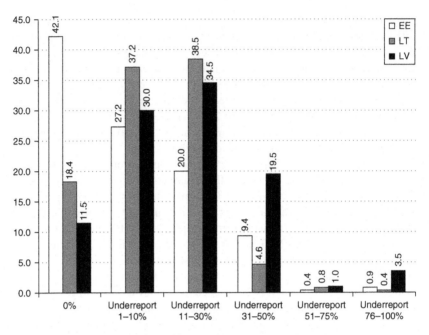

Note: The vertical axis measures the percentage of each country's respondents underreporting within the range given on the horizontal axis.

Figure 3.4   Underreporting of income (percentage of actual profits) in 2014

per cent of actual profits are reported by 11.5 per cent and 18.4 per cent of respondents, respectively.

Figures 3.5 and 3.6 illustrate the level of underreporting of the number of employees. Figure 3.5 suggests that underreporting of employees in all three Baltic countries has decreased slightly in 2014. Similar to previous years, a relatively low proportion of respondents claim that underreporting of employees in 2014 represents more than 50 per cent of employees (Figure 3.6).

Figure 3.7 indicates that, on average, envelope wages as a proportion of total wages have also decreased in all Baltic countries in 2014. The biggest decrease compared to 2013 is in Latvia (from 25.2 per cent to 20.3 per cent), whereas in Lithuania and Estonia the proportion of envelope wages in 2014 are estimated as 12.2 per cent and 13.6 per cent of total wages, respectively. Figure 3.8 shows that in 2014 most frequently companies from Latvia and Lithuania underreport 11–30 per cent of actual salaries, whereas in Estonia the figure is 1–10 per cent.

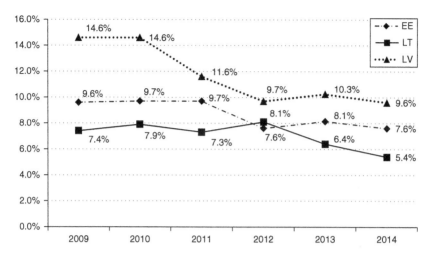

Figure 3.5   Underreporting of the number of employees (percentage of the actual number of employees), 2009–14

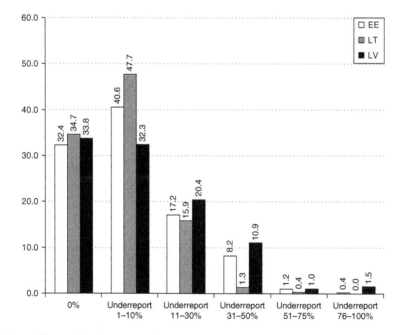

Note: The vertical axis measures the percentage of each country's respondents underreporting within the range given on the horizontal axis.

Figure 3.6   Underreporting of the number of employees in 2014

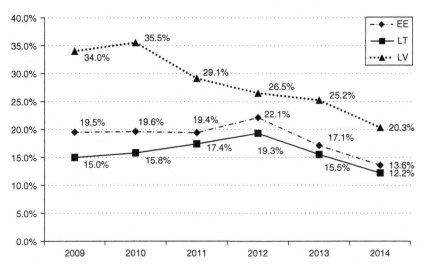

Figure 3.7　Underreporting of salaries (percentage of actual salaries), 2009–14

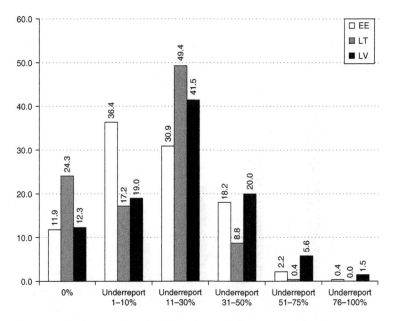

Note:　The vertical axis measures the percentage of each country's respondents underreporting within the range given on the horizontal axis.

Figure 3.8　Underreporting of salaries in 2014

Figure 3.9 indicates that during 2014 Lithuanian and Latvian companies paid proportionally more in bribes (revenues spent on 'getting things done') than Estonian companies. The level of bribery in Latvia and Lithuania during 2014 is rather similar – around 10 per cent, whereas in Estonia it has decreased to 3.4 per cent. The level of bribery in the Baltic countries during 2014, expressed as the percentage of each country's respondents making unofficial payments 'to get things done' within a given range, is further presented in Figure 3.10.

Figures 3.11 and 3.12 illustrate the percentage of the contract value that firms typically offer as a bribe to secure a contract with the government. Similar to the general level of bribery reported in Figure 3.9, the level of government bribery has decreased in Estonia. We also observe a decrease compared to 2013 in Latvia. The estimated level of the government bribery, however, has substantially increased in Lithuania, reaching 10.9 per cent of the contract value in 2014, compared to 6.2 per cent in 2013. Consistent with these findings, Figure 3.12 illustrates that the most frequent size of government bribes (proportion of the contract value) in Lithuania is higher than in the other two Baltic countries.

Table 3.4 reports estimates of the proportion of unregistered enterprises in the Baltic countries. According to our data, the proportion of unregistered enterprises in 2014 is slightly higher in Estonia, compared to Latvia and Lithuania (6.3 per cent, compared to 5.6 per cent and 5.2 per cent of

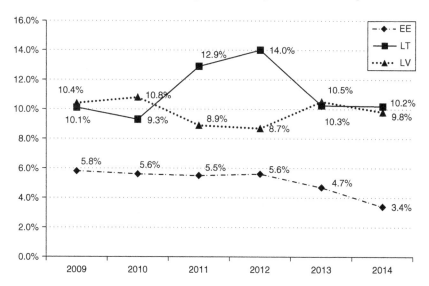

Figure 3.9   Bribery (percentage of revenue spent on payments 'to get things done'), 2009–14

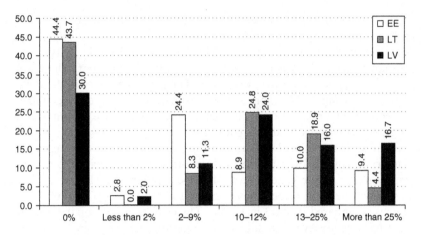

Note: The vertical axis measures the percentage of each country's respondents making unofficial payments 'to get things done' within the range given on the horizontal axis.

Figure 3.10   Bribery in 2014 as a percentage of revenue

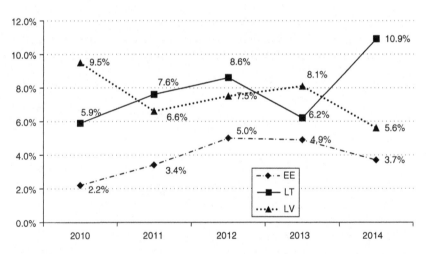

Figure 3.11   Percentage of the contract value paid to government to secure the contract, 2010–14

all enterprises, respectively – see Table 3.4). The differences across the three Baltic countries are not statistically significant. The proportion of unregistered enterprises is highest in the construction sector in all three Baltic countries. In Lithuania, a high proportion of unregistered enterprises is also observed in the wholesale sector (Figure 3.13).

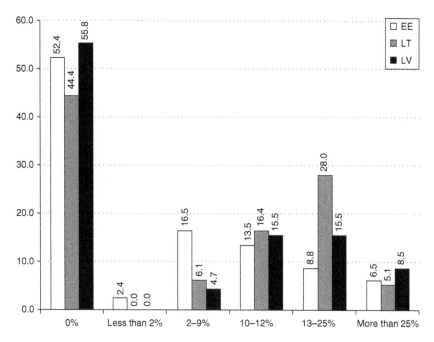

Note: The vertical axis measures the percentage of each country's respondents paying bribes within a given range of the contract value to secure contracts with government.

Figure 3.12   Bribing government in 2014

Table 3.4   Proportion of unregistered enterprises in the Baltic countries, 2013–2014

	Estonia	Latvia	Lithuania
2013	7.6%	6.2%	5.4%
	(5.4%, 9.9%)	(5.3%, 7.1%)	(4.2%, 6.6%)
2014	6.3%	5.6%	5.2%
	(4.5%, 8.2%)	(4.5%, 6.7%)	(4.5%, 6.0%)

Note: This table reports point estimates and 95% confidence intervals of unregistered enterprises as a percentage of all enterprises in Estonia, Latvia and Lithuania.

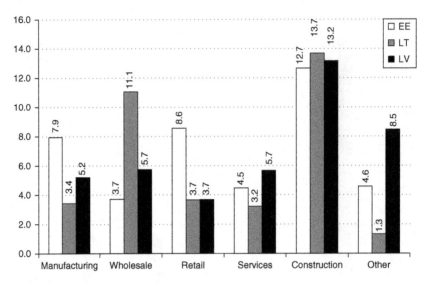

Figure 3.13   Proportion of unregistered enterprises in the Baltic countries in 2014 by industry

4   DETERMINANTS OF SHADOW ACTIVITY

We use regressions to analyze the determinants of firms' involvement in the shadow economy. For the regressions, we use pooled data from the past five survey rounds, which gives a panel that spans the years 2010–14 and has a cross-section of approximately 1500 firms per year. The dependent variable in all regressions is the level of the firm's involvement in the shadow economy. The independent variables are various firm-level characteristics, attitudes, sector dummy variables, region and year fixed effects.

The regression results are reported in Appendix 3A.2. Model 1 includes most of the measured determinants of shadow activity and dummy variables for Estonian and Lithuanian firms (Latvian firms are the base case). It excludes variables that measure the firm's perceived probability of being caught for involvement in the shadow economy (*DetectionProbability*) and the firm's perceived penalties for being caught (*PenaltyForDetection*) in order to make use of data from 2010 (the variables *DetectionProbability* and *PenaltyForDetection* are only collected from 2011 onwards). Model 2 includes the full set of determinants of shadow activity and thus restricts the sample to 2011–13. Model 3 replaces the country dummy variables with region dummy variables (with Kurzeme, Latvia, as the omitted category). Model 4 adds year fixed effects. Model 5 replaces *Satisfaction* with a dummy variable for whether the interview is conducted in the Russian language.

The country dummy variables suggest that during the sample period, the size of the shadow economy is smaller in Estonia and Lithuania relative to Latvia, after controlling for a range of explanatory factors, and the differences are statistically significant. Tolerance towards tax evasion is positively associated with the firm's stated level of income/wage underreporting, that is, entrepreneurs that view tax evasion as a tolerated behavior tend to engage in more informal activity. The measures of tolerance also serve the important role of controlling for possible understating of the extent of shadow activity (untruthful responses) due to the sensitivity of the topic.[7]

The regression coefficients indicate that the effect of perceived detection probabilities and penalties on the tendency for firms to engage in deliberate misreporting is consistent with the predictions of rational choice models; that is, the higher the perceived probability of detection and the larger the penalties, the lower the amount of tax evasion and misreporting. The effect of detection probability in particular stands out as being a remarkably strong deterrent of shadow activity. This evidence suggests a possible policy tool for reducing the size of the shadow economies, namely increasing the probability of detection of misreporting. This could be done via an increased number of tax audits, whistle-blower schemes that provide incentives to report information to authorities about non-compliant companies, and investment in tax evasion detection technology.

Empirical studies find that the actual amount of tax evasion is considerably lower than predicted by rational choice models and the difference is often attributed to the second, broader, set of tax evasion determinants: attitudes and social norms. These factors include perceived justice of the tax system, that is, attitudes about whether the tax burden and administration of the tax system are fair, attitudes about how appropriately taxes are spent and how much firms trust the government. Finally, tax evasion is also influenced by social norms such as ethical values and moral convictions, as well as fear of feelings of guilt and social stigmatization if caught. We measure firms' attitudes using four questions about their satisfaction with the State Revenue Service, the government's tax policy, business legislation and the government's support for entrepreneurs.

The regression results indicate that a firm's satisfaction with the tax system and the government is negatively associated with the firm's involvement in the shadow economy; that is, dissatisfied firms engage in more shadow activity, satisfied firms engage in less. This result is consistent with previous research on tax evasion, and offers an explanation of why the size of the shadow economy is larger in Latvia than in Estonia and Lithuania; namely that Latvian firms engage in more shadow activity because they are more dissatisfied with the tax system and the government. Analyzing each of the four measures of satisfaction separately, we find that shadow activity is most strongly related to dissatisfaction with business legislation and the State Revenue Service, followed by the government's tax policy and support for entrepreneurs.

A natural question to ask is why Latvian companies are more dissatisfied. One explanation is that the business environment (actions of the government and SRS) is less favorable to companies in Latvia. It may also be that the ethnic composition of the country plays a role, as minority groups may feel less engaged in society and involved in the country-level decision making. To test this hypothesis, specifically with respect to the Russian-speaking population in each of the countries, in Model 5 we replace the *Satisfaction* variable with a dummy variable for whether the interview is conducted in the Russian language. Consistent with the hypothesis, Model 5 indicates that the companies of Russian-speaking respondents tend to be involved in a slightly higher (3.6 percentage points) level of shadow activity, controlling for other factors. This effect is moderately statistically significant. Given that Latvia has a proportionally larger Russian-speaking population than Estonia and Lithuania, this result suggests that the mix of ethnicities may contribute to the difference in the size of the shadow economies in the Baltic countries.

Another strong (and statistically significant) determinant of involvement in the shadow economy is firm size, with smaller firms engaging in more shadow activity than larger firms, although the descriptive statistics suggest the relation may be non-monotonic. The statistically significant coefficient on firm age suggests that younger firms engage in more shadow activity than older firms. A possible explanation for these two relations is that small, young firms use tax evasion as a means of being competitive against larger and more established competitors. The sector dummy variables suggest that firms in the construction sector and services tend to engage in more shadow activity than firms in other sectors such as retail. The association between shadow activity and the average wage paid by a firm or a firm's change in profits (or employees or turnover) is not significant across all specifications.

5   ENTREPRENEURS' ATTITUDES REGARDING SHADOW ACTIVITIES

In addition to estimating the size of shadow economy and its influential factors, we also elicit entrepreneurs' opinions regarding various aspects of the shadow economy in the Baltic countries. We believe that some of these data might be useful to policy makers, at least as complementary information.

We ask entrepreneurs a number of questions about the motivation for participating in tax evasion. Entrepreneurs are presented with various statements, which they are asked to assess on a 1–7 scale, where '1' represents 'completely agree' and '7' represents 'completely disagree'. The results are summarized in Figure 3.14. The key finding in 2014 is that

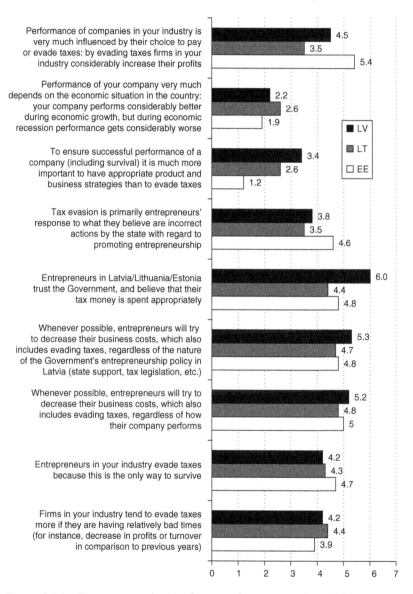

Figure 3.14   Entrepreneurs' attitudes regarding tax evasion, 2014

Latvian entrepreneurs disagree more with the statement that they trust the government and believe that tax money is spent adequately. Entrepreneurs in Latvia also disagree more strongly than entrepreneurs in Lithuania and Estonia that to ensure competitiveness it is more appropriate to invest in new products and strategies rather than to evade taxes.

6   DISCUSSION AND CONCLUSIONS

This chapter estimates the size, structure and determinants of the shadow economy using surveys of entrepreneurs in the Baltic countries. Our method uses a number of surveying and data collection techniques shown in previous studies to be effective in eliciting relatively truthful responses. The Shadow Economy Index combines estimates of misreported business income, unregistered or hidden employees, as well as unreported 'envelope' wages to obtain estimates of the shadow economies as a proportion of GDP, and we separately estimate the proportion of unregistered enterprises.

Our first key finding is about recent trends in the Baltic shadow economies. During 2014, Estonia and Lithuania have continued their long-term trend of gradually reducing the size of their shadow economies. Our estimates suggest that the Estonian and Lithuanian shadow economies contracted by approximately 2.5–2.8 percentage points and now account for 12.5 per cent to 13.2 per cent of GDP. The contraction has been across all components of the shadow economies (misreported business income, 'envelope' wages and unregistered employees). In contrast, the Latvian shadow economy has remained largely unchanged in aggregate compared to the previous year and is estimated at around 23.5 per cent of GDP. The different dynamics of the shadow economies means that there is now a large difference in their size – the Latvian shadow economy is almost double the size of those in neighboring countries. According to our data, unregistered companies make up around 5 per cent to 8 per cent of all enterprises. They are most widespread in the construction sector.

Although in aggregate the size of the shadow economy in Latvia has not changed much in 2014, its composition has changed. Envelope wages have declined, but their contraction is offset by a corresponding increase in corporate tax evasion – companies in Latvia misreport a larger proportion of their business income in 2014 compared to the previous two years. Unreported business income has overtaken envelope wages and now makes up around 46 per cent of the total Latvian shadow economy. By far the worst sector is construction, where shadow activity in Latvia is estimated to be as high as 48.9 per cent (it is also the sector with the highest level of shadow activity in Estonia and Lithuania, but with more modest levels of 21 per cent and 19 per cent). As the Latvian economy continues to recover from the crisis, real estate prices have risen from their post-crisis lows and the construction sector is regaining activity after having almost ground to a halt. The recovery in the construction sector with its high level of shadow activity has offset the declining levels of shadow activity in other sectors.

In addition to providing rich information about the structure of the shadow economy (how the different components have changed through time), another advantage of our direct method of measuring the shadow economy is the ability to analyze the factors that make Baltic entrepreneurs more likely to operate in the shadow sector. We find that firms that are dissatisfied with the tax system or the government tend to engage in more shadow activity; satisfied firms engage in less. This result is consistent with previous research on tax evasion, and has implications for policy measures to reduce the size of the shadow economy. We also find that smaller, younger firms engage in proportionally more shadow activity than larger, older firms, consistent with the anecdotal evidence that tax evasion is used by firms to gain a competitive edge, and that having an edge is important in competing in an established market. Finally, the level of tax evasion and deliberate misreporting among Baltic companies is responsive to the perceived probabilities of being caught and to the expected penalties for being caught. In particular, companies that perceive the probability of being caught as being higher tend to engage in less shadow activity.

Our results have several noteworthy implications. For policy makers, our results highlight the need for continued reforms and actions that combat the shadow economy, in particular in Latvia. We believe the widening shadow economy gap between Latvia and neighboring countries (after the gap was nearly closed in 2012) partly reflects the slow-down in Latvian policy maker efforts in combating shadow activity. The data from 2011 and 2012 support the notion that large-scale and serious efforts to combat the shadow economy can make a difference and reduce the size of the shadow economy. In exchange for financial assistance during the crisis, the Latvian government undertook over 60 different policy actions to combat the informal economy between 2010 and 2013, with most of the reforms front-loaded, that is, taking effect in 2010 and 2011. Our estimates of the size of the Latvian shadow economy in previous years are consistent with the notion that the deliberate policy efforts aimed at reducing shadow sector activity were indeed successful; Latvia experienced a large decline in the size of its shadow economy from a peak of 38 per cent of GDP in 2010 to a low of 21 per cent in 2012. However, following the completion of this substantial package of policy actions, Latvian policy maker efforts targeting the shadow economy have substantially subsided. The reduced regulatory/policy effort is likely to have contributed to the ending of the consecutive contractions in the size of the Latvian shadow economy and serves as a strong signal that reducing the shadow economy requires continued effort from policy makers and enforcement agencies such as the State Revenue Service. Now is the time for Latvian policy makers to implement a second large-scale and serious policy package targeting the shadow economy, as was done during 2010–13. The reforms could focus on misreporting of business income, as well as the construction sector, as these are the most problematic parts of the shadow economy.

Our results on the determinants of shadow activity in the Baltic countries suggest a number of approaches for policy makers to reduce the size of the Baltic shadow economies. First, reducing dissatisfaction with the tax system is likely to decrease the size of the shadow economies. Addressing this issue could involve actions such as making tax policy more stable (less frequent changes in procedures and tax rates), making taxes more 'fair' from the perspective of businesses and employees, and increasing the transparency with which taxes are spent. Second, increasing the probability of detection is expected to reduce shadow activity. This could be achieved via an increased number of tax audits, whistle-blower schemes that provide incentives to report information to authorities about non-compliant companies, and investment in tax evasion detection technology. Third, we find that the mix of ethnicities also has an impact on the level of shadow economy, possibly as a result of minorities feeling less engaged in society and country-level decision making. Therefore, addressing social cohesion and integration of minorities may also lead to a reduction in the shadow economy.

NOTES

1. This definition corresponds to what the Organisation for Economic Co-operation and Development (OECD) in their comprehensive 2002 handbook 'Measuring the Non-observed Economy' as well as the System of National Accounts (SNA 1993) refer to as 'underground production'. It is also consistent with definitions employed by other researchers (for example, the World Bank study of 162 countries by Schneider et al. (2010)). We elaborate further on the components of the unobserved economy in section 2.
2. For example, Gerxhani (2007), Kazemier and van Eck (1992), and Hanousek and Palda (2004).
3. Because we do not measure shadow activity in the state (public) sector, our estimates refer to private sector shadow activity as a percentage of private sector domestic output.
4. Question 7 asks 'Please estimate the approximate degree of underreporting business income by firms in your industry in the previous year'.
5. Question 11 asks 'Please estimate the approximate degree of underreporting salaries paid

to employees by companies in your industry in the previous year (for instance, if in reality an employee receives EUR 400, but the reported salary is EUR 100, then underreporting is 75%; if EUR 400 and EUR 200, then underreporting is 50%)'. Question 9 asks 'Please estimate the approximate degree of underreporting number of employees by firms in your industry in the previous year'.

6. For details on this procedure see the *Global Competitiveness Report 2011–2012* (Box 3, p. 64), which is available at: http://www3.weforum.org/docs/WEF_GCR_Report_2011-12.pdf.

7. For example, consider two firms that underreport income/wages by 40 per cent each, but the first operates in an environment in which tax evasion is considered highly unethical and is not tolerated, whereas the second operates in an environment in which tax evasion is relatively tolerated. The first firm might state that its estimate of underreporting is around 20 per cent (a downward biased response due to the more unethical perception of tax evasion) whereas the second firm might answer honestly that underreporting is around 40 per cent. This example illustrates that failure to control for the sensitivity of tax evasion (proxied here by tolerance) can lead to biased comparisons.

REFERENCES

Gerxhani, K. (2007), '"Did you pay your taxes?" How (not) to conduct tax evasion surveys in transition countries', *Social Indicators Research*, **80**, 555–81.

Hanousek, J. and Palda, F. (2004), 'Quality of government services and the civic duty to pay taxes in the Czech and Slovak Republics, and other transition countries', *Kyklos*, **57** (2), 237–52.

Kazemier, B. and van Eck, R. (1992), 'Survey investigations of the hidden economy', *Journal of Economic Psychology*, **13**, 569–87.

Putniņš, T.J. and Sauka, A. (2015), 'Measuring the shadow economy using company managers', *Journal of Comparative Economics*, **43** (2), 471–90.

Sauka, A. (2008), *Productive, Unproductive and Destructive Entrepreneurship: A Theoretical and Empirical Exploration*, Frankfurt am Main: Peter Lang.

Schneider, F., Buehn, A. and Montenegro, C. (2010), 'New estimates for the shadow economies all over the world', *International Economic Journal*, **24** (4), 443–61.

APPENDIX 3A.1

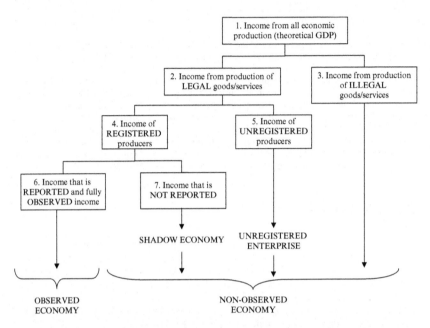

Notes: Income refers to both business income and employee income. Illegal production (3) includes production of goods/services that are illegal regardless of who produces them (e.g., narcotics, prostitution) and production of goods that themselves are legal but the production is illegal because it is carried out by an unauthorized producer (e.g., unlicensed surgeons, unlicensed production of alcohol). Goods/services that are produced legally (2) can still involve breaches of the law at the registration or reporting stage (e.g., intentional underreporting of profit to evade taxes). Most of the income generated from producing legal goods is reported by registered firms and therefore fully captured in official GDP (6). However, some proportion of income is intentionally hidden from authorities either by not registering the enterprise (5) or by misreporting wages or company earnings (7). Following other studies, we refer to the latter (7) as the 'shadow economy', and use the term 'non-observed' economy in a broader sense referring to illegal goods/services, activities of unregistered enterprises and the shadow economy.

Figure 3A.1   Observed and non-observed components of GDP

Table 3A.1   Determinants of firms' involvement in shadow activity

	Model 1	Model 2	Model 3	Model 4	Model 5
Intercept	36.955***	41.197***	39.625***	36.378***	34.585***
	(15.53)	(12.83)	(10.50)	(9.53)	(9.10)
D_EE	-6.395***	-6.467***			
	(-6.31)	(-5.04)			
D_LT	-9.430***	-5.688***			
	(-8.89)	(-4.00)			
Tolerance_TaxEvasion	1.570***	1.208***	1.202***	1.129***	1.388***
	(4.90)	(3.18)	(3.14)	(2.94)	(3.71)
Satisfaction	-1.591***	-1.815***	-1.772***	-1.818***	
	(-4.32)	(-4.03)	(-3.81)	(-3.96)	
DetectionProbability		-2.196***	-2.155***	-2.057***	-2.230***
		(-4.29)	(-4.18)	(-4.01)	(-4.40)
PenaltyForDetection		-1.130**	-1.114**	-0.995**	-0.777*
		(-2.49)	(-2.48)	(-2.23)	(-1.74)
ln(FirmAge)	-3.891***	-4.582***	-4.430***	-4.016***	-3.852***
	(-4.96)	(-5.07)	(-4.80)	(-4.37)	(-4.20)
ln(Employees)	-0.818***	-1.096***	-1.109***	-1.454***	-1.384***
	(-2.71)	(-3.23)	(-3.22)	(-4.20)	(-4.12)
AverageWage	-0.001*	-0.001**	-0.002**	-0.001**	-0.002***
	(-1.96)	(-2.29)	(-2.54)	(-2.35)	(-2.72)
ChangeInProfit	0.011***	0.017**	0.017**	0.014*	0.016**
	(2.99)	(2.10)	(2.06)	(1.66)	(1.98)
D_Wholesale	0.385	0.338	0.078	-0.636	-0.553
	(0.32)	(0.25)	(0.06)	(-0.46)	(-0.41)

Table 3A.1 (continued)

	Model 1	Model 2	Model 3	Model 4	Model 5
D_Retail	1.025	1.507	1.447	1.147	1.582
	(0.83)	(1.05)	(1.00)	(0.80)	(1.12)
D_Services	1.717	2.097*	1.844	1.807	1.938
	(1.64)	(1.75)	(1.51)	(1.50)	(1.63)
D_Construction	4.596***	5.416***	5.624***	5.552***	5.774***
	(3.49)	(3.64)	(3.75)	(3.73)	(3.90)
D_OtherSector	−0.764	1.321	1.323	0.830	0.870
	(−0.47)	(0.65)	(0.64)	(0.40)	(0.43)
D_RU					3.595*
					(1.68)
Region fixed effects	No	No	Yes	Yes	Yes
Year fixed effects	No	No	No	Yes	Yes
Data	2010–2014	2011–2014	2011–2014	2011–2014	2011–2014
R-squared	10.5%	13.0%	13.9%	15.3%	14.8%

Notes: This table reports coefficients from regressions of firms' unreported proportion of production (dependent variable; see section 2 for details of calculation) on various determinants of shadow activity, using the pooled sample of Estonian, Latvian and Lithuanian firms, between 2010 and 2014. *D_EE* and *D_LT* are dummy variables for Estonian and Lithuanian firms, respectively (Latvian firms are the omitted category). *Tolerance_ TaxEvasion* is the firm's response to Question 5, with higher scores indicating more tolerance. *Satisfaction* is the first principal component of the firm's responses to Questions 1–4, with higher scores indicating higher satisfaction with the country's tax system and government. *DetectionProbability* and *PenaltyForDetection* measure the firm's perception of the probability of being caught for shadow activity and the severity of penalties conditional on being caught (calculated as the first principal component of responses to Questions 17(i)–16(iv), and the response to Question 18, respectively). ln(*FirmAge*) and ln(*Employees*) are the natural logarithms of the firm's age in years and its number of employees. *AverageWage* is the average monthly salary in EUR paid by the firm. *ChangeInProfit* is the firm's percentage change in net sales profit relative to the previous year. *D_Wholesale* to *D_OtherSector* are sector dummy variables with manufacturing as the omitted category. *D_RU* is a dummy variable that takes the value one if the respondent elected to answer the questionnaire in the Russian language. ***, ** and * indicate statistical significance at the 1%, 5% and 10% levels. T-statistics are reported in parentheses.

4. The participation of the self-employed in the shadow economy in the European Union[1]

Colin C. Williams, Ioana A. Horodnic and Jan Windebank

INTRODUCTION

Is it common for the self-employed to participate in the shadow economy? Are some groups of the self-employed more likely to participate than others? And if so, who among the self-employed display a greater propensity to participate in the shadow economy? The aim of this chapter is to seek answers to these questions. Over the past decade or so, there has been a growth in the literature which examines how the self-employed have a greater propensity to participate in the shadow economy and how much of the work in the shadow economy is undertaken on a self-employed basis (Barbour and Llanes, 2013; Copisarow, 2004; Copisarow and Barbour, 2004; ILO, 2013; Llanes and Barbour, 2007; Williams, 2015a, 2015b; Williams and Horodnic, 2015; Williams et al., 2011). Until now, however, two competing perspectives have prevailed regarding which groups of the self-employed are most likely to participate in the shadow economy. On the one hand, and the predominant perspective, is that the self-employed participating in the shadow economy are those who might loosely be referred to as the 'marginalized' self-employed, such as those who enter self-employment because they cannot find formal employment (Barbour and Llanes, 2013; Brill, 2011; Katungi et al., 2006; Llanes and Barbour, 2007). This is here referred to as the 'marginalization thesis'. On the other hand, an alternative view here referred to as the 'reinforcement thesis' argues the opposite, namely that it is less marginalized groups of the self-employed who benefit most from the shadow economy and thus that the shadow economy reinforces, rather than decreases, the economic inequalities found within the self-employed (Pahl, 1984; Williams et al., 2011). So far, however, no known studies have evaluated the validity of these competing viewpoints. The intention in this chapter is therefore to fill that gap by examining their validity in relation to the European Union.

To do this, in the first section, we review the competing viewpoints regarding which groups of the self-employed participate in the shadow economy, namely the dominant marginalization thesis, which asserts that it is predominantly marginalized groups, and the emergent reinforcement thesis, which asserts that relatively affluent, better educated and more professional groups of the self-employed are the ones who benefit more from the shadow economy. Finding that no studies have so far evaluated these competing perspectives, this gap begins to be filled in the second section by introducing the data and methods used to examine who amongst the self-employed participates in the shadow economy. Reporting a multi-level mixed-effects logistic regression analysis of data on the participation of the self-employed in the shadow economy derived from a 2013 Eurobarometer survey conducted across the 28 member states of the European Union (EU-28), the third section then reports the descriptive findings on which groups of the self-employed display a greater propensity to participate in the shadow economy. The fourth section then reports the results of the multilevel mixed-effects logistic regression analysis, which identifies the self-employed groups most likely to participate in the shadow economy when other characteristics are held constant. The fifth and final section then brings the chapter to a close by discussing the theoretical and policy implications of these findings. This displays the need for not only a more nuanced theoretical understanding but also a more variegated and finer-grained approach by policy-makers when targeting the self-employed in order to tackle the shadow economy.

Before commencing, however, it is necessary to outline briefly how the shadow economy is defined in this chapter. Reflecting the broad consensus in both the scholarly and policy literature, the shadow economy is here seen to include paid activities not declared to the authorities for tax, social security and/or labour law purposes (Dekker et al., 2010; European Commission, 2007; OECD, 2012; Schneider, 2008; Schneider and Williams, 2013; Williams, 2005, 2006). If there are other absences or deficiencies, then the activities are not generally defined as part of the shadow economy. For example, if the goods and/or services being exchanged are illegal (for example, illegal drugs), then such activities will be defined as part of the wider 'criminal' economy rather than the shadow economy (McElwee et al., 2014; Smith and McElwee, 2013), and if there is no payment then they will be part of the separate unpaid economy. Nevertheless, and as with any definition, blurred boundaries remain, such as whether to include work rewarded in the form of gifts or in-kind reciprocal favours, rather than money. In this chapter, however, activities rewarded with gifts or in-kind favours are excluded. Only paid activities not declared to the authorities for tax, social security and/or labour law purposes are included.

SELF-EMPLOYMENT, THE SHADOW ECONOMY AND THE MARGINALIZATION THESIS

To understand the contrasting views on which groups of the self-employed participate in the shadow economy, it is first necessary to understand the wider theories from which these views are derived. For much of the twentieth century, the 'modernization thesis' dominated discourse on the shadow economy, whereby there was seen to be a natural and inevitable shift towards the formalization of goods and services provision as societies become more 'advanced'. From this viewpoint, therefore, all economies are considered to witness the same linear and unidimensional trajectory of economic development whereby shadow work steadily disappears and is replaced by formal goods and services provision. To witness the dominance of this conceptualization of economic development, one has only to consider how it lies at the heart of the view that different nations are at varying stages of economic development. The degree to which economies are formalized, that is to say, is frequently taken as the measuring rod used to define 'third world' countries as 'developing', and 'first world' nations as 'developed'. From the viewpoint of the modernization thesis, in consequence, the existence of supposedly traditional informal activities is taken as a manifestation of 'backwardness' and it is assumed that they will disappear with economic progress (modernization). In this conceptualization, the shadow economy is primitive or traditional, stagnant, marginal, residual, weak and about to be extinguished. It is a leftover of pre-capitalist formations and the inexorable and inevitable march of modernization will eradicate such work. Such a view of the shadow economy as some kind of traditional outdated type of work that is in long-term terminal decline and will vanish with the pursuance of modernization, however, has come under considerable criticism in recent years, not least due to the recognition that in the contemporary era, it remains a persistent and extensive feature of the global economy (ILO, 2002a, 2002b, 2013; Jütting and Laiglesia, 2009; Schneider, 2008; Williams, 2013, 2014b). Indeed, of the 3 billion people in the global workforce, an OECD report suggests that nearly two-thirds (1.8 billion) have their main employment in the shadow economy (Jütting and Laiglesia, 2009).

Rather than depict the shadow economy as some leftover or a 'a mere "lag" from traditional relationships of production' (Castells and Portes, 1989: 13), an alternative view that has emerged is one that reads such work as a new form of advanced capitalist exploitation that is a direct product of the neo-liberal project of deregulation taking hold (for example, Castells and Portes, 1989; Sassen, 1996; Taiwo, 2013). The argument has been that the processes associated with economic globalization are causing an expansion of the shadow economy. In this economic reading, economic globalization refers to a dangerous cocktail of deregulation and increasing global competition that produces an expansion of shadow work. This exploitative form of employment is thus seen to have emerged as a new facet of contemporary capitalism. From this perspective therefore, participation in the shadow economy is viewed to result from people's 'exclusion' from state benefits and the formal labour market. Viewing the shadow economy as an inherent feature of contemporary capitalism and a direct result of employers seeking to reduce costs, such as by sub-contracting to businesses employing informal labour under 'sweatshop-like' conditions and the 'precarious' or 'false' self-employed, shadow workers are characterized as marginalized populations conducting such work out of necessity and as a last resort (Davis, 2006; Slavnic, 2010).

In recent decades, however, another view has emerged. In this view, there is recognition that much work in the shadow economy is conducted on a self-employed basis. This was first recognized in a developing world context where a vast swathe of micro-entrepreneurs, street hawkers and petty traders participate in the shadow economy (Cross, 2000; Cross and Morales, 2007; De Soto, 1989, 2001; ILO, 2002a; Williams and Shahid, 2014). As the ILO (2002b) find, 70 per cent of those operating in the shadow economy are doing so on a self-employed basis in sub-Saharan Africa, 62 per cent in North Africa, 60 per cent in Latin America and 59 per cent in Asia. This understanding that much shadow work is conducted on a self-employed basis then spread to analyses of post-socialist transition economies (Chavdarova, 2014; Round et al., 2008; Williams et al., 2012, 2013) and the western world (Evans et al., 2006; Katungi et al., 2006; Small Business Council, 2004; Snyder, 2004; Williams, 2005, 2006, 2007, 2010; Williams et al., 2011).

One result has even been the emergence of a new sub-discipline of entrepreneurship scholarship termed 'informal entrepreneurship', which focuses upon this previously ignored group of entrepreneurs conducting some or all of their transactions in the shadow economy (Aidis et al., 2006; Barbour and Llanes, 2013; Bureau and Fendt, 2011; Dellot, 2012; Kus, 2014; Mróz, 2012; Thai and Turkina, 2013; Webb et al., 2013; Williams, 2006). This burgeoning sub-field of entrepreneurship has not only sought to understand the magnitude of entrepreneurship in the shadow economy (Autio and Fu, 2015; Williams, 2013) and the extent to which they operate in the shadow economy (De Castro et al., 2014; Williams and Shahid,

2014) but also their reasons for participating in the shadow economy (Adom, 2014; Chen, 2012; Hudson et al., 2012; Williams, 2009; Williams et al., 2012).

Examining the reasons for the self-employed participating in the shadow economy, two broad competing views can be identified. On the one hand, an 'exclusion' perspective portrays those participating in shadow self-employment as doing so out of necessity and as a last resort in the absence of alternative means of livelihood (Copisarow, 2004; Llanes and Barbour, 2007). On the other hand, an 'exit' perspective depicts them as voluntarily exiting the formal economy. Conventionally, such commentators have depicted informal workers as heroes casting off the shackles of a burdensome state so as to avoid the costs, time and effort of formal registration (Cross, 2000; Gërxhani, 2004; Maloney, 2004; Snyder, 2004). More recently, however, this 'exit' perspective has also been argued by a wider collection of both public choice scholars (for a review, see Gërxhani, 2004) and institutional theorists arguing that shadow work arises due to the asymmetry between the codified laws and regulations of a society's formal institutions and the norms, values and beliefs that constitute its informal institutions (Webb et al., 2009, 2013, 2014; Welter and Smallbone, 2011; Williams and Shahid, 2014; Williams and Vorley, 2014). Based on these competing views of their motives, two competing perspectives can be identified regarding the characteristics of the self-employed participating in the shadow economy, namely the marginalization and reinforcement theses.

Marginalization Thesis

Based on the exclusion perspective, the 'marginalization thesis' posits that the self-employed participating in the shadow economy are predominantly marginalized populations (Barbour and Llanes, 2013; Brill, 2011; Dellot, 2012; Katungi et al., 2006). Here, the self-employed are viewed as more likely to operate in the shadow economy when they live in deprived urban neighbourhoods (Barbour and Llanes, 2013; Brill, 2011; Dellot, 2012; Katungi et al., 2006), peripheral rural regions (Button, 1984; Williams, 2010), poorer nations (Schneider and Williams, 2013) and poorer regions of the global economy (ILO, 2012; Williams, 2013). It is similarly the case when discussing which groups of the self-employed participate in the shadow economy. The marginalization thesis believes that the self-employed participating in the shadow economy are predominantly marginalized populations. For example, adherents to this thesis assert that the propensity to participate in the shadow economy is greater among the self-employed with greater financial difficulties and/or among the lower-income groups of the self-employed (Barbour and Llanes, 2013; Brill,

2011; Katungi et al., 2006) and women who are self-employed rather than men in self-employment (ILO, 2013; Leonard, 1994; Stănculescu, 2005).

Reinforcement Thesis

Recently, however, a reinforcement thesis has begun to emerge which challenges this dominant marginalization thesis. This argues that such work is not conducted purely out of necessity solely by marginalized populations, but rather that the participation of the self-employed in the shadow economy is lower among marginalized populations. Instead, such work is more likely to be conducted out of choice and it is for instance relatively affluent, better educated, more professional groups of the self-employed who are seen as more likely to participate in the shadow economy (Kaitelidou et al., 2011; MacDonald, 1994; Moldovan and Van de Walle, 2013; Pahl, 1984; Williams, 2014a; Williams et al., 2013). Seen through this lens therefore, the shadow economy does not reduce the disparities produced by the formal economy amongst the self-employed but instead reinforces these inequalities (Ferrer-i-Carbonell and Gërxhani, 2011). For example, it can be argued that the self-employed in affluent neighbourhoods, localities and regions are more likely to participate in the shadow economy than the self-employed in less affluent neighbourhoods, localities and regions (Foudi et al., 1982; Hadjimichalis and Vaiou, 1989; Krumplyte and Samulevicius, 2010; Mingione, 1991; Surdej and Ślęzak, 2009; Van Geuns et al., 1987). Similarly, it is asserted that women who are self-employed display a lower propensity to engage in the shadow economy than men (Lemieux et al., 1994; McInnis-Dittrich, 1995) and that those self-employed with financial difficulties are less likely to engage in such endeavours than more affluent self-employed (Williams et al., 2013; Williams and Martinez-Perez, 2014b, 2014c).

Examining the evidence to support either the marginalization or reinforcement thesis, it becomes quickly apparent that no known studies have evaluated these competing theses. Instead, many studies of the participation of the self-employed in the shadow economy simply assume that one or other thesis is valid. Brill (2011), for instance, studies only people living in a deprived neighbourhood of Salford in the UK who operate on a self-employed basis in the shadow economy, grounded in the assumption that this is where shadow self-employment is concentrated. This is similarly the case in numerous other studies of the participation of the self-employed in the shadow economy (Barbour and Llanes, 2013; Katungi et al., 2006; Llanes and Barbour, 2007). Indeed, the only known attempts to determine which groups of the self-employed participate in the shadow economy have been limited to evaluating whether different groups of business owners started up their businesses in the shadow economy. The finding is that women were less likely than men to have done so and that businesses with low current annual turnovers were more likely to have done so (Williams and Martinez, 2014a, 2014d). Until now, therefore, there have been no evaluations of the validity of the marginalization and reinforcement theses. Neither has there been any evaluation of whether these are competing or substituting hypotheses, or whether they can be complementary.

This chapter fills that gap. Here, we report a contemporary extensive survey of which groups of the self-employed participate in the shadow economy in the EU-28. The objective in doing so is to evaluate the following two hypotheses:

Marginalization hypothesis (H1): The self-employed participating in the shadow economy are predominantly marginalized populations, when other characteristics are taken into account and held constant.

Reinforcement hypothesis (H2): The participation of the self-employed in the shadow economy is lower among marginalized groups of the self-employed, when other characteristics are taken into account and held constant.

METHODOLOGY

To evaluate these hypotheses, we here use data collected in Special Eurobarometer survey no. 402 conducted in April and May 2013 as part of wave 79.2 of the Eurobarometer survey across the 28 member states of the European Union. Of the 27 563 face-to-face interviews conducted, some 1969 were with people self-reporting themselves as self-employed. It is these interviews which are here analysed, all of which were conducted face-to-face in the national language with adults aged 15 years and older. In each country, a multi-stage random (probability) sampling methodology was employed so as to ensure that on the variables of gender, age, region and locality size, each country is representative in terms of the proportion of interviews undertaken with each group. In the univariate analysis therefore, we have employed the sample weighting scheme as the literature suggests (Sharon and Liu, 1994; Solon et al., 2013; Winship and Radbill, 1994). For the multivariate analysis, however, and reflecting the majority of the literature on whether or not to use a weighting scheme (Pfeffermann, 1993; Sharon and Liu, 1994; Solon et al., 2013; Winship and Radbill, 1994), we have not done so.

Given that asking participants about engagement in the shadow economy is a sensitive topic, the schedule of the interview adopted a gradual approach by first building a rapport with the participants before posing more sensitive questions regarding their participation in the shadow economy. The interview schedule thus started by asking participants about their attitudes towards shadow work followed by questions on whether they had purchased goods and services from the shadow economy. Only then were questions put regarding their participation in the shadow economy. Analysing interviewers' post-interview responses regarding the perceived reliability of the interviews with the people reporting that they were self-employed, the finding is that cooperation was deemed bad in only 0.5 per cent of the interviews. Cooperation was deemed excellent in 64.3 per cent, fair in 30.0 per cent and average in just 5.2 per cent. As discussed elsewhere (Ram and Williams, 2008), there is thus little reason to assume that participants are hiding their shadow work from the interviewer.

To analyse the data, descriptive statistics are produced on the level of participation in shadow work of different groups of the self-employed, whilst multilevel mixed-effects logistic regression analysis is used to analyse the characteristics of the self-employed who engage in the shadow economy. To do this, the dependent variable measures whether those reporting that they are self-employed participated in the shadow economy based on the question 'Have you yourself carried out any undeclared paid activities in the last 12 months?' To analyse which self-employed engaged in the shadow economy meanwhile, the following independent socio-demographic, socio-economic and spatial variables are considered.

Socio-demographic Independent Variables

- *Gender:* a dummy variable for the gender of the self-employed person, with value 1 for men and 0 for women.
- *Age:* a categorical variable for the age of the self-employed person, with value 1 for those aged 15 to 24 years old, value 2 for those aged 25 to 39, value 3 for those aged 40 to 54, value 4 for those 55 years old or over.
- *Marital status:* a categorical variable for the marital status of the self-employed person, with value 1 for married/remarried individuals, value 2 for single living with a partner, value 3 for singles, value 4 for those separated or divorced, and value 5 for widowed and for other forms of marital status.
- *Social class:* a categorical variable for the self-employed person's perception regarding the social class to which s/he belongs, with value 1

for the working class, value 2 for middle class, value 3 for upper class, and value 4 for other class or none.

- *Age when stopped full-time education:* a categorical variable for age the self-employed person stopped full-time education, with value 1 for 15 years old and under, value 2 for 16–19 years old, value 3 for 20 years old or over.
- *People 15+ years in own household:* a categorical variable for the number of people 15+ years in the self-employed person's household (including the respondent), with value 1 for one person, value 2 for two persons, value 3 for 3 persons, and value 4 for 4 persons or more.
- *Children* (up to 14 years old in the household): a categorical variable for number of children, with value 1 for self-employed people with no children, value 2 for the presence of children less than 10 years old living in their household, value 3 for the presence of children aged 10 to 14 years old living in their household and value 4 for the presence of children less than 10 years old and children aged 10 to 14 years old living in their household.
- *Tax morality index:* a constructed index of their attitude towards tax non-compliance. Participants were asked to rate how acceptable they viewed six tax non-compliant behaviours using a 10-point scale where 1 means 'absolutely unacceptable' and 10 means 'absolutely acceptable'. These are: someone receives welfare payments without entitlement; a firm is hired by another firm and does not report earnings; a firm hires a private person and all or part of their salary is not declared; a firm is hired by a household and doesn't report earnings; someone evades taxes by not or only partially declaring income; and a person hired by a household does not declare earnings when they should be declared. The tax morality index for each individual is calculated using the mean score across these six attitudinal questions.

Socio-economic Independent Variables

- *Occupation of self-employed:* a categorical variable grouping self-employed respondents by their occupation, with value 1 for farmer/fisherman, value 2 for professional (lawyer, etc.), value 3 for owner of a shop, craftsmen, etc., and value 4 for business proprietors, etc.
- *Difficulties paying bills:* a categorical variable for whether the self-employed person witnessed difficulties in paying bills, with value 1 for having difficulties most of the time, value 2 for occasionally, and value 3 for almost never/never.

Spatial Independent Variables

- *Area respondent lives:* a categorical variable for the area where the self-employed person lives, with value 1 for rural area or village, value 2 for small or middle sized town, and value 3 for large urban area.
- *EU region:* a categorical variable for the EU region where the self-employed person lives, with 1 for East-Central European countries, value 2 for Western European countries, value 3 for Southern European countries and value 4 for Nordic Nations.

Below, the findings are reported.

FINDINGS

Across the EU-28, governments have funnelled resources into detecting shadow economic activity amongst the self-employed grounded in the belief that the self-employed have a greater propensity to participate in the shadow economy (Dekker et al., 2010; Vanderseypen et al., 2013; Williams, 2014a). To determine whether this focus upon the self-employed is valid, Table 4.1 reports the participation rates of the self-employed, unemployed and employees in the shadow economy. This reveals that 6 per cent of the self-employed participate in the shadow economy, which is a higher participation rate than employees and the economically inactive (excluding the registered unemployed). However, just 12 per cent of all shadow work is conducted by the

Table 4.1　Extent of participation of the population of the EU-28 in the shadow economy: by economic status, 2013

	% engaging in shadow economy	% of all shadow work conducted by:	% of surveyed population	Mean annual shadow income/ shadow worker (€)	% of total all shadow income earned by:
EU-28	4	100	100	723	100
Self-employed	6	12	8	1214	14
Unemployed	9	20	9	696	18
Other economically inactive	3	30	42	511	24
Formal employees	3	38	41	767	44

self-employed (who constitute 8 per cent of the surveyed population) and just 14 per cent of all shadow income is earned by this group. Therefore even if governments successfully deterred the self-employed from taking up shadow work, this would not solve the problem of the shadow economy. Nevertheless, a clear rationale remains for focusing greater resources on the self-employed. As Table 4.1 shows, they display a greater propensity to participate in the shadow economy than the majority of the population and earn significantly more when they do participate than other population groups: an average of €1214 per annum compared with €723 for the average EU person participating in the shadow economy.

Which groups of the self-employed therefore display a greater propensity to engage in the shadow economy? Is it, as the marginalization thesis posits, marginalized groups of the self-employed who have a greater propensity to operate in the economy? Or is it, as the reinforcement thesis asserts, that the propensity to operate in the shadow economy is lower among marginalized groups of the self-employed?

Table 4.2 reports the descriptive statistics regarding the propensity of different groups of the self-employed to participate in the shadow economy. First, and supporting the marginalization thesis, some marginalized groups of the self-employed do display a greater propensity to operate in the shadow economy. Younger age groups, who are more likely to be unemployed in the contemporary European labour market (European Commission, 2013), display a greater propensity to participate in the shadow economy than older self-employed people. So too do those self-reporting themselves as working class compared with those self-reporting themselves as middle class, and those having difficulties paying their bills most of the time compared with those self-employed who rarely have such difficulties. This is similarly the case with those self-employed whose education ended at 15 years old or younger. Moreover, self-employed craftspeople and shop owners are more likely to participate in the shadow economy than the self-employed who belong to the professions (for example, doctors, lawyers) and business proprietors.

There is also evidence, however, to support the reinforcement thesis. The propensity of the self-employed to participate in the shadow economy is lower among some marginalized populations. The self-employed in less affluent European regions for instance are less likely to operate in the shadow economy than those in relatively affluent Nordic nations. Self-employed women are also less likely to operate in the shadow economy than self-employed men, and the self-employed reporting themselves as working class less likely than the self-employed reporting themselves as belonging to the upper classes. Those whose formal education ended at

Table 4.2 *Participation of the self-employed in the shadow economy in the EU-28: socio-demographic, socio-economic and spatial variations*

	% engaged in shadow economy	Annual earnings from shadow economy:						Mean (€)
		€1–100 (%)	€101–200 (%)	€201–500 (%)	€501–1000 (%)	€1000+ (%)	Don't remember/ know, refusal (%)	
All EU 28	6	18	13	6	10	19	34	1214
Gender								
Men	6	23	6	7	7	19	38	941
Women	5	4	31	2	17	20	26	1784
Age								
15–24	15	0	0	14	8	49	29	1436
25–39	10	16	12	2	15	8	47	917
40–54	4	32	14	11	1	17	25	1388
55+	3	3	23	4	13	46	11	1408
Marital status								
Married/remarried	4	22	11	10	12	15	30	987
Unmarried/ cohabiting	13	21	18	5	4	9	43	1253
Unmarried/single	6	4	15	1	17	33	30	1554
Divorce/separated	6	14	3	0	5	56	22	1540
Widowed/other	8	15	0	0	0	0	85	74

Social class								
Working class	7	13	20	0	4	10	53	743
Middle class	4	2	10	12	17	33	26	1898
Higher class/other/none	12	96	0	1	0	1	2	100
Age education ended								
<15	8	20	15	0	1	0	64	125
16–19	5	19	7	5	10	14	45	1027
20+	6	18	18	9	14	25	16	1500
Adults in household								
One	6	11	14	1	14	35	25	1557
Two	5	11	14	10	5	13	47	1097
Three	6	28	18	2	18	14	20	1515
Four and more	6	32	3	4	8	24	29	623
Children								
<10 years old	6	28	8	0	21	20	23	1314
10–14 years old	6	17	24	15	5	0	39	251
<10 and 10–14	15	26	29	0	0	3	42	249
No children	4	12	6	7	10	30	35	1699
Occupation of self-employed								
Farmer/fisherman	5	8	18	3	2	29	40	743
Professional (lawyer, etc.)	4	0	8	25	9	46	12	1969

Table 4.2 (continued)

	% engaged in shadow economy	Annual earnings from shadow economy:						
		€1–100 (%)	€101–200 (%)	€201–500 (%)	€501–1000 (%)	€1000+ (%)	Don't remember/ know, refusal (%)	Mean (€)
Occupation of self-employed								
Owner of a shop, craftsmen, etc.	7	21	11	1	15	12	40	1273
Business proprietors, etc.	6	30	17	3	6	9	35	664
Difficulties paying bills								
Most of the time	10	34	13	2	0	15	36	784
From time to time	7	7	7	4	13	28	41	1895
Almost never/never	4	21	20	9	12	8	30	624
Area								
Rural area or village	6	15	8	5	9	24	39	1535
Small or middle sized town	5	4	27	7	13	18	31	1091
Large town	6	42	1	6	6	13	32	872
EU Region								
East-Central Europe	6	6	5	13	4	2	70	499
Western Europe	6	27	19	7	5	29	13	972
Southern Europe	4	9	9	0	18	20	44	2355
Nordic nations	13	27	20	0	25	17	11	664

20 years old or over, moreover, are slightly more likely to participate in the shadow economy than those whose education ended between 16 and 19 years old.

These descriptive statistics thus tentatively suggest that the marginalization thesis applies in relation to age, education, marital status and income levels; younger age groups, those with a lower level of education, the self-employed who are unmarried or cohabiting and those having difficulties paying household bills are more likely to participate in the shadow economy. However, the marginalization does not apply when discussing women compared with men, occupations, EU regions and those living in rural areas compared with urban areas. Instead, the reinforcement thesis tentatively appears valid. Analysing these descriptive statistics therefore, the tentative conclusion is that it is not possible to assert that either the marginalization or reinforcement thesis is universally applicable at all spatial scales and across all socio-demographic and socio-economic groups. Instead, the marginalization thesis appears applicable when discussing some population groups but the reinforcement thesis seems applicable for others.

ANALYSIS

Here, we analyse whether these variations in the participation of the self-employed in the shadow economy by socio-demographic group (gender, age, marital status, age when stopped full-time education, people 15+ years in own household, number of children, tax morality index), socio-economic group (occupation, difficulty in paying bills) and geographic location (urban/rural area, EU region) continue to be valid when all other variables are held constant. Given the hierarchical structure of the data (individuals nested within countries), for this multivariate analysis, we employ a multilevel model. As the dependent variable is dichotomous, we use a multilevel mixed-effects logistic regression (Snijders and Bosker, 2012). The binary response variable is whether a self-employed person participated in the shadow economy in the 12 months prior to interview. Indeed, the likelihood-ratio test for the null hypothesis that there are no variations in the participation of the self-employed in the shadow economy reports that this hypothesis can be safely rejected. Therefore, the multilevel mixed-effects logistic regression is used.

To analyse the effect of these independent variables on the participation of the self-employed in the shadow economy when the other variables are held constant, an additive model is used. The first stage model (M1) includes solely the socio-demographic factors to examine their effects, the second stage model (M2) adds socio-economic factors alongside the socio-demographic factors, while the third stage model (M3) adds spatial factors to the socio-demographic and socio-economic factors to examine their influence on participation in the shadow economy. Table 4.3 reports the results.

Model 1 in Table 4.3 shows that the marginalization thesis is valid when analysing various socio-demographic variables. Not only are the younger self-employed more likely to participate in the shadow economy but so too are those who are widowed. In addition, those holding non-conformist attitudes towards tax compliance are more likely to participate in such endeavours, suggesting that those self-employed who are marginalized in the sense that their norms, values and beliefs (that is, their individual morality) do not align with the codified laws and regulations (that is, state morality) display a significantly greater propensity to participate in the shadow economy.

Contrary to the marginalization thesis and in support of the reinforcement thesis, however, men are found to be significantly more likely to participate in the shadow economy than women. Nevertheless, no evidence is found to support the marginalization (or reinforcement) thesis when analysing the age the self-employed stopped their full-time education, the number of people aged 15+ in the household and the number of children in the household. As such, when evaluating the socio-demographic characteristics of the self-employed, the finding is that a finer-grained understanding of the validity of the marginalization thesis is needed. The marginalization thesis is valid for some marginalized socio-demographic groups (for example, younger people, widowed or other categories and the self-employed whose individual morality does not align with state morality), but not others (for example, women).

When Model 2 adds socio-economic factors (that is, occupational characteristics and financial circumstances of the self-employed) to their socio-demographic characteristics, there are no major changes in the influence of the socio-demographic variables on the propensity of the self-employed to participate in the shadow economy. However, the additional finding is that the occupation of the self-employed has a significant influence. Compared with self-employed farmers and fishermen, self-employed shop owners and craftspeople are more likely to participate in the shadow economy. Moreover, the self-employed who have difficulties paying household bills most of the time (that is, an indicator of their financial circumstances) are more likely to participate in the shadow economy than those who seldom have difficulties. The marginalization thesis, therefore, is valid not only for younger people, widows and those whose individual morality does not

Table 4.3   Multilevel mixed-effects logistic regression of the participation of the self-employed people in the shadow economy in the European Union

Variables	Model 1	Model 2	Model 3
Gender (CG: Women)			
Men	0.827*** (0.249)	0.971*** (0.260)	0.954*** (0.260)
Age (CG: 15–24):			
25–39	−1.164** (0.474)	−1.210** (0.494)	−1.234** (0.495)
40–54	−1.951*** (0.492)	−2.039*** (0.513)	−2.089*** (0.515)
55+	−1.977*** (0.543)	−2.029*** (0.569)	−2.109*** (0.571)
Marital status: (CG: Married/remarried)			
Single living with partner	0.369 (0.309)	0.350 (0.318)	0.355 (0.318)
Single	−0.583 (0.416)	−0.572 (0.425)	−0.571 (0.424)
Divorced or separated	0.342 (0.425)	0.232 (0.444)	0.200 (0.451)
Widow/other	1.294** (0.550)	1.393** (0.570)	1.310** (0.575)
Social class, self-assessment (CG: The working class of society)			
The middle class of society	−0.179 (0.244)	−0.111 (0.261)	−0.0988 (0.261)
The higher class of society/other/none	−0.648 (0.524)	−0.522 (0.553)	−0.515 (0.551)
Age stopped full-time education (CG: 15 years):			
16–19	−0.292 (0.422)	−0.566 (0.440)	−0.621 (0.444)
20+	0.0192 (0.435)	−0.217 (0.462)	−0.288 (0.465)
Number 15+ years in household (CG:1 person):			
2 persons	−0.170 (0.370)	−0.215 (0.383)	−0.255 (0.388)
3 persons	−0.199 (0.406)	−0.204 (0.419)	−0.217 (0.422)
4+ persons	0.314 (0.419)	0.335 (0.435)	0.317 (0.439)

Table 4.3 (continued)

Variables	Model 1	Model 2	Model 3
Number of children: (CG: No children)			
Children < 10	0.0293 (0.312)	−0.116 (0.324)	−0.130 (0.325)
Children 10–14	0.163 (0.369)	0.175 (0.377)	0.166 (0.379)
At least one child < 10 and at least one 10–14	0.418 (0.435)	0.290 (0.460)	0.143 (0.463)
Tax morality	0.513*** (0.0597)	0.531*** (0.0620)	0.534*** (0.0626)
Occupation (CG: Farmer/fisherman)			
Professional (lawyer, etc.)		0.605 (0.459)	0.760 (0.469)
Owner of a shop, craftsmen, etc.		0.699* (0.402)	0.867** (0.407)
Business proprietors, etc.		0.268 (0.429)	0.424 (0.437)
Difficulties paying bills last year (CG: Most of the time)			
From time to time		−0.550 (0.344)	−0.623* (0.344)
Almost never/never		−1.182*** (0.362)	−1.318*** (0.364)
Area respondent lives (CG: Rural area or village):			
Small/middle sized town			−0.395 (0.262)
Large town			−0.272 (0.291)

EU region (CG: East Central Europe)

Western Europe			−0.0241 (0.436)
Southern Europe			−0.770 (0.497)
Nordic Nations			1.460** (0.585)
Constant	−2.951*** (0.761)	−2.528*** (0.871)	−2.207** (0.900)
Observations	1675	1661	1661
Number of groups	28	28	28
Random-effects Parameters			
Identity: Country			
Variance (constant)	0.567***	0.844***	0.458***

Notes: Standard errors in parentheses; *** p < 0.01, ** p < 0.05, * p < 0.1.

align with state morality, but also for those having difficulties paying the bills (that is, the self-employed who are less affluent).

When spatial factors are added in Model 3, there are again no major changes to the significance of the socio-demographic and socio-economic characteristics of the self-employed which influence participation in the shadow economy. However, no evidence is found to support either the marginalization or reinforcement thesis regarding those in peripheral rural areas compared with those in more urban areas. Evidence is found to support the reinforcement thesis, nevertheless, when the European region is analysed; the self-employed living in Nordic Nations are more likely to participate in the shadow economy compared with those in East Central Europe.

DISCUSSION AND CONCLUSIONS

To evaluate the marginalization thesis, which views the propensity of the self-employed to operate in the economy as greater among marginalized groups, this chapter has reported the results of a 2013 survey of the participation of the self-employed in the shadow economy in the EU-28 involving 1969 face-to-face interviews with self-employed people. Using multilevel mixed-effects logistic regression analysis, and as Table 4.4 summarizes, the marginalization thesis has been found to be valid in relation to

Table 4.4   Validity of marginalization and reinforcement theses: by socio-demographic, socio-economic and spatial variations

Variables	Type of self-employed significantly more likely to participate in shadow economy	Thesis supported
Gender	Men	Reinforcement
EU region	Affluent EU regions	Reinforcement
Age	Younger age groups	Marginalization
Marital status	Widows	Marginalization
Occupation of self-employed	Shop owners and craftspeople	Marginalization
Tax morale	Not conforming to state morality	Marginalization
Household financial circumstance	Those having difficulties	Marginalization
Educational level	No significant association	Neither
No. of children in household	No significant association	Neither
Urban/rural area	No significant association	Neither

some marginalized population groups. The younger self-employed display a significantly greater propensity to participate in the shadow economy, as do those who are widowed, shop owners and craftspeople, those whose individual morality does not align with state morality, and those who have difficulties paying household bills. The reinforcement thesis, meanwhile, has been found to be valid in relation to other groups. Self-employed men display a significantly greater propensity to participate in the shadow economy than women, as do those living in the more affluent EU region of the Nordic nations. No evidence is found to support the marginalization (or reinforcement) thesis, nevertheless, in relation to educational level, the number of children in the household or the urban–rural divide.

Analysing the theoretical implications, the finding is that a finer-grained reading of the marginalization thesis is required when discussing the participation of the self-employed in the shadow economy. The marginalization thesis applies when examining socio-demographic and socio-economic characteristics such as their age, marital status, tax morality, occupation and household financial circumstances. However, when gender and regional variations are analysed, the reinforcement thesis is valid; participation in the shadow economy reinforces the gender and European regional disparities found amongst the self-employed in the formal economy. When other characteristics are examined, furthermore, such as the urban–rural divide, educational level and number of children, there is no evidence to support either the marginalization or reinforcement thesis.

Examining the policy implications, these results show the specific spaces and populations that require targeting when tackling the self-employed participating in the shadow economy. In recent years in the EU-28, for example, an emphasis has been put on targeting poorer EU regions such as East-Central and Southern Europe when allocating resources through European structural funds to tackle the shadow economy (Dekker et al., 2010; European Commission, 2013; Vanderseypen et al., 2013). This chapter, nevertheless, displays that the self-employed in these poorer EU regions are not disproportionately engaged in the shadow economy. Indeed, the self-employed in affluent European regions have significantly higher participation rates in the shadow economy, intimating the need to rethink the spatial allocation of European funds when tackling the shadow economy among the self-employed. Nonetheless, this chapter does display that the focus of many national governments on the self-employed when tackling the shadow economy is not a mistake (European Commission, 2007; Vanderseypen et al., 2013; Williams, 2014a). The self-employed display a significantly greater propensity to participate in the shadow economy. Popular policy initiatives such as seeking to facilitate the formalization of the self-employed are therefore worthwhile

(Barbour and Llanes, 2013). Nevertheless, given that the self-employed undertake just 12 per cent of all shadow work and only 14 per cent of shadow income is earned by this group, care needs to be taken not to pay too much attention to the self-employed. This survey also reveals that it may be worthwhile targeting some groups of the self-employed when tackling the shadow economy, such as men, younger people, widows, shop owners and craftspeople, those who have difficulties paying household bills, the self-employed in Nordic nations and those whose individual morality differs from state morality. In other words, this analysis provides a useful preliminary risk assessment at the EU-28 level of which groups of the self-employed are most likely to participate in the shadow economy. As shown, however, this is not necessarily always marginalized groups (for example, women, those living in rural areas and deprived EU regions, the less educated).

The question which then arises of course is what policy measures should be used to reduce the shadow economy when targeting these population groups. Until now, there has been a tendency to focus upon the use of direct controls which seek to ensure that the benefits of operating in the legitimate economy outweigh the costs of working in the shadow economy. However, this chapter reveals that there is a strong significant association between the level of tax morale and participation in the shadow economy. The intimation, therefore, is that there should perhaps be greater emphasis given to indirect controls that focus upon improving the social contract between the state and its citizens by fostering a high trust, high commitment culture among those engaged in entrepreneurship.

In sum, this chapter has revealed the need for a finer-grained, more variegated understanding of the marginalization thesis which asserts that self-employed people participating in the shadow economy in the EU-28 are predominantly marginalized populations. Whether this is the case in individual nations, and also whether similar groups are identified, now requires evaluation, not least because most policy is implemented at the national level. If this chapter stimulates such national evaluations, then it will have achieved one of its intentions. If it also leads governments to start adopting a more nuanced approach that targets particular segments of the self-employed when tackling the shadow economy, and not always solely marginalized groups of the self-employed, then this chapter will have achieved its wider intention.

NOTE

1. This chapter is a derived version of Williams and Horodnic (2015).

REFERENCES

Adom, K. (2014), 'Beyond the marginalization thesis: an examination of the motivations of informal entrepreneurs in sub-Saharan Africa: insights from Ghana', *International Journal of Entrepreneurship and Innovation*, **15** (2), 113–25.

Aidis, R., F. Welter, D. Smallbone and N. Isakova (2006), 'Female entrepreneurship in transition economies: the case of Lithuania and Ukraine', *Feminist Economics*, **13** (2), 157–83.

Autio, E. and K. Fu (2015), 'Economic and political institutions and entry into formal and informal entrepreneurship', *Asian Pacific Management Journal*, **32** (1), 67–94.

Barbour, A. and M. Llanes (2013), *Supporting People to Legitimise their Informal Businesses*, York: Joseph Rowntree Foundation.

Brill, L. (2011), *Women's Participation in the Informal Economy: What Can We Learn from Oxfam's Work?*, Manchester: Oxfam.

Bureau, S. and J. Fendt (2011), 'Entrepreneurship in the informal economy: why it matters', *International Journal of Entrepreneurship and Innovation*, **12** (2), 85–94.

Button, K. (1984), 'Regional variations in the irregular economy: a study of possible trends', *Regional Studies*, **18** (3), 385–92.

Castells, M. and A. Portes (1989), 'World underneath: the origins, dynamics and effects of the informal economy', in A. Portes, M. Castells and L.A. Benton (eds), *The Informal Economy: Studies in Advanced and Less Developing Countries*, Baltimore: Johns Hopkins University Press, pp. 11–39.

Chavdarova, T. (2014), 'Risky businesses? Young people in informal self-employment in Sofia', *International Journal of Urban and Regional Research*, **38** (6), 2060–77.

Chen, M. (2012), *The Informal Economy: Definitions, Theories and Policies*, Manchester: Women in Informal Employment Global and Organising.

Copisarow, R. (2004), *Street UK – A Micro-Finance Organisation: Lessons Learned from its First Three Years' Operations*, Birmingham: Street UK.

Copisarow, R. and A. Barbour (2004), *Self-Employed People in the Informal Economy –Cheats or Contributors?*, London: Community Links.

Cross, J. (2000), 'Street vendors, modernity and postmodernity: conflict and compromise in the global economy', *International Journal of Sociology and Social Policy*, **20** (1), 29–51.

Cross, J. and A. Morales (2007), 'Introduction: Locating street markets in the modern/postmodern world', in J. Cross and A. Morales (eds), *Street Entrepreneurs: People, Place and Politics in Local and Global Perspective*, London: Routledge, pp. 1–14.

Davis, M. (2006), *Planet of Slums*, London: Verso.

De Castro, J.O., S. Khavul and G.D. Bruton (2014), 'Shades of grey: how do informal firms navigate between macro and meso institutional environments?', *Strategic Entrepreneurship Journal*, **8** (1), 75–94.

De Soto, H. (1989), *The Other Path*, London: Harper and Row.

De Soto, H. (2001), *The Mystery of Capital: Why Capitalism Triumphs in the West and Fails Everywhere Else*, London: Black Swan.

Dekker, H., E. Oranje, P. Renooy, F. Rosing and C.C. Williams (2010), *Joining up the Fight against Undeclared Work in the European Union*, Brussels: DG Employment, Social Affairs and Equal Opportunities.

Dellot, B. (2012), *Untapped Enterprise: Learning to Live with the Informal Economy*, London: Royal Society of the Arts.

European Commission (2007), 'Stepping up the fight against undeclared work', Document COM(2007) 628 final, Brussels: European Commission.

European Commission (2013), *Employment and Social Developments in Europe 2013*, Brussels: European Commission.

Evans, M., S. Syrett and C.C. Williams (2006), *Informal Economic Activities and Deprived Neighbourhoods*, London: Department for Communities and Local Government.

Ferrer-i-Carbonell, A. and K. Gërxhani (2011), 'Financial satisfaction and (in) formal sector in a transition country', *Social Indicators Research*, **120** (2), 315–31.

Foudi, R., F. Stankiewicz and N. Vanecloo (1982), *Chomeurs et Economie Informelle*, Cahiers de l'observation du changement social et culturel no. 17, Paris: CNRS.

Gërxhani, K. (2004), 'Tax evasion in transition: outcome of an institutional clash? Testing Feige's conjecture in Albania', *European Economic Review*, **48** (7), 729–45.

Hadjimichalis, C. and D. Vaiou (1989), 'Whose flexibility? The politics of informalisation in Southern Europe', paper presented to the IAAD/SCG Study Groups of the IBG Conference on *Industrial Restructuring and Social Change: The Dawning of a New Era of Flexible Accumulation?*, Durham.

Hudson, J., C.C. Williams, M. Orviska and S. Nadin (2012), 'Evaluating the impact of the informal economy on businesses in South East Europe: some lessons from the 2009 World Bank Enterprise Survey', *The South-East European Journal of Economics and Business*, **7** (1), 99–110.

ILO (2002a), *Women and Men in the Informal Economy: A Statistical Picture*, Geneva: International Labour Organisation.

ILO (2002b), *Decent Work and the Informal Economy*, Geneva: International Labour Organisation.

ILO (2012), *Statistical Update on Employment in the Informal Economy*, Geneva: International Labour Organisation.

ILO (2013), *Measuring Informality: A Statistical Manual on the Informal Sector and Informal Employment*, Geneva: International Labour Organisation.

Jütting, J.P. and J.R. Laiglesia (2009), 'Employment, poverty reduction and development: what's new?', in J.P. Jütting and J.R. Laiglesi (eds), *Is Informal Normal? Towards More and Better Jobs in Developing Countries*, Paris: OECD, pp. 1–19.

Kaitelidou, D., C.S. Tsirona, P.A. Galanis, O. Siskou, P. Mladovsky, E.G. Kouli, P.E. Prezerakos, M. Theodorou, P. Sourtzi and L. Liaropolous (2011), 'Informal payments for maternity health services in public hospitals in Greece', *Health Policy*, **109** (1), 23–40.

Katungi, D., E. Neale and A. Barbour (2006), *People in Low-Paid Informal Work*, York: Joseph Rowntree Foundation.

Krumplyte, J. and J. Samulevicius (2010), 'Complex research on undeclared work: theoretical aspects and empirical application in Lithuania', *Inzinerine Ekonomika – Engineering Economics*, **21** (3), 283–94.

Kus, B. (2014), 'The informal road to markets: neoliberal reforms, private entrepreneurship and the informal economy in Turkey', *International Journal of Social Economics*, **41** (4), 278–93.

Lemieux, T., B. Fortin and P. Frechette (1994), 'The effect of taxes on labor supply in the underground economy', *American Economic Review*, **84** (1), 231–54.

Leonard, M. (1994), *Informal Economic Activity in Belfast*, Aldershot, UK: Avebury.

Llanes, M. and A. Barbour (2007), *Self-Employed and Micro-Entrepreneurs: Informal Trading and the Journey Towards Formalization*, London: Community Links.

MacDonald, R. (1994), 'Fiddly jobs, undeclared working and the something for nothing society', *Work, Employment and Society*, **8** (4), 507–30.

Maloney, W.F. (2004), 'Informality revisited', *World Development*, **32** (7), 1159–78.

McElwee, G., R. Smith and P. Somerville (2014), 'Developing a conceptual model of illegal rural enterprise', in A. Fayolle (ed.), *Handbook of Research in Entrepreneurship*, Cheltenham, UK and Northampton, MA, USA: Edward Elgar Publishing, pp. 367–88.

McInnis-Dittrich, K. (1995), 'Women of the shadows: Appalachian women's participation in the informal economy', *Affilia: Journal of Women and Social Work*, **10** (4), 398–412.

Mingione, E. (1991), *Fragmented Societies: A Sociology of Economic Life Beyond the Market Paradigm*, Oxford: Basil Blackwell.

Moldovan, A. and S. van de Walle (2013), 'Gifts or bribes: attitudes on informal payments in Romanian healthcare', *Public Integrity*, **15** (4), 383–95.

Mróz, B. (2012), 'Entrepreneurship in the shadow: faces and variations of Poland's informal economy', *International Journal of Economic Policy in Emerging Economies*, **5** (3), 197–211.

OECD (2012), *Reducing Opportunities for Tax Non-Compliance in the Underground Economy*, Paris: OECD.

Pahl, R.E. (1984), *Divisions of Labour*, Oxford: Blackwell.

Pfeffermann, D. (1993), 'The role of sampling weights when modelling survey data', *International Statistical Review*, **61** (2), 317–37.

Ram, M. and C.C. Williams (2008), 'Making visible the hidden: researching off-the-books work', in D. Buchanan and A. Bryson (eds), *Handbook of Organizational Research Methods*, London: Sage, pp. 141–60.

Round, J., C.C. Williams and P. Rodgers (2008), 'Corruption in the post-Soviet workplace: the experiences of recent graduates in contemporary Ukraine', *Work, Employment & Society*, **22** (1), 149–66.

Sassen, S. (1996), 'Service employment regimes and the new inequality', in E. Mingione (ed.), *Urban Poverty and the Underclass*, Oxford: Basil Blackwell, pp. 142–59.

Schneider, F. (ed.) (2008), *The Hidden Economy*, Cheltenham, UK and Northampton, MA, USA: Edward Elgar Publishing.

Schneider, F. and C.C. Williams (2013), *The Shadow Economy*, London: Institute of Economic Affairs.

Sharon, S.L. and J. Liu (1994), 'A comparison of weighted and unweighted analyses in the National Crime Victimization Survey', *Journal of Quantitative Criminology*, **10** (4), 343–60.

Slavnic, Z. (2010), 'Political economy of informalization', *European Societies*, **12** (1), 3–23.

Small Business Council (2004), *Small Business in the Informal Economy: Making the Transition to the Formal Economy*, London: Small Business Council.

Smith, R. and G. McElwee (2013), 'Confronting social constructions of rural criminality: a case story on "illegal pluriactivity" in the farming community', *Sociologia Ruralis*, **53** (1), 112–34.

Snijders, T.A. and R.L. Bosker (2012), *Multilevel Analysis: An Introduction to Basic and Advanced Multilevel Modelling*, London: Sage.

Snyder, K.A. (2004), 'Routes to the informal economy in New York's East village: crisis, economics and identity', *Sociological Perspectives*, **47** (2), 215–40.

Solon, G., S.J. Haider and J. Wooldridge (2013), 'What are we weighting for?', NBER Working Paper No. 8, Washington, DC: National Bureau of Economic Research.

Stănculescu, M. (2005), 'Working conditions in the informal sector', *South East Europe Review for Labour and Social Affairs*, **10** (3), 79–93.

Surdej, A. and E. Ślęzak (2009), 'Formal and informal work in a transition economy: the case of Poland', in B. Pfau-Effinger, L. Flaquer and P.H. Jensen (eds), *Formal and Informal Work: The Hidden Work Regime in Europe*, London: Routledge, pp. 89–116.

Taiwo, O. (2013), 'Employment choice and mobility in multi-sector labour markets: theoretical model and evidence from Ghana', *International Labour Review*, **152** (3–4), 469–92.

Thai, M.T.T. and E. Turkina (eds) (2013), *Entrepreneurship in the Informal Economy: Models, Approaches and Prospects for Economic Development*, London: Routledge.

Van Geuns, R., J. Mevissen and P. Renooy (1987), 'The spatial and sectoral diversity of the informal economy', *Tijdschrift voor Economische en Sociale Geografie*, **78** (5), 389–98.

Vanderseypen, G., T. Tchipeva, J. Peschner, P. Rennoy and C.C. Williams (2013), 'Undeclared work: recent developments', in European Commission (ed.), *Employment and Social Developments in Europe 2013*, Brussels: European Commission, pp. 231–74.

Webb, J.W., R.D. Ireland and D.J. Ketchen (2014), 'Towards a greater understanding of entrepreneurship and strategy in the informal economy', *Strategic Entrepreneurship Journal*, **8** (1), 1–15.

Webb, J.W., G.D. Bruton, L. Tihanyi and R.D. Ireland (2013), 'Research on entrepreneurship in the informal economy: framing a research agenda', *Journal of Business Venturing*, **28** (4), 598–614.

Webb, J.W., L. Tihanyi, R.D. Ireland and D.G. Sirmon (2009), 'You say illegal, I say legitimate: entrepreneurship in the informal economy', *Academy of Management Review*, **34** (3), 492–510.

Welter, F. and D. Smallbone (2011), 'Institutional perspectives on entrepreneurial behavior in challenging environments', *Journal of Small Business Management*, **49** (1), 107–25.

Williams, C.C. (2005), 'The undeclared sector, self-employment and public policy', *International Journal of Entrepreneurial Behaviour and Research*, **11** (4), 244–57.

Williams, C.C. (2006), *The Hidden Enterprise Culture: Entrepreneurship in the Underground Economy*, Cheltenham, UK and Northampton, MA, USA: Edward Elgar Publishing.

Williams, C.C. (2007), 'Small businesses and the informal economy: evidence from the UK', *International Journal of Entrepreneurial Behaviour and Research*, **13** (6), 349–66.

Williams, C.C. (2009), 'The hidden enterprise culture: entrepreneurs in the underground economy in England, Ukraine and Russia', *Journal of Applied Management and Entrepreneurship*, **14** (2), 44–60.

Williams, C.C. (2010), 'Spatial variations in the hidden enterprise culture: some lessons from England', *Entrepreneurship and Regional Development*, **22** (5), 403–23.

Williams, C.C. (2013), 'Beyond the formal economy: evaluating the level of employment in informal sector enterprises in global perspective', *Journal of Developmental Entrepreneurship*, **18** (4), 1–18.

Williams, C.C. (2014a), *Confronting the Shadow Economy: Evaluating Tax Compliance and Behaviour Policies*, Cheltenham, UK and Northampton, MA, USA: Edward Elgar Publishing.

Williams, C.C. (2014b), 'Out of the shadows: a classification of economies by the size and character of their informal sector', *Work, Employment and Society*, **28** (5), 735–53.

Williams, C.C. (2015a), *Informal Sector Entrepreneurship*, Paris: OECD.

Williams, C.C. (2015b), 'Explaining cross-national variations in the commonality of informal sector entrepreneurship: an exploratory analysis of 38 emerging economies', *Journal of Small Business and Entrepreneurship*, **27** (2), 191–212.

Williams, C.C. and I. Horodnic (2015), 'Self-employment, the informal economy and the marginalisation thesis: some evidence from the European Union', *International Journal of Entrepreneurial Behaviour and Research*, **21** (2), 224–42.

Williams, C.C. and A. Martinez-Perez (2014a), 'Is the informal economy an incubator for new enterprise creation? A gender perspective', *International Journal of Entrepreneurial Behaviour and Research*, **20** (1), 4–19.

Williams, C.C. and A. Martinez-Perez (2014b), 'Why do consumers purchase goods and services in the informal economy?', *Journal of Business Research*, **67** (5), 802–806.

Williams, C.C. and A. Martinez-Perez (2014c), 'Entrepreneurship in the informal economy: a product of too much or too little state intervention?', *International Journal of Entrepreneurship and Innovation*, **15** (4), 227–37.

Williams, C.C. and A. Martinez-Perez (2014d), 'Do small business start-ups test-trade in the informal economy? Evidence from a UK small business survey', *International Journal of Entrepreneurship and Small Business*, **22** (1), 1–16.

Williams, C.C. and M.S. Shahid (2014), 'Informal entrepreneurship and institutional theory: explaining the varying degrees of (in)formalization of entrepreneurs in Pakistan', *Entrepreneurship and Regional Development*, available at: http://dx.doi.org/10.1080/08985626.2014.963889.

Williams, C.C., S. Nadin and M. Baric (2011), 'Evaluating the participation of the self-employed in undeclared work: some evidence from a 27-nation European survey', *International Entrepreneurship and Management Journal*, **7** (3), 341–56.

Williams, C.C., S. Nadin and P. Rodgers (2012), 'Evaluating competing theories of informal entrepreneurship: some lessons from Ukraine', *International Journal of Entrepreneurial Behaviour and Research*, **18** (5), 528–43.

Williams, C.C., J. Round and P. Rodgers (2013), *The Role of Informal Economies in the Post-Soviet World: The End of Transition?*, London: Routledge.

Williams, N. and T. Vorley (2014), 'Institutional asymmetry: how formal and informal institutions affect entrepreneurship in Bulgaria', *International Small Business Journal*, doi: 10.1177/0266242614534280.

Winship, C. and L. Radbill (1994), 'Sampling weights and regression analysis', *Sociological Methods and Research*, **23** (2), 230–57.

APPENDIX 4A.1

Table 4A.1 Variables used in the analysis: definitions and descriptive statistics

Variables	Definition	Mode or mean	Min./Max.
Shadow economy (dependent variable)	Dummy variable of whether participated in shadow economy in the last 12 months	No shadow activities (94.04%)	0/1
Gender	Dummy for the gender of the respondent	Male (66.13%)	0/1
Age	Respondent age in intervals	40–54 years old (45.67%)	1/4
Marital status	Respondent marital status in categories	Married/remarried (61.46%)	1/5
Social class	Respondent perception regarding social class of society to which it belongs in categories	Middle class of society (59.60%)	1/3
Age when stopped full time education	Respondent age when stopped full-time education in categories	16–19 years old (47.80%)	1/3
People 15+ years in own household	People 15+ years in respondent's household (including the respondent) in categories	Two people (47.83%)	1/4
Children	Presence of children (up to 14 years old) in the household in categories	No children (64.97%)	1/4
Tax morality index	Constructed index of self-reported tolerance towards tax non-compliance	2.31	1/10
Occupation	Respondent occupation in categories	Owner of a shop, craftsmen, etc. (38.30%)	1/4
Difficulties paying bills	Respondent difficulties in paying bills in categories	Almost never/never (59.50)	1/3
Area respondent lives	Size of the area where the respondent lives in categories	Rural area or village (38.93%)	1/3
EU Region	Region where the respondent lives in categories	Western Europe (39.69%)	1/4

Source: Eurobarometer 79.2 (2013): Undeclared Work in the European Union.

PART II

Entrepreneurship and the Shadow Economy
in Various Contexts

5. Informal entrepreneurship and informal entrepreneurial activity in Russia

Alexander Chepurenko

INTRODUCTION

The aim of this chapter is to examine the rationales and motives for conducting informal activities in transitional economies like Russia. To do this, it seeks to explore the roots and character of informal entrepreneurial activity in contemporary Russia using a set of in-depth interviews with a panel of start-ups and entrepreneurs in Moscow collected in two waves, in 2013 and 2014. In doing so, this chapter adds to the relatively sparse literature on entrepreneurship development in weak institutional environments undergoing transition. The main idea underpinning the chapter is that informal entrepreneurial activity in the contemporary Russian economy and in similar transitional environments is only partly a result of the heritage of the Socialist era. In many ways, informal behaviour of start-ups and SMEs is the result of the realms established during the transition itself.

While it is well established within the body of small business literature that 'context matters', when considering the nature of entrepreneurship and entrepreneurial behaviour (Welter, 2011), the full impact of historical, cultural and social contexts of entrepreneurship in transitional contexts still requires additional consideration (Blackburn and Kovalainen, 2009). This is true also for informal entrepreneurial activity and informal entrepreneurship in Russia and similar economies with a fragile institutional setting, imperfect competition and 'limited access order' (North et al., 2013).

By adopting such an approach, this chapter argues that the dominance of rent-seeking behaviour and 'unproductive entrepreneurship' (Baumol, 1990) impacts on entrepreneurial motivation and strategy. It strongly posits that there is a lack of understanding of the heterogeneity of informal entrepreneurship in Russia, due to insufficient reflection on the different push/pull factors for entrepreneurial activity and small business development within the country. To address this, the chapter develops a typology of Russian bottom-up entrepreneurs, based on their attitude towards informal practices, to demonstrate, in terms of motivation and strategy, their diversity.

To achieve this, the chapter is structured as follows. First, it briefly outlines how it defines informal entrepreneurial activity and informal entrepreneurship and second, it provides the outline of the institutional and social contexts within which the entrepreneurs operate and which determine the motivation of entrepreneurial activity, including the informal activities of many Russian small businesses. The chapter then explores, based on a set of cases collected by the author, the diversity of resources, motives and strategies with which the different actors operate. The chapter then concludes by calling for a more accurate formulation of policy to 'combat' informal entrepreneurial activity in Russia and for further research into the role of context in entrepreneurship and small business development.

LITERATURE REVIEW: 'INFORMAL ENTREPRENEURIAL ACTIVITY' AND 'INFORMAL ENTREPRENEURSHIP'

Within the scope of the literature dealing with the informal economy (Castells and Portes, 1989; De Soto, 1989; Andrews et al., 2011; Godfrey, 2011; Williams et al., 2013), our aim is to focus on the narrower theme, informal entrepreneurial activity (Webb et al., 2013; Dau and Cuervo-Cazurra, 2014).

There are many partly diverging definitions of what is meant when discussing 'informal entrepreneurial activity', especially under transition (for more detail see Gërxhani, 2004), and this chapter draws upon the approach of De Soto (1989) and his followers (see also Portes and Haller, 2005; La Porta and Shleifer, 2008), as it provides the following definition: activities, while being illegal, remain legitimate for many entrepreneurs' counterparts (consumers and suppliers, employees and so on). Phenomena embraced by such a definition include the use of undocumented hiring of employees, counterfeiting, ticket scalping, unregistered and/or tax-avoiding businesses, bootlegging, the skirting of environmental regulations, 'street entrepreneurship' and so on (Webb et al., 2013; Dau and Cuervo-Cazurra, 2014).

This definition might also be formulated as follows: informal economic practices are unreported (or in other ways hidden from the state) activities of entrepreneurs/entrepreneurial firms whose business is not 'antisocial in intent' (De Soto, 1989) and who produce goods and services not forbidden by law. Such endeavours are to be distinguished from, for example, actors such as so-called violent entrepreneurs who use violence as a source of rent extraction (Volkov, 1999), or illegal entrepreneurial activity (Aidis and van Praag, 2007).

First of all, therefore, it needs to be stressed that informal economy, informal entrepreneurial activity and informal entrepreneurship are to be treated as related but different terms. This chapter focuses both on informal entrepreneurial activity and informal entrepreneurship, and the variety of its forms and motives in Russia, a specific post-socialist society characterized by the deep embeddedness of such practices. Consequently, it is important to define the area. According to Gimpelson and Zudina (2011), those who act informally in any economy can be broadly placed into five categories:

- entrepreneurs without any registration of their businesses;
- self-employed who are registered but who act partially informally;
- informal wage and salary workers hired by private persons;
- informal wage and salary workers hired by formal firms and working without any sign of a written contract;
- irregular workers.

Only the first two categories are the actors under investigation in the present chapter. It is widely accepted, as supported by both official statistics and academic estimations, that the share of 'shadow', 'grey' or informal entrepreneurial activity in the majority of former socialist economies is relatively large (Estrin and Mickiewicz, 2011). In these post-socialist societies, the informal economy grew rapidly during the first decade of economic reform due to the chaotic nature of the processes (Schneider and Enste, 2000). For example, during the rapid marketization process, many employees of former state-owned plants were pushed into 'street entrepreneurship' (Earle and Sakova, 2000) or suitcase or shuttle trading (Eder et al., 2003; Yakovlev et al., 2007) as wage arrears became a mass strategy of former state enterprises, thus forcing employees to earn an income informally.

According to some measurements, as much as 40 per cent of economic activity in the Russian Federation could be informal in nature, significantly greater than in OECD countries and many other emerging economies (Schneider et al., 2010). Consequently, some experts argue that 'some of the gap in formal SME and entrepreneurship activity in the Russian Federation, as counted in official business registers, is the reflection of a relatively large informal sector' (OECD, 2015, p. 6). This fact is sometimes used by Russian officials as a reason to elaborate measures to combat, downsize or eliminate 'informal entrepreneurship'.

Meantime, it is important not to conflate the informal economy with informal entrepreneurial activity, as for instance subsistence economy, homeworking, mutual neighbours' services and so on form a part of the informal economy, but not of informal entrepreneurial activity. Taking into consideration the geography of Russia where many inhabitants of rural areas and even of small towns are participating in the subsistence economy which is informal by definition but has nothing in common with entrepreneurship or business, we presume that the share of these two groups among the variety of the informally active population groups cannot be as large, especially if we refer to the GEM data. The results of this quite reliable project should confirm such doubts, as the share of early entrepreneurs in Russia is among the lowest in the world during the whole period of observation (2006–14), and does not exceed 3–4 per cent of the adult population.[1] It is important to stress, nevertheless, that the GEM method does not differentiate between formal and informal entrepreneurial activity. Hence, the informal part of entrepreneurial activity cannot be bigger than the total early stage entrepreneurial activity.

However, this does not mean that informal entrepreneurial activity is totally harmless and should not attract the attention of researchers. But it should be understood as a part of entrepreneurial activity in the country being a result of some institutional and societal specifics. On this basis, it could help to explain the nature of informal entrepreneurial activity in Russia and to elaborate more relevant policy recommendations on how to deal with it.

Second, we insist that informal entrepreneurial activity is a broader term than informal entrepreneurship. Many registered and mainly formally acting firms – and not only in transitional economies – occasionally or regularly use informal practices, such as off-the-books transactions with suppliers and customers or the hiring of employees without written contracts. Purely informal entrepreneurship is a much narrower niche, the domain of so-called one-day firms or silent money lenders providing funding to relatives and friends who are starting a new venture, or even to strangers, without any permission or registration needed to do business on a regular basis formally.

The literature on entrepreneurship under the so-called systemic transition, the complex and enduring process of systemic change in the former socialist countries of Central and Eastern Europe (CEE) and the Commonwealth of Independent States (CIS), has been growing since the middle of the 1990s (McMillan and Woodruff, 2002; Smallbone and Welter, 2001, 2009; Djankov et al., 2005; Ovaska and Sobel, 2005; Welter, 2005; Aidis et al., 2008; Manolova et al., 2008; Welter and Smallbone, 2011; Williams et al., 2013). It is widely accepted that in the course of systemic transition, several institutional factors predetermined a significant growth of informal entrepreneurial activity, including the specifics of privatization (Feige, 1997; Scase, 1997; 2003; Spicer et al., 2000) and the societal realms (Rehn and Taalas, 2004).

In mature market economies, operating informally is often a temporary strategy of start-ups, to test a product/idea/service informally to gauge the market. If the start-up stage is realized more or less successfully, these enterprises seek to formalize to have better access to customers, financial sector services and to gain the social benefits formality brings. In contrast, in transitional environments, informal entrepreneurial activity is often the single possibility for business survival (Chepurenko, 2014). Why? As Williams (2008) notes, there are four main theoretic lenses to explain informal entrepreneurial activity. First, the modernization perspective presents a dichotomous view that states that as an economy matures, informality will die away. It is also argued that a significant cause of informal entrepreneurial behaviour is the legacy of the 'socialist past' – an attempt to use notions of 'path dependency' to explain contemporary economic development in transition countries and its institutional forms (Ellman, 1994; Johnson et al., 2000; Puffer and McCarthy, 2001; Estrin et al., 2006). However, this chapter argues that to fully understand the persistence and self-reproduction of informal entrepreneurial practices, more than 20 years after the Soviet Union's collapse, requires a greater appreciation of the institutional frameworks of the transition itself. Furthermore, in the existing literature there is a lack of reflection on the variety of forms and practices of informal entrepreneurship – a result of an insufficient examination of different factors pushing/pulling people to engage in such behaviour, their motivations, self-reflections, self-perceptions and so on, within fragile and rapidly shifting business environments.

The second, structuralist, perspective argues that when individuals are excluded from formal labour markets they will turn to informal activities, including when starting up a business activity, despite the lack of protection and low benefits this provides (Castells and Portes, 1989; Sassen, 1997). A third, neo-liberal viewpoint, argues that informal entrepreneurship results from state inefficiencies, corruption and/or over-regulation (De Soto, 1989). Fourthly, a post-structuralist perspective views informal entrepreneurial activity as an alternative space in which participants transform their work identity and/or reveal their true selves such as by establishing informal lifestyle businesses (down-shifters and freelancers becoming entrepreneurs) for a multitude of reasons.

In contemporary Russia, as well as in some similar transitional economies, a mix of all four arguments can be justified (with cases partly reflecting them below, in the empirical part of the chapter). First, the impact of informal entrepreneurship as a reaction to the shocks and massive decon-struction of the formal economy is decreasing (the rise and then a quick decline of the shuttle-trading; see Yakovlev et al., 2007); second, the reason for informal entrepreneurial activity persistence is the structural exclusion of those without the political connections and/or relevant skills and capital to do business formally, especially immigrants, rural inhabitants and other less adaptive groups; third, the neo-liberal arguments are true when con-sidering formally established SMEs aiming to avoid the excessive bureauc-racy; fourth, in post-structural terms many people decide it is safer to be 'hidden' from rent-seekers and to become freelancers acting semi-formally. There are many person-related factors and reasons which may influence the decision to do business informally, at least partly. Very generally, silent money lenders, entrepreneurial employees and self-employed; those driven by empathy or being motivated by necessity; those characterized by the combination of low human capital plus low social capital; strangers and foreigners are more inclined to start up and even to do business informally, or at least semi-formally (Table 5.1; see also Chepurenko, 2014, for details of its 'fuzziness'). Hence, any empirical investigation of the reasons and strategies used by entrepreneurs to act informally should take this fuzziness into consideration.

The balance between formal and informal entrepreneurial activities is not only driven by personal factors but is also context dependent (Welter, 2011), that is, dependent on the specific set and configuration of institutions. Among these institutions, as shown in institutional theory, property rights protection and/or state interference, and easy and equal entry are especially important to ensure that entrepreneurs are active and operate formally. There are different approaches to delineate the differences in institutional settings among countries, with North et al.'s (2013) generalist approach, which highlights 'free access' and 'limited access' orders, an appropriate tool for examining the role of context in entrepreneurial activity and small business development. We assume that, in spite of the fact that North et al. themselves constructed the concept of a 'limited access order' while studying some societies in Latin America and South-Eastern Asia, this concept is fully applicable to Russia and similar 'transitional' societies because they are character-ized by exactly the same characteristic features of the state, its role in society, uneven access of representatives of different strata to policy and law protection, and the dominant role of some groups of interest ('oligarchs', 'siloviki' etc.). This is already clearly evident in the literature (Elster et al., 1998; Remington, 2000; Renz, 2006: Rivera and Rivera, 2006; Treisman, 2006; Aidis et al., 2008; Gelman, 2010a, 2010b, 2011) and is supported by the scores Russia obtains in different comparative

Table 5.1 Variety of personal factors influencing informal entrepreneurial activity

By character of entrepreneurial activity	By reasons to become entrepreneurial	By motivation	By set of capital	By origin	By gender
Silent money lenders	Empathy	Reciprocity	Money capital	Core ethnicity	Male
Entrepreneurial employees	Seeking additional income source	Necessity driven	High human capital + high social capital	Immigrant	Female
	Gaining start-up experience				
Self-employed	Traditional ('street entrepreneurs' etc.)	Improvement driven opportunity	Low human capital + high social capital		
	Freelancers	Life style			
		Protest at system			
		Linked to ability			
Solo owners	Survival		Low human capital + low social capital		
Entrepreneurial firms	Growth				

rankings (for example, Index of Economic Freedom; Doing Business; Global Competitiveness Index).

Under such circumstances, unproductive entrepreneurship, that is seeking and exploitation of opportunities to extract administrative or political rent, becomes dominant, as has already been described based on CEE countries' experience (Sauka and Welter, 2007). When unproductive and destructive entrepreneurship become commonplace there are significant implications for entrepreneurs. First, trust in the state is extremely low as entrepreneurs view it as a hawkish, unfair competitor and societal support for informal entrepreneurial activities increases (Welter, 2005). Tolerance of tax evasion becomes embedded and the reliance on informal shared norms and contacts rather than on legal frameworks becomes stronger (for more detail see Batjargal, 2006; 2010; Ledeneva, 1998; Puffer et al., 2010; Raiser et al., 2003; Smallbone and Welter, 2001; 2009; Tonoyan et al., 2010). Under such conditions, informal entrepreneurial activity is rather a form of rational compromise than of avoidance and deviance (Oliver, 1991). This rationality impacts upon the societal image of informal behaviour, which also differs according to context.

Contrary to established market economies, engaging in informal economic practices in Russia does not necessarily affect the social status of people engaged in it (Zudina, 2013; Round et al., 2008). Whilst commentators have often sought to explain the existence of informal entrepreneurship according to a single logic, recently there have been calls for a greater integration of these four theorizations taking into account the fact that different motives may co-exist for entrepreneurs (Aidis and Van Praag, 2007) and also an individual's motives can change over time (Welter and Smallbone, 2011).

DATA AND METHODOLOGY

The theme of the survey is quite a sensitive topic, and the general parameters of the sample uncertain. Therefore, the preference was made for choosing an appropriate quantitative method (Atkinson and Flint, 2001), while establishing a small sample for a 3 to 4-year survey. Thus, the study is based on a series of cases collected in accordance with the 'typical cases' approach. Below, some findings of the first two waves of semi-structured interviews conducted in 2013 and 2014 in Moscow are presented. The panel was formed in the middle of 2013 among Moscow self-employees, entrepreneurs and start-up founders using the snowball technique to establish a sample (see Table 5.2).

In the initial sample there were respondents included who represented

Table 5.2 *Structure of the panel by socio-demographic issues, employment status and entrepreneurial experience (as at the beginning of the study)*

		Employment status			Beginning of entrepreneurial activity		
		Self-employed	Entrepreneur	Start-up (or seed stage)	1990–1999	2000–2012	At the time of the survey
Gender	Man	2	6	2	2	7	3
	Woman	1	1	1	1	–	–
Age	21–30	1	1	1			
	31–45		2				
	46–60	1		7			
Education	Not completed secondary school			1	1		
	Secondary school		1			1	
	Not completed higher school	1					1
	Higher school		10		3	7	
Ethnical business			1		1		

both already established business owners and freelancers as well as start-up projects and even seed-stage entrepreneurs, men and women between 24 and 60 years and older, with education from secondary school up to university degree, both born and bred Muscovites and those who had moved to the capital from other Russian regions and the CIS, belonging to different branches (productive sector, business services as well as B2C, catering).

A short portrait of respondents is as follows:

- No. 1: man, over 30 years old, secondary school, Russian, born and raised in Uzbekistan, in Moscow since the end of the 1990s, main business repairing apartments and offices as well as cottage development, more than 10 years of business experience;
- No. 2: man, about 45 years old, from a military family, left a military higher school before graduating, in Moscow since the mid-1990s, self-employed, main business repairing apartments, business experience over 20 years;
- No. 3: man, 50 years old, higher school in engineering, Muscovite, business: engineering in building construction and management, business experience over 20 years;
- No. 4: man, about 60 years old, higher school in economics, Muscovite, business in consumption goods import (food), business experience over 20 years;
- No. 5: woman, about 25 years old, higher school, humanities education, born and brought up in North Caucasus, catering, business experience more than 1 year;
- No. 6: man, 60 years old, higher school in engineering and physics, coming from one of the CIS republics in the Caucasus, in Moscow since the beginning of the 1990s, business in construction, business experience over 20 years;
- No. 7: man about 35 years old, secondary school not completed, Muscovite, IT in trade and services, business experience about 20 years;
- No. 8: man about 30–32 years old, higher school, economics, Muscovite, business in transportation and logistics, experience of about 5 years;
- No. 9: woman, about 27 years old, higher school, humanities education, in Moscow since 2005, catering, business experience about 2 years;
- No. 10: woman of pension age (in Russia: over 55), higher school, humanities education, Muscovite, business services and printing, business experience over 15 years;

- No. 11: man, about 40 years old, Muscovite, higher education in engineering and physics as well as in economics, business: initially Internet trade, then business brokering, business experience about 15 years;
- No. 12: man, about 60 years old, Muscovite, higher education in engineering, PhD degree, business experience in consulting, including political consulting, project development in mining extraction, business experience over 20 years;
- No. 13: man, about 30 years old, Muscovite, higher school, humanities education, printing services, business experience about 3 years.

Interviews were semi-structured; no recording was used according to the wishes of most of the respondents, but after decoding the notes, the written versions were sent to the respondents and checked by them to avoid any factual misunderstandings.

In the first wave in the Autumn of 2013, the interviews mostly raised questions on life and business experience, family, its role in the business, description of the current business, partners, ownership structure, goals, attitudes towards state regulation, team and its structure, employees and forms of hiring and sales, future plans and strategies.

In the Autumn of 2014, the second wave of semi-structured interviews was conducted, which mostly raised questions on the change of status and the businesses of the interviewees, as well as questions concerning factors relating to changes in the business climate and so on, estimations of the prospects of their current business and their own life prospects. Within such a context, questions were also asked during the first and second waves of interviews about the respondents' current experience in dealing with the state and state servants, use of different forms of taxation, tax optimization (and possible frauds), as well as on forms of hiring of employees, which could provide some in-depth information about the tools and schemes of informal entrepreneurial activity that were used as well as on the reasons for engaging in informal activity and self-perception of informal activity (if mentioned).

As a rule, an interview in the first wave took close to 2 hours; in the second wave it took 40 minutes to 1.5 hours, with a few longer talks with some interviewees.

RESULTS OF TWO WAVES OF INTERVIEWS (2013 AND 2014)

The two waves of the survey brought some evidence about the forms of informal practices and reasons for using them when hiring employees, developing payment practices between the entrepreneur and his/her clients and suppliers, as well as when communicating with state authorities. Moreover, there are some assessments of the economic situation in Russia and business morals, and self-perceptions of the factors behind the informal activities which were being assessed.

This part of the chapter is organized according to the logic of the interviews as follows: (a) hiring of personnel and related informal practices (according to our expectations, this was the most common and least sensitive issue); (b) relations with customers (here, we assumed there would be less willingness to report informal activities); (c) relations with state officials (which we initially believed to be the most emotional part of the interview).

Hiring of Personnel and Informal Practices

Informal hiring without a proper work contract as well as informal payment practices when the whole or a significant part of the salary is paid off-the-books exist, according to the interviewees, almost everywhere. However, the major difference between the formally registered and totally informal firms is whether all or only a proportion of the employees receive their payment in cash or off-the-books.

Respondent No. 9 expressed this when laughing: 'If any salary is to be paid, it is paid "white" – in white envelopes'. Sometimes, there are no informal payments, as for instance at the firm of respondent No. 10, where most interpreters hired for big events are registered as solo entrepreneurs. That is why no salary relation exists, as they are in effect subcontracted. Only those who do not have the formal status of a solo entrepreneur receive their contract payment through a third party, contracted solo entrepreneurs, in cash.

If the firm is under the exceptional control of the state authorities, the usage of only formal hiring and payment practices becomes unavoidable. This is the case in respondent No. 4's firm where until 2009 part of the salary was paid informally, and 'nobody worried about it, but after the conflict with the Customs and Tax administration began, wage arrears occurred. After August 2013 we switched to only white salary, as we did not have any non-accounted goods and transactions any more'. Thus, in his family business there is no core personnel turnover at all in spite of the relatively modest salaries: 65–70 000 roubles per month if the business is running well, while sales managers have a fixed part of their salary (30–40 per cent) and the rest consists of special bonuses for fulfilling certain key performance indicators (KPIs). Before the incident with the state authorities, this bonus, according to the interviewee, was also paid in envelopes. However, there are no unregistered workers. 'Even the workers from Central Asian republics working in the depot (it is impossible to hire any non-alcoholics among Russian citizens for this kind of work) have official registration permits', says the interviewee, as well as written contracts with carefully formulated terms and conditions.

Forms of the self-legitimation of informal hiring and payment to employees differ: some respondents argue it is a form of control; some add also that it is a form of partial risk transfer to the personnel. The single argument which was not at all mentioned by the respondents is the minimizing of tax costs.

Certainly, often respondents told us that they engage in these practices because all the entrepreneurs are doing it, and the most important reason for this situation is corruption. As respondent No. 2 mentioned, 'there are about 10 per cent of entrepreneurs in Moscow who work entirely legally. Others are using 'black' cash. Otherwise, you will have only troubles; one inspection goes out, the next is coming in. And all insist on donations. The change of the Governor of the city [in 2010, the old Governor Lushkov, known for his highly bureaucratic and corrupt system of city governance, was suspended by the President 'for loss of trust' and a new Governor Sobyanin from the Kremlin administration was assigned] did not change much in this situation'.

Respondent No. 1:

> Sure, all employees are working on the basis of oral agreements only. As soon as the contract with the client is received, I make the initial calculation. Then, I make an initial calculation of salaries. I do not pay any advance, the first payment comes after 5 to 7 days of working on the job; I have to prove first whether it is OK there. After it I pay regularly, in small instalments, and my residual is about 10 per cent.

As he stated:

> Now, it is more and more difficult to find workers for the simplest kinds of work. That is, it is hard with the black people. We call them avatars. Because they are able only for the simplest types of work. But they are not drinking, unlike Russians, and do not have many other harmful habits, they only are chewing their *nasvay*.[2] . . . Who is responsible for it? The Federal Migration Service and we, Russian racists. Russians are, to my feeling, big racists. In [Central] Asia, according to Russian employers' demand, there is already a firmly established slave trade; there are many courtyards where prospective workers are coming. You may come and choose somebody who is fatter or leaner. Then, you say: I will take this guy and another guy; if you need, you may take even 70 persons or more. Then, you have to pay a tax to the authorities, they are sending all of them to you, and you are using them as a cheap labour. They are very submissive; it is easy to oppress them morally and to let them do what you wish. And

Russians, they do not like to work, besides, they have their habits to drink, to smoke etc. And all of them, even those who are not able to do anything, wish to become bosses.

As respondent No. 11 said:

Now, we have around 50 persons in our firm. There are drivers, call-centre people, IT personnel (outside of the official staff), storekeepers, purchasing managers, quality control, accountants. Some of them are working on a labour contract, some have agency agreements. For instance, our IT people are residing in the Ukraine, and there is one individual on an agency agreement who is paid for their work.

Those who are formally hired receive a fixed salary and some rewards according to the financial results.

In such a way, we try to transfer part of our financial risks to employees. Sure, a part of the salary is paid off-the-books. But it is so in all small enterprises. Medium sized firms cannot work in such a manner. And as for the big firms, for them it is maybe impossible.

Especially interesting was the statement of respondent No. 7. He does not accept any shadow transactions, as this is against his moral principles, but he shows a certain understanding for other entrepreneurs, as 'the Russian legislation is a draconian legislation. That is why entrepreneurs try to avoid taxes'.

To avoid salary taxation, which in Russia is the employer's responsibility, apart from a simple off-the books technique, there are several other methods used. One method is, however, a clear separation of core and periphery workers as regards their employment status and level of formality. For instance, as respondent No. 1 mentioned in the second wave of interviews:

my formal staff consists of only three persons, as officially we provide only services but not works in furnishing and construction. Then, which questions could be raised to me [from the tax authorities]? All my workers 'graze' outside of the wall. Really, I have around 70 employees now, 4 teams, each with its own master; besides that, we hire from outside when needed. All the questions concerning salary, its form, level etc., the masters clarify by themselves.

Immigrant workers dominate. 'A whole international team is working there, Dagestan people, Uzbeks, Tajiks, Tartars, Gagauz people, Ukrainians, we even have one Jewish man who is breaking old walls; nobody believes me when I am telling about him'.

A similar picture was painted by respondent No. 6. At his firm,

> besides the masters and workers who change steadily and receive a piecework payment, there are 8 core staff members: director, chief engineer, deputy director, accountant, 2 consultants, 2 chief masters. All of them receive a fixed 'white' salary and may receive some bonuses, if we are able to pay them. No envelopes. That is my principle. Maybe, because I am unable to dodge? Two times in my life I tried to bribe, and both times I was caught; it seems to me that it is written on my face when I try to cheat [he smiles].

The fact that masters and workers belong to the personnel, too, and that the hiring and payment practices with this category seem to be not as formal as with the core team, seems not to be reflected by the respondent as a problem.

The above examples let us assume that within the entrepreneurial community in Russia certain differences exist, not only in the level of salary but also in the level of formality of hiring between the core and the periphery. Second, the informal hiring of the periphery seems not to appear to be a problem for the entrepreneurs themselves, either regarding the legal aspect or the moral state of things.

Another method used is the establishment of a model of business in which most members of the team are formally independent solo entrepreneurs, so no employment relation formally exists. For instance, most workers of respondent No. 8 are formally his franchisees; a similar story is told by respondent No. 10. However, in her case, many interpreters who initially were individual entrepreneurs decided to quit the business, as the social tax for solo owners was doubled in 2014 by the Russian government. After this, she complained, many of the interpreters decided to work only off-the-books, while transferring the fiscal claims of the government to her firm: she was forced to register her son and daughter as solo entrepreneurs and to pay them according to contract. In reality, the honoraria were paid in cash to the persons who really managed the work.

The self-legitimation of the informal payment of a (sometimes significant) part of the salary usually consists in the argument that in such a way the respondent is trying to minimize taxation. This argument, however, sometimes contradicts the fact that the taxation system for some of the interviewees should, on the contrary, stimulate them to show all costs properly. For instance, this was the case for respondent No. 13, whose micro-business uses the simplified tax system where the amount of tax is calculated as a share from the difference between turnover and total costs. It seems that, without stating it openly, the respondent used such a form of payment in order to control the labour and the loyalty of his small staff (three people) to the firm. Or, another possible explanation is that it is an instinctive attempt to portray the business as being as small as possible in order not to attract inspections and to avoid a business takeover by low-level state bureaucrats. And certainly it is a strategy used by those of the interviewees who will never try to sell their businesses. As respondent No. 11 stated, 'when the true goal of the business is not the operation profit but the price of the company, you must be transparent. Thus, the motivation is changing'. His firm has five employees, all of them receiving fixed 'white' salaries.

Relations to Customers and Informal Practices

In relations with customers, fully formalized practices usually exist, with the exception of such trust-based areas as construction and repair, where deals mainly rely upon an already existing personal acquaintance with the prospective serviceman or upon recommendations of well trusted people who informally play a role of 'due diligence'.

As respondent No. 2 stated:

> I have my own market, as the clients recommend me to third parties, and I am working mostly with teachers and academic scholars. It is a very charming audience. And the demand is not going down, and in 2008[3] it even increased. Why? Maybe because many of them already had bad experience with legal firms, where prices are higher, and simply due to different frauds.

He works only in Moscow, as it is a larger market and the travel distances are shorter for him than in the greater Moscow area.

Informant No. 1 says that the use of formal or informal practices is client dependent:

> It looks different with different types of clients. If I have to deal with juridical entities, I usually use any one day firm, all scope of works are to be registered with this firm, but in reality all services are provided by my firm. If there is an individual, then I act according to the customer's desire; if he or she wishes, we make a formal agreement on paper, but do not register it and do not show it anywhere. If the customer already knows us and has trust in our services, then we don't do that. We simply agree upon the total price and start working.

The same story is confirmed by respondent No. 2:

> For sure, with clients we always agree orally. Somebody introduces me to the client, and I cherish my own reputation very much. In the event of any defect, I remove it without additional payment as I guarantee the quality. Therefore, people have trust in me and are ready to refuse any written contract.

However, respondent No. 6, who also works in construction, considers a close cooperation with big firms which are juridical entities as a reason to resort to different stratagems including informal practices: 'Under the circumstances described above [see pp. 136–7] it is very difficult not only to plan but also to pay salary to the workers regularly. From here we have to deal with the "optimization" of taxation, hiring without written contracts etc.'

It is evident that the level of formalization of the main business plays a role. Unlike entrepreneurs and the self-employed in construction, in the retail trade the level of formalization of relations with customers is much higher. As respondent No. 3, who is a co-owner of a retail shop dealing with cladding panels, mentioned, they deal with customers only with advance payment; therefore this kind of relationship is carefully documented, after payment on delivery they only deal with a small number of reliable customers who already have significant experience in cooperating with his firm.

> Our principle is never to provoke our clients. Even if the client wishes to return an item for any reason, we agree although we are not required to do so if nothing is corrupted or damaged, because we are aware that in this case the client will choose us next time again.

However, as the respondent mentioned, if the entrepreneurs tried to avoid accepting returned items, 'he will never accept reclamations, and no bailiffs would help because no firm responsible would exist there at that time'.

The legal form of the entity is important, too, as it is possible to use the simplified tax regimes. As respondent No. 5 mentioned,

> as we are using the simplified tax regime, we tried to have for all our purchases any receipts or cash-cheques etc. For instance, the rental of a truck was included in the estimates of the project. But concerning the revenue it is not so . . . If you are working according to the simplified tax rule, it is always in your interest to show all your expenses in full – but not all your benefits.

Informant No. 9 confirmed that when the payments are by bank transfer (through a third juridical entity, as the individual firm is in the process of registration), 'in such a case all is made in accordance with the law'.

Why do entrepreneurs like oral agreements with customers? Informant No. 3 explained that there is no choice:

> Otherwise, where will we receive the cash from which we need to pay salary to our staff and to ourselves? There are no risks, as when we let our staff collect payment from clients for services, it is not such a huge amount of money to run away with. There are other risks: last year, my bag with a big amount of money was stolen; it was the black revenue of the firm.

As regards the customers, their reasons are similar, according to respondent No. 2:

> We discuss all details orally. Customers are eager to do so because they also receive only 10–12 per cent of their wages officially, the rest of their income is off-the-books. And the renovation may cost up to 1–2 billion roubles. Therefore, nobody is interested in showing his/her real incomes!! To buy materials we use cash, and we report the expenses showing the invoices from the market.

It should be stressed, however, that in spite of the fact that it seems to be a quite realistic explanation, it is not really; in Russia, there is no obligation to register such kinds of civil-law contracts; moreover, tax inspectors working with documents of private entrepreneurs have no powers to analyse the sources of revenue of households who are customers of the controlled firms.

However, in other fields the situation might differ. For instance, in consumption goods retail trade, according to respondent No. 4: 'Actually, we simply do not need such a practice – 90 per cent [of turnover] goes through our bank; we rarely use our own cash. Because, why should we need it? If we need a small amount of cash, we may show a natural decrease (shrinkage, spillage, damage etc.), of up to 10 per cent [of costs]'.

In printing and publishing the situation is mixed. As respondent No. 10 mentioned, 'most transactions flow through the bank, among them from individuals, but somebody who knows and believes in us and our reputation, simply brings cash. Anyway, all is dealt with according to the customer's wish'. In other words, the firm itself has no preferences, and is equally eager to work with bank transfers or cash.

And respondent No. 9 insisted that oral agreements could even cause a financial crash of the business: 'our main customers are big firms (tourist agencies etc.), and they are not inclined to work with "black" cash; moreover, the agreement is a guarantee for us against any attempt to cheat from the side of bigger companies'. Here, we see a contradictory statement: on one hand, the respondent argues, it is the strategy of clients to avoid any informal payments, but on the other hand, she confirms that an agreement is rather an instrument of self-protection of the small firm. Anyway, she described some evident reasons not to use any informal off-the-books transactions between two businesses.

Meanwhile, in construction it also depends on the typology of customers. Clients of respondent No. 6 are mostly big construction companies. Therefore, 'such forms are not used, rather we have to count with the possibility that they will not pay the full price, or with cases when payment is suddenly suspended. For instance now we are still waiting to see whether a very big customer would pay, all the same'. Such an exploitation of smaller firms serving as suppliers of big companies that dominate the market formally does not imply any informal transactions in B2B relations; however, to survive under such circumstances, the supplier is pushed to minimize costs, for instance using informal hiring.

If oral agreements are a usual practice, it is mainly not a tactic used to avoid taxation but simply because the business itself is based upon a variety of very quick logistical services for different firms and individuals – respondent No. 8's business is delivery of goods, therefore, 'oral agreements are typical, also with business companies like Internet-shops where delivery is to be organized just in time; so, we simply don't have time to deal with many papers'.

Relations with State Officials

Respondents mainly tried to avoid talking about the state and its politics, except the representatives of the older cohort whose long entrepreneurial experience enables them to discuss the evolution of the state approach to entrepreneurs and small business. With one exception, this evolution is considered very negatively.

First, respondents assess the state approach to small business as a fiscal one. Characteristically, respondent No. 7 lamented, concerning taxation:

> you should give back 60 per cent from the profit but for what kind of services from the state? Seventy per cent of entrepreneurs according to my own estimations do not want to pay to such a state, 20 per cent came on the market to earn fast money and would not pay to any state at all, 10 per cent are still starting up and are still unable to pay any taxes.

For instance, the company where at the moment of the interview the respondent is employed is paying all taxes and respecting all rules, but it is big enough, while small businesses are objectively unable to fulfil all the tax regulations. Accountants recognize this fact and sell them tax optimization schemes for 2000–3000 roubles. As for him, 'solo entrepreneurs with up to 100 billion roubles annual turnover should be free of any taxation at all, otherwise they would not be able to establish new jobs, at least legally'.

Second, state policy is repressive. Meanwhile, identifying and combating economic crimes of some firms is often used as an excuse to extort rent from 'partners in crime'. The following is a story told by respondent No. 4:

> My firm specialises in import of consumption goods; there are constantly trucks arriving, and a necessary element of such business is customs clearance. But my firm is located in Moscow and the customs where we usually import is located in St Petersburg. Under the existing conditions, we are pushed to

cooperate with those customs brokers whom we find on advice of certain circles around the customs; at one time they recommended some closely related intermediaries, and we worked with this firm over a period. In 2010 it suddenly turned out that this firm was caught smuggling (at that time this still was a criminal, not an administrative issue), then it was caught evading tax. After the firm was investigated, they started to accuse our firm, as if our firm was the real initiator of the affair, and they were simply being our 'agent', and we had organized all the deals. As the customs officers were closely involved in these dirty affairs, the firm, to avoid prosecution, started a war against us: they did not allow our goods into the country, and we had serious losses. Subsequently, three big customers who made up a big part of our turnover left us, because we were unable to provide them with all the required range of goods and on time. Then, Moscow customs began to chase us. Our account was suspended, but we had managed to open an account at another bank beforehand. In that way, we saved a part of our turnover. Then, there was a certain hiatus, and some representatives of, let us call them, law enforcement bodies contacted us and asked us to pay 300 000 USD, although without any guarantees that the prosecution would be terminated. As we denied it, they told us that we would be sorry. Then, an arbitrage court was engaged by the tax inspectors, and after that, to increase the pressure, the criminal court; meanwhile, the criminal case was instituted by the Investigation Committee in 2012 without any claims from the tax authority.

Meanwhile, estimations of the tax and of the police were very different; the tax was 34 billion roubles in overdue payments, but the police were asking only 13 billion roubles. The fact that during the same period of three years the firm had paid, apart from the payments made in Moscow, more than 200 billion roubles in VAT through the customs in St Petersburg was ignored, as well as the independent economic expertise results provided by the firm; not one (!) petition was taken into consideration either by the investigator, or by the judge. According to formal regulations, a criminal case should be discontinued on expiry of the limitation period. But the investigator decided, relying on the opinion of the tax inspector (who gave the tax inspector the right to interpret the law?) that the VAT paid through the customs office should not be included in the total sum of taxes paid to the state (?!) and proposed article 2 of article 199 'overdue tax payments in large scale'. And the court stamped this proposal without any doubts.

As a result, after two and a half years of battling with the tax authority and the Investigation Committee, in July 2013 we were enforced to pay 250 000 roubles in penalties (and X thousand USD passed through our lawyer to the judge, otherwise I had to count on two years of prison, as the Prosecutor requested). And the output: it is naive to expect an objective treatment from any state branch. If they want, they will find any possibility to crush you. Business in Russia is an enemy of the existing regime. But also its source of enrichment.

Now the respondent has a criminal record. In spite of the fact that the firm now formally belongs to his wife, it has no more access to bank credit, whereas earlier they had received credit from the Sberbank without any problems. No new credit cards can be issued for him. Moreover, living some years under such a pressure has left its mark; first he had a hypertensive crisis, and now he has chronic heart disease and other illnesses.

Some of the respondents even made generalizations like: 'Putin – it is the Soviet Union! He is rebuilding it. We hope he will leave a small piece that we do not have to die in a gutter . . . ' (respondent No. 3).

Meanwhile, younger entrepreneurs and start-ups did not have any tensions with state authorities at all, and this theme seemed to be irrelevant for them, in contrast to those with longer business and life experience. The statements of the latter concerning their communications with state officials were, as a rule, filled not so much with condemnation or resentment but rather with indifference and disgust.

In the context of relations with public authorities corruption was mentioned occasionally. So, respondent No. 7 mentioned:

I got acquainted with one former KGB officer. And he asked me whether I am thinking about my life after becoming retired. But it seemed to me that he had something quite different in mind than me. Even because I am thinking over my retirement, I am doing business but not theft on state procurement. All people who make me a certain offer, I send to one colonel from the FSEP [Federal Service of Execution of Punishments]. All my relatives are somehow connected with the Army, and they still have some views on the officer's honour and how things should be. In general, I try not to do any deals with officers, only with generals; they have already solved all their problems and they do not raise bad questions.

The comparison of experience with other countries where corruption is assumed to be high might help to make cynical judgements, as respondent No. 12 does. He is involved in different business projects in several African countries, and he said:

What is the difference between officials in Africa and in Russia? In Africa, corruption is not personalized; they understand that a bribe is paid not to the person X, but to the deputy minister. It implies that if the person is suspended and you start to work with their successor the new person will never require his 'slice of the pie'. In Russia now we started to combat against corruption; but there are no non-corrupt institutions, and the result of such a combat will consist in a total stagnation of business life. In a country where there are no non-corrupt schemes of the industry policy, it is impossible to start to combat corruption!

Corruption is not always combined with the state; as respondent No. 1 mentioned, corrupt behaviour is rather typical of representatives of big customers or contractors:

With officials I did not have such an experience, but with contractors. First, often they simply do not have specialists speaking professional language, as construction and furnishing is something outside of their main competences. Therefore, sometimes people responsible for working with us from the side of the contractor are not aware of any technical or economic issues they have to supervise. But they are fully aware of what they want to receive personally in the process of procurement . . . So, we have to negotiate . . . [smiling].

The same story was told by respondent No. 3:

We participated in two subcontracting deals, because one firm we have been cooperating with for a long time asked us to participate in two big tenders by a big state-owned contractor. Because of this deal we actually have some income. But with tenders, what kind of deal is it usually? To give you an example: one tender I know about was to service 130 air conditioners for 130 000 roubles annually. We don't play such games. Because you have to work with only one air conditioner for at least three hours when you are making a proper service, and 130 000 will cover the salary of one serviceman for no longer than two months, the minimal price of such kind of procurement should be no less than 300 000! But I have no doubt that somebody took part in this tender and won it. Really, no service was provided at all, but the responsible person on the side of the contractor has earned something. Moreover, a significant part of the employees received no bonuses, because a significant part of that money was used to pay for a proper service of air conditioners.

A legal small business is very vulnerable in such kinds of relations imposed by firms which are affiliated with state institutions; although there are usually more advantageous price conditions offered, the risk of the participation in illegal schemes being detected is also very high. For example, respondent No. 4 referred to:

Some goods we import not by ourselves but receive them [already in Russia] from a big import company closely affiliated with the CEO of the customs; they sell them to us at a very cheap price because the costs of customs clearance for them are equal to zero. Why do they sell them to us? Not because we are very close to them, but because we are specializing in such a segment of goods which is very narrow, so they simply do not know who could be included in their scheme in place of our firm.

If an entrepreneur is working completely in the 'shadows', he or she has no tension with corrupt state officials or contractors' representatives. That is the case of respondent No. 2, who admitted that he does business entirely informally:

I do not have any contact with inspections and other state institutions. Sometimes it happens that neighbours complain, then the police inspector is coming, but he has no powers. He only can ask me to keep silence outside of normal working hours or request my passport. But my passport is OK. And what else can he control? Even large construction and repair companies usually make contracts with clients without specifying the full amount or even without any amount of the contract.

Hence, the respondent justifies his behaviour with reference, first, to the cost reduction, and second to the usual practices of firms in that field.

It is noteworthy that both of the two senior individuals in the sample mentioned that they try to avoid, if possible, any contact with state officials. So, respondent No. 4 claimed on annoying bailiffs:

> In accordance with the decision of the court I have already paid all the penalties in January. But in April I recognized that I am still on the stop-list on the bailiffs' website as a debtor. With the regional bailiffs department there were no worries; I have called them and sent a scan of the payment order; they have withdrawn all my data from the database. But it was about penalties, but I had to confirm the payment of the customs itself, and it was to do with the municipal bailiffs' service. They had no website, the phone given on the website of the region's office website was invalid, and they even had no fax. I had to visit them personally twice; both times I handed the copies of the payment orders out against receipt, but no changes in the database were made. The third time I went there close to the end of the summer, shortly before leaving for a business trip abroad.[4] 'My' bailiff was absent, and there was a queue both to the chief and deputy chief of some dozens of people. I managed to catch the chief in the hallway and to explain the reason to him. He ordered another person to make improvements to the database. All in all, it took me several days.
>
> Earlier, when things got better, I even had a special deputy in administration matters to negotiate with officials, because I do not like them at all and cannot speak quietly to them, as I immediately fall into a rage from their unique mixture of aplomb and ignorance.

A similar view was shared by respondent No. 6:

> Immediately [with officials], I do not contact officials, try to avoid them. But also clerks of commercial organizations are trying to dress like bureaucrats when you are visiting them with any commercial offer. But what is the difference, who is the guest and who is the visitor? What is important, it is the issue to be discussed. But no, they are so proud . . .

In the context of people's own sad experience of relations with concrete state institutions and their representatives, very critical comments were made concerning the general current socio-economic situation and political system. It should be noted that such characteristics are formulated by the respondents who declared the rejection of informal business activity. So, for instance, respondent No. 6 noticed:

> Total control over a personality, they act according to [Stalin's] principle; it is important to get a person, and then we will find any article in the law. That is the credo of legislators. And Bastrykin[5] is simply like a vice-premier in economics!
>
> The more oppressed is the personality, the lower will be the business activity of self-made people. For an infusion of a new blood into business, under such circumstances, any stimuli are absent . . .

It began already under Yeltsin, in the second half of the 1990s. In Moscow it was especially evident, because Luzhkov managed to establish his own power vertical[6] earlier. Large corporations are 'built in', therefore they behave not like private business, but rather like conductors of bureaucratic interests. If you follow the intonations and accents of officials who make statements in the press it is evident that today only those people may try to enter business who cannot imagine an alternative existence. We're rolling downhill. Actually, already in the mid-1990s there were security services who governed the business; nobody could persuade me that I am wrong. Exceptions were already rare at that time; only people who managed to explore a proper niche from the very beginning and who were already grown before the security services captured them. For example, Yevtushenkov;[7] he is neither Gates nor Jobs. He was 'allowed'. I think, even in China the share of entrepreneurs who grow freely is higher than here.

EVIDENCE AND POLICY RECOMMENDATIONS

The chapter has sought to explain that the labels 'informal entrepreneurship' and 'informal entrepreneurial activity' should be used more accurately, taking into consideration a wide variety of both motivations for undertaking entrepreneurial activities partly or totally on an informal basis within the nexus of opportunity/necessity-driven motivation within imperfect transitional economies like Russia. The chapter points out such crucial constraints of informal entrepreneurial activity as low visibility, financial traps as well as absence of possibilities to transfer the business to the new generation of the family.

The self-legitimization of doing business totally or partly informally is very different. Some of the respondents speak about their lack of entrepreneurial experience, some of them argue that they have to save on taxes, while for others it is the necessity to have unrecorded cash to bribe officials or representatives of contractors. As there is no single reason for informal entrepreneurial activity, there can no single recipe to reduce informal entrepreneurial activity. The 'typical cases' analysed in the chapter show that usually there is a set of external and internal factors pushing or pulling the entrepreneur to use informal practices, namely, the size of the business, field, market structure (open or closed), as well as with the strategy of personal hiring. Hence, state policy aiming to diminish the impact of informal entrepreneurial activity should try to accept this complexity; otherwise, it will not achieve its goals.

Micro-business owners and start-ups in the B2C sphere interviewed in the course of the project insisted that they are unwilling pawns of the economy, pushed to act informally. But it seems that here we are not dealing with any transitional specifics or even peculiarities of the Russian market, as some fields such as construction and household repair services are informal by nature; facts and arguments mentioned by the interviewees could be found in any other economy including established market economies. As such, businesses are creating only a few jobs and primarily for the kinds of employees who are not inclined or even not able to compete for jobs in the formal labour market, such a form of informal entrepreneurial activity should be rather tolerated or welcomed in societies with weak social protection systems and low pensions, because it provides these categories of adults with temporary jobs and salaries.

It is to be stressed that in the course of the project we dealt with some cases where the markets are constituted in such a way that micro- and small businesses are very dependent on procurements of either the state institutions or large firms, and this circumstance may become a crucial pushing factor to skip to informal practices to minimize the costs because of regular overdue payments, or simple underpayment from the side of the mighty and influential contractor dominating the market. In such situations, or when the contractors enforce them to minimize the price of their services, the subcontractors are forced to hire some of the personnel on an informal basis, and to do part of their transactions off-the-books to both reduce the salary fund and to have some cash to pay minimal salaries until the contract is paid. Such a practice becomes more regular during a crisis when currency is depreciating; as contractors have fixed budgets and are involved in the realization of several state-controlled programmes, they try (a) to decrease the payment compared with the initial contract, and (b) to pay as late as possible to gain benefits from the depreciation of the rouble. Having much weaker positions on the market, the small subcontractors have a choice either to tolerate such voluntary behaviour of contractors, or to quit the market. Even big and prosperous Russian firms may become hostages of such situations when being involved in huge politically prioritized projects in contemporary Russia.[8] Meanwhile, the state concern in Russia is to attract as many SMEs as possible to participate in state procurement. The experience of some of our respondents, however, shows that taking into consideration the disparity of market power and quite rational reasons for payment arrears and so on on the part of the contractors, for many SMEs becoming subcontractors of bigger firms could become an additional factor of uncertainty and rather encourage them in informal behaviour, or lead them to bankruptcy, especially under the conditions of a long-lasting crisis.

The most common informal practice mentioned by the respondents is no doubt the off-the-books salary payment, especially in the case of peripheral personnel. Even those among the respondents who describe their business as something fully formalized are limiting the area of purely formal contracting of their employees to the core only. As regards the periphery (construction workers, maintenance workers and so on), by default, the hiring of them is purely informal, and this fact is not perceived by respondents as a problem. In the course of this project, it was not possible to collect opinions from the employees themselves about their satisfaction with such a status. But from other research papers (Zudina, 2013) we know that being employed informally does not negatively affect the life satisfaction or the self-perception of their social status. It is a quite rational attitude taking into consideration a short life expectation, uncertainty of the prospects of the pension system, low quality of free state medical care and so on. Hence, the embeddedness of semi-formal or informal hiring practices is, on one side, protecting the entrepreneurs against the volatility of external market conditions and a regulatory framework; on the other hand, it finds an acceptance from the employees themselves. In conclusion, without serious changes to the environmental conditions (social services of the state for the formally employed population), any attempts to diminish the sweep of informal hiring in the SME sector will hardly become efficient.

However, to pay part of the salary on a steady basis off-the-books, entrepreneurs need to have some unreported turnover; its sources seem to be the most sensitive part of the interviews. To have unreported cash, interviewees mostly used a limited number of techniques: starting from informal oral agreements with clients in services; taking loans from relatives and friends; shrinkage and outage in retail trade with consumption goods; and finishing with participation in 'simulated' state procurement, which is already criminal. Of all these usual practices, only the last one is really illegal and should be suppressed; but under a dominance of 'unproductive entrepreneurship' this seems not to be realistic.

Informal entrepreneurial activity is reflected as something negative by those respondents who are growing their business for sale. In situations when the main purpose of running a business is simply to secure the well-being of the owner and his/her family, the attitude toward informal activity is more tolerant. As a general improvement of the economy should increase the share of serial entrepreneurs aiming to sell their successful businesses, it automatically would strengthen the positions of those inclined to do business entirely formally.

The start-up respondents had, in parallel with the observed business, either some freelance experience or an ongoing freelance project. Some of them respect freelancing, and sometimes even employment, as a necessary supplement of their business; freelance activity is a source of existence while business is something dealing with self-realization. Nota bene: those combining freelance activities with a start-up never have spoken about any necessity to do business informally, or to have some amount of grey money with which to bribe officials and so on.

An attitude toward entrepreneurship as something creative, even as a game, is a remarkable trait of the younger respondents; a possible failure is taken into account but rather as a result of lack of business experience. However, for representatives of older cohorts a business failure may become a trauma due to circumstances, or due to a bad environment or state policy. Older respondents, regardless of the size and nature of their business, are more inclined to condemn the bad macroeconomic situation or the state for their failures or even regarding doing (parts of) their business informally. Younger respondents, however, are more likely to recognize that when choosing informal activities it is their own decision, and they are more tolerant toward the regulatory functions of state authorities, and, when trying to avoid unnecessary contact with officials, they have more respect for their functions. Consequently, a possible failure and quitting a business is perceived much more deeply by the older generation of entrepreneurs, and they are more likely to introduce informal activities to avoid such a negative scenario. Moreover, a starting point is important and has a strong impact on the business nature and the embeddedness of informal practices. Those respondents who started a venture in the early 1990s achieved their first efforts while using a very modest amount of initial capital and informal networking to establish the business. In contrast to this, start-ups of the late 2000s tried to behave formally, both to attract external resources as well as to develop their businesses. Therefore, among respondents less than 30 years old, we could not find anybody aiming to do business totally informally, in contrast to representatives of older cohorts. It seems that, first, better entrepreneurial skills and, second, a natural process of generational change may improve the situation in Russia; younger generations grown in the atmosphere of state interventionism are taking it 'as it is' and are protesting less; hence, from a moral point of view, they are less inclined to legitimate informal activity as a protest against the intervening state.

CONSTRAINTS AND FUTURE RESEARCH POSSIBILITIES

The most evident constraints of the study are the small number of respondents (hence, the validity of the results might be questionable) and the very short distance of time between the two waves, taking into consideration the fact that entrepreneurial behaviour changes because a reaction to both the external and internal situation of the related business may take much more time. It would be advisable to carry out a longitudinal survey in a longer perspective to examine the role of different factors such as motivation, self-efficacy, set of capitals and strategy as well as of the macro-conditions in the country in the possible change of the intensity and forms of informal activities of respondents.

If such a study could be based on quantitative surveys with a sample representing the adult population structure (using the PSEDI method of initial sample formation), the results could also be used to discover cross-regional differences and the role of the urban factor, among others.

NOTES

1. See http://www.gemconsortium.org/teams/79/russia.
2. A mix of different organic components which has a slightly stimulating and saturating effect, like coca leaves, used by the native population in some Central Asian countries.
3. The beginning of the previous crisis in Russia.
4. In Russia, if a person has not paid fiscal debts or penalties, they may be added to the stop-list of the border police.
5. Head of the Federal Investigation Committee of the Russian Federation.
6. President Putin's term for a centrally governed hierarchy he has been establishing in the country since the beginning of the 2000s.
7. Multibillionaire, head of the mighty 'Systema' holding, imprisoned and then released in 2014 in the course of an investigation of an old privatization case.
8. CEO of the second largest IT-holding in Russia, 'Lanit', Georgi Gens, claimed in an interview: 'A serious risk of payment arrears occurs. We had some bad contracts which had a very strong impact on the company as a whole. There are, for instance, gross non-payments on some big projects of strategic importance for the country which we finished last year, among them in Sochi. We were being urged to do it as quickly as possible, then we were thanked. But a part of the objects remained unpaid until now... there were subcontracts. Taking the specifics of the construction of Olympic games projects, many issues of agreements execution were solved in an emergency mode ... Our personnel worked perfectly, they always tried to fulfil the contractor's wishes, even if certain services were not the subject of our agreement. All people understood how important it was. Nevertheless, more than one year ago we still do not have the final instalment. It is more than 50 billion rubles. We are forced to sue. But it is the constructing firm who was the contractor we were subcontracted by with ... who did not receive money, or did not receive in full' (Vedomosti, 10 March, 2015, available at: http://www.vedomosti.ru/newspaper/characters/2015/03/09/na-primere-irana-yasno-chto-sanktsii-mogut-stat-zatyazhnoi-problemoi).

REFERENCES

Aidis, R. and M. van Praag (2007), 'Illegal entrepreneurship experience: does it make a difference for business performance and motivation?', *Journal of Business Venturing*, **22** (2), 283–310.

Aidis, R., S. Estrin and T. Mickiewicz (2008), 'Institutions and entrepreneurship development in Russia: a comparative perspective', *Journal of Business Venturing*, **23** (6), 656–72.

Andrews, D., A. Caldera Sánchez and Å. Johansson (2011), 'Towards a better understanding of the informal economy', OECD Economics Department Working Papers, No. 873.

Atkinson, R. and J. Flint (2001), 'Accessing hidden and hard-to-reach populations: snowball research strategies', *Social Research Update*, **33**, 1–4.

Batjargal, B. (2006), 'The dynamics of entrepreneurs' networks in a transitioning economy: the case of Russia', *Entrepreneurship & Regional Development*, **18** (4), 305–20.

Batjargal, B. (2010), 'Network dynamics and new ventures in China: a longitudinal study', *Entrepreneurship & Regional Development*, **22** (2), 139–53.

Baumol, W. (1990), 'Entrepreneurship: productive, unproductive, and destructive', *Journal of Political Economy*, **98** (5), 893–921.

Blackburn, R. and A. Kovalainen (2009), 'Researching small firms and entrepreneurship: past, present and future', *International Journal of Management Reviews*, **11** (2), 127–48.

Castells, M. and A. Portes (1989), 'World underneath: the origins, dynamics and effects of the informal economy', in A. Portes, M. Castells and L.A. Benton (eds), *The Informal Economy: Studies in Advanced and Less Developed Countries*, Baltimore, MD: Johns Hopkins University Press, pp. 11–37.

Chepurenko, A. (2014), 'Informal entrepreneurship under transition: causes and specific features', in D. Boegenhold (ed.), *Soziologie des Wirtschaftlichen*, Wiesbaden: Springer Fachmedien, pp. 361–82.

Dau, L.A. and A. Cuervo-Cazurra (2014), 'To formalize or not to formalize: entrepreneurship and pro-market institutions', *Journal of Business Venturing*, **29** (5), 668–86.

De Soto, H. (1989), *The Other Path: The Invisible Revolution in the Third World*, New York: HarperCollins.

Djankov, S., E. Miguel, Y. Qian, G. Roland and E. Zhuravskaya (2005), 'Who are the Russian entrepreneurs?', *Journal of European Economic Association Papers and Proceedings*, **3** (23), 587–97.

Earle, J. and Z. Sakova (2000), 'Business start-ups or disguised unemployment? Evidence on the character of self employment from transition economies', *Labour Economics*, **7** (5), 575–601.

Eder, M., A. Yakovlev and A. Garkoglu (2003), 'Suitcase trade between Turkey and Russia: Microeconomics and institutional structure', preprint WP4/2003/07, Higher School of Economics, Moscow.

Ellman, M. (1994), *Socialist Planning*, Cambridge: Cambridge University Press.

Elster, J., C. Offe and U. Preuss (with F. Boenker, U. Goetting and F.W. Rueb) (1998), *Institutional Design in Post-Communist Societies: Rebuilding the Ship at Sea*, Cambridge: Cambridge University Press.

Estrin, S. and T. Mickiewicz (2011), 'Entrepreneurship in transition economies: the role of institutions and generational change', in M. Minniti (ed.), *Dynamics of Entrepreneurship*, Oxford: Oxford University Press, pp. 181–208.

Estrin, S., K. Meyer and M. Bytchkova (2006), 'Entrepreneurship in transition economies', in M. Casson, B. Yeung, A. Basu and N. Wadesdon (eds), *Oxford Handbook of Entrepreneurship*, Oxford: Oxford University Press, pp. 693–709.

Feige, E. (1997), 'Underground activity and institutional change: productive, protective and predatory behavior in transition economies', in J. Nelson, C. Tilly and L. Walker (eds) *Transforming Post-Communist Political Economies*, Washington, DC: National Academy Press, pp. 21–35.

Gelman, V.Y. (2010a), 'Dead end: authoritarian modernisation in Russia', *Osteuropa*, **60** (1), 3–13.

Gelman, V.Y. (2010b), 'Regime changes despite legitimacy crises: exit, voice, and loyalty in post-communist Russia', *Journal of Eurasian Studies*, **1** (1), 54–63.

Gelman, V.Y. (2011), 'State power, governance, and local regimes in Russia', *Russian Politics and Law*, **49** (4), 42–52.

Gërxhani, K. (2004), 'The informal sector in developed and less developed countries: a literature survey', *Public Choice*, **120** (3/4), 267–300.

Gimpelson, V. and A. Zudina (2011), '"Neformaly" v rossiyskoy ekonomike: skolko ikh i kto oni?' ('"Non-formals" in the Russian economy: how many and who are they?'), *Voprossy Ekonomiki*, **10**, 53–76 (in Russian).

Godfrey, P.C. (2011), 'Toward a theory of the informal economy', *The Academy of Management Annals*, **5** (1), 231–77.

Johnson, S., J. McMillan and C. Woodruff (2000), 'Entrepreneurs and the ordering of institutional reform', *Economics of Transition*, **8** (1), 1–36.

La Porta, R. and A. Shleifer (2008), 'The unofficial economy and economic development', *Brookings Papers on Economic Activity*, **39** (2), 275–363.

Ledeneva, A. (1998), *Russia's Economy of Favours*: Blat, *Networking, and Informal Exchange*, Cambridge: Cambridge University Press.

McMillan, J. and C. Woodruff (2002), 'The central role of entrepreneurs in transition economies', *Journal of Economic Perspectives*, **16** (3), 153–70.

Manolova, T., R. Eunni and B. Gyoshev (2008), 'Institutional environments for entrepreneurship: evidence from emerging economies in Eastern Europe', *Entrepreneurship Theory and Practice*, **32** (1), 203–18.

North, D.C., J.J. Wallis, S.B. Webb and B. Weingast (2013), 'Limited access orders: an introduction to the conceptual framework', in D.C. North, J.J. Wallis, S. Webb and B. Weingast (eds), *Politics, Economics, and Problems of Development: In the Shadow of Violence*, Cambridge: Cambridge University Press, pp. 1–23.

OECD (2015), *Russian Federation: Key Issues and Policies*, OECD Studies on SMEs and Entrepreneurship, Paris: OECD Publishing.

Oliver, C. (1991), 'Strategic responses to institutional processes', *Academy of Management Review*, **16** (1), 145–79.

Ovaska, T. and R. Sobel (2005), 'Entrepreneurship in post-Socialist economies', *Journal of Private Enterprise*, **21** (1), 8–28.

Portes, A. and W. Haller (2005), 'The informal economy', in N. Smelser and R. Swedberg (eds), *Handbook of Economic Sociology*, New York: Princeton University Press, pp. 403–25.

Puffer, S. and D. McCarthy (2001), 'Navigating the hostile maze: a framework for Russian entrepreneurship', *Academy of Management Executive*, **15** (4), 24–36.

Puffer, S., D. McCarthy and M. Boisot (2010), 'Entrepreneurship in Russia and China: the impact of formal institutional voids', *Entrepreneurship Theory and Practice*, **34** (3), 441–67.

Raiser, M., A. Rousso and F. Steves (2003), *Trust in Transition: Cross-country and Firm Evidence*, London: European Bank for Reconstruction and Development.

Rehn, A. and S. Taalas (2004), 'Znakomstva i svyazi (Acquaintances and connections): *Blat*, the Soviet Union, and mundane entrepreneurship', *Entrepreneurship and Regional Development*, **16** (3), 235–50.

Remington, T.F. (2000), 'Russia and the "strong state" ideal', *East European Constitutional Review*, **9** (1/2), 65–9.

Renz, B. (2006), 'Putin's militocracy? An alternative interpretation of Siloviki in contemporary Russian politics', *Europe-Asia Studies*, **58** (6), 903–24.

Rivera, S.W. and D.W. Rivera (2006), 'The Russian elite under Putin: militocratic or bourgeois?', *Post-Soviet Affairs*, **22** (2), 125–44.

Round, J., C. Williams and P. Rodgers (2008), 'Corruption in the post-Soviet workplace: the experiences of recent graduates in post-Soviet Ukraine', *Work, Employment and Society*, **22** (1), 149–66.

Sassen, S. (1997), *Informalization in Advanced Market Economies*, Geneva: International Labour Office.

Sauka, A. and F. Welter (2007), 'Productive, unproductive and destructive entrepreneurship in an advanced transition setting: the example of Latvian small enterprises', in M. Dowling and J. Schmude (eds), *Empirical Entrepreneurship in Europe*, Cheltenham, UK and Northampton, MA, USA: Edward Elgar Publishing, pp. 87–111.

Scase, R. (1997), 'The role of small businesses in the economic transformation of Eastern Europe: real but relatively unimportant', *International Small Business Journal*, **16** (1), 113–21.

Scase, R. (2003), 'Entrepreneurship and proprietorship in transition: policy implications for the SME sector', in R. McIntyre and B. Dallago (eds), *Small and Medium Enterprises in Transitional Economies*, New York: Palgrave Macmillan, pp. 64–77.

Schneider, F. and D. Enste (2000), 'Shadow economies: size, causes and consequences', *Journal of Economic Literature*, **38** (1), 77–114.

Schneider, F., A. Buehn and C. Montenegro (2010), 'New estimates for the shadow economies all over the world', *International Economic Journal*, **24** (4), 443–61.

Smallbone, D. and F. Welter (2001), 'The distinctiveness of entrepreneurship in transition economies', *Small Business Economics*, **16** (4), 249–62.

Smallbone, D. and F. Welter (2009), *Entrepreneurship and Small Business Development in Post-Socialist Economies*, London and New York: Routledge.

Spicer, A., G. McDermott and B. Kogut (2000), 'Entrepreneurship and privatization in Central Europe: the tenuous balance between destruction and creation', *Academy of Management Review*, **25** (3), 630–49.

Tonoyan, V., R. Strohmeyer and M. Habib (2010), 'Corruption and entrepreneurship: how formal and informal institutions shape small firm behavior in transition and mature market economies', *Entrepreneurship Theory and Practice*, **34** (5), 803–31.

Treisman, D. (2006), 'Putin's silovarchs', *Orbis*, **51** (1), 141–53.

Volkov, V. (1999), 'Violent entrepreneurship in post-Communist Russia', *Europe-Asia Studies*, **51** (5), 741–54.

Webb, J.W., G.D. Bruton, L. Tihanyi and R.D. Ireland (2013), 'Research on entrepreneurship in the informal economy: framing a research agenda', *Journal of Business Venturing*, **28** (5), 598–614.

Welter, F. (2005), 'Entrepreneurial behaviour in differing environments', in D. Audretsch, H. Grimm and C.W. Wessner (eds), *Local Heroes in the Global Village*, New York: Springer, pp. 93–112.

Welter, F. (2011), 'Contextualizing entrepreneurship: conceptual challenges and ways forward', *Entrepreneurship Theory and Practice*, **35** (1), 165–84.

Welter, F. and D. Smallbone (2011), 'Institutional perspectives on entrepreneurial behavior in challenging environments', *Journal of Small Business Management*, **49** (1), 107–25.

Williams, C.C. (2008), 'Beyond necessity-driven versus opportunity-driven entre-preneurship: a study of informal entrepreneurs in England, Russia and Ukraine', *International Journal of Entrepreneurship and Innovation*, **9** (3), 157–65.

Williams, C., J. Round and P. Rodgers (2013), *The Role of Informal Economies in the Post-Soviet World: The End of Transition?*, London and New York: Routledge.

Yakovlev, A., V. Golikova and N. Kapralova (2007), 'Rossiyskie "chelnoki" – ot vynuzhdennogo predprinimatelstva k integracii v rynochnuyu ekonomiku' ('Russian "shuttles" – from necessity driven entrepreneurs to the integration into the market economy'), *Mir Rossii*, **2**, 84–106 (in Russian).

Zudina, A. (2013), 'Do informal workers make an underclass? An analysis of subjective social status', Working Paper by NRU Higher School of Economics, Series SOC 'Sociology', 24.

6. The shadow economy and entrepreneurship in Ukraine

Elena Denisova-Schmidt and Yaroslav Prytula

INTRODUCTION

The phenomenon of the 'shadow economy' (the informal or unofficial economy), defined as 'economic activities that take place outside the framework of bureaucratic public and private sector establishments' (Hart, 2008), has existed in Ukraine for a long time. The feeding system (*systema hoduvan'*) – the rewards given by citizens to state officials, which dates as far back as the late ninth century in Kievan Rus – is corruption according to Transparency International: 'the abuse of entrusted power for private gain'.

In the Soviet command economy (Denisova-Schmidt and Kryzhko, 2015), the phenomenon of the 'shadow economy' meant 'all economic activities that are either undertaken directly for private gain or are knowingly illegal in some substantial way' (Grossman, 1977). 'The shadow economy [in the USSR (1924–91)] was based on more entrepreneurial and efficient business. However, since it was dependent upon illegal use of state material and financial resources, it was essentially parasitic by its character' (Apressyan, 1997).

This heritage still influences modern Ukrainian entrepreneurship, including the misuse of state power by oligarchs (Åslund, 2001, 2005, 2014; Kuzio, 2014), tax evasion (Bilotkach, 2006), unofficial employment (Rodgers et al., 2008), evasion of payment for the usage of state facilities (Leipnik and Kyrychenko, 2013), corporate raiding (Rojansky, 2014) and other forms (Fuxman, 1997; Markovskaya et al., 2003; Onoshchenko and Williams, 2014).

DATA AND ESTIMATION RESULTS

This chapter is based on two different original data sets. The first is a representative survey of Ukrainian firms done in early 2013. The sample encompasses 625 firms, which are stratified according to region and size;

Table 6.1   Firm characteristics

Firm size	2013 survey (all Ukraine)			2015 survey (Western Ukraine)		
	Small	Medium	Large	Small	Medium	Large
Number of employees	29.14	97.20	655.08	13.72	108.41	545.60
Number of female employees	11.33	40.89	294.87	5.43	25.82	296.80
Change in the number of employees over the last 3 years (1: reduced by more than 20%, 2: reduced by 5–20%, 3: did not change, 4: increased by 5–20%, 5: increased by more than 20%)	2.75	2.88	2.88	3.08	3.05	4.00
Year of firm establishment	1999.62	1995.12	1991.31	2005.00	2000.30	1997.78
Foreign ownership (binary)	0.02	0.08	0.12	0.06	0.14	0.40
Business-to-Customer business model (binary)	0.76	0.73	0.69	0.89	0.82	0.60
% products/services sold domestically	97.13	91.06	87.13	90.81	84.50	74.60
% products/services bought domestically	95.26	88.40	83.08	67.10	42.52	39.67
Business development in last 3 years (1: very bad . . . 5: very good)	3.27	3.52	3.63	3.55	3.23	3.60
Business development expectations in next 3 years (1: very bad . . . 5: very good)	3.68	3.80	3.88	3.99	3.50	4.20
Corruption is a problem for development (1: never . . . 5: systematically)	2.79	2.80	2.69	3.14	3.40	2.90
Number of observations	126	311	188	88	22	10

25 firms were sampled in each of Ukraine's 25 administrative regions (24 oblasts and the Republic of Crimea). In each region, 20 percent of the sample were small businesses (20 to 50 employees), 50 percent were mid-sized companies (51 to 250 employees), and 30 percent were large enterprises (251 to 1000 employees). Additionally, firms were stratified by sectors of the economy in proportion to each sector's contribution to Ukraine's GDP in 2010 (Table 6.1).[1] The second data set is from a representative survey of Ukrainian firms conducted in early 2015. The sample includes 120 firms located in the western part of Ukraine; 73 percent of the sample firms were small businesses (20 to 50 employees), 19 percent were mid-sized companies (51 to 250 employees), and 8 percent were large

enterprises (251 to 1000 employees)[2] (Table 6.1). Apart from a wide range of firm-specific characteristics (financial indicators, ownership structure, employee quantity and structure and so on), the survey contains information on and judgments regarding the respondents' (firm owner or top manager) perception of the occurrence and severity of corruption and informal practices among their peers and with the relevant authorities.

In our study, we follow the approach developed and tested by Shekshnia et al. (2013, 2014) for business corruption in Russia.[3] The scholars examined the existing typologies for corruption in post-communist societies (Tanzi, 1998; Karklins, 2005; Knack, 2006; Ledeneva, 2006, 2009a, 2009b, 2013) and conducted a content analysis of the media in order to identify corrupt practices that correspond to these types. Inspired by the concept of obliquity developed by John Kay (2011), who stated that 'goals are best achieved indirectly', they coded the negatively connoted word 'corruption' into the more neutral 'informal practices' – the practical norms that CEOs and managers often use to get things done (Table 6.2a and Table 6.2b).

The data from the 2013 survey show that the most popular informal practices include the use of unfair tender procedures and the payment of salaries and bonuses in cash. Indeed, excluding 'hard to answer' or 'don't know' answers, almost 46 percent of the firms surveyed admitted the frequent informal selection of tender winners by their peers, out of which 25 percent use it sometimes, 16 percent use it often, and 5 percent use it systematically. At the same time, 38 percent of firms admitted the frequent informal, cash payment of salaries and bonuses to avoid paying taxes and social fees by their peers, of which 21 percent use this practice sometimes, 12 percent use it often, and 6 percent use it systematically. The data from the 2015 survey confirm these tendencies and show a considerable increase of about one standard deviation in the usage of these two informal practices. The average of the respondents' opinions on the frequency of selecting vendors, contractors or the winners of open tenders on the basis of informal relationships and agreements increased from 2.3 to 3.3 on a scale of 1 to 5, and paying salaries and bonuses to staff in cash without paying taxes or social fees increased from 2.23 to 3.4 on the same scale. In our opinion, such results are indications of a continuing social and economic crisis, which resulted from the military conflict in Donbas and the nearly defaulted state of the economy. The situation is pushing many businesses to the edge of survival, making informal or corrupt practices the only option to survive. As was indicated by our respondents, the practice of using informal relations to select tender winners reduces the time and resources necessary for formal tender arrangements. Respondents also consider the paying of salaries and bonuses in cash or evading of taxes as a means of improving productivity and a socially accepted way of increasing the

Table 6.2a   Informal practices

Informal practices as known to participants	Survey 2013				Survey 2015			
	1	2	3	4	1	2	3	4*
Selecting vendors/contractors/winners of open tenders on the basis of informal relationships or agreements	45.9% n = 287	21.3% n = 133	17.6% n = 110	15.2% n = 95	15.7% n = 19	29.8% n = 36	31.4% n = 38	23.1% n = 28
Receiving kickbacks or other informal rewards (for example, expensive gifts) from vendors, suppliers, or buyers	54.4% n = 340	20.2% n = 126	9.4% n = 59	16% n = 100	44.6% n = 54	24% n = 29	15.7% n = 19	15.7% n = 19
Paying salaries and bonuses to staff in cash without paying taxes or social fees	53% n = 331	18.4% n = 115	15.2% n = 95	13.4% n = 84	15.6% n = 31	19.8% n = 24	43% n = 52	11.6% n = 14
Receiving kickbacks or other material benefits from job candidates	66.3% n = 414	11% n = 69	6.6% n = 41	16.2% n = 101	73.6% n = 89	12.4% n = 15	5% n = 6	9.1% n = 11
Using company funds, facilities or staff for personal gain	66.4% n = 415	11.4% n = 71	8.3% n = 44	15.2% n = 95	56.2% n = 68	22.3% n = 27	10.8% n = 13	10.7% n = 13
Using unethical informal tools such as *kompromat* against competitors	65.9% n = 412	13% n = 81	5.4% n = 34	15.7% n = 98	72.7% n = 88	10.7% n = 13	4.2% n = 5	12.4% n = 15

Note: * 1 – never or rarely; 2 – sometimes; 3 – often or systematically; 4 – hard to say.

Table 6.2b   Firms' usage of corrupt informal practices in doing business in Ukraine, survey 2013

Question: How often do firms comparable to your own face the informal practices listed below? (Scale from 1 – never to 5 – systematically)

Informal practices as known to participants	Forms of corruption in the Transparency International classification	Mean	St. dev.	No. of answers
Selecting vendors/ contractors/winners of open tenders on the basis of informal relationships or agreements	Cronyism, nepotism, lobbying	2.37	1.24	530
Receiving kickbacks or other informal rewards (for example, expensive gifts) from vendors, suppliers or buyers	Gift, conflict of interest	2.02	1.11	525
Paying salaries and bonuses to staff in cash without paying taxes or social fees	Fraud	2.19	1.27	541
Receiving kickbacks or other material benefits from job candidates	Gift, conflict of interest	1.67	1.01	524
Using company funds, facilities or staff for personal gain	Abuse of power or office	1.70	1.02	530
Using unethical informal tools such as *kompromat* against competitors	Influence peddling	1.68	1.01	527

Sources: Denisova-Schmidt and Prytula (2015a, 2015b).

benefits of employees (Denisova-Schmidt and Prytula, 2015a and 2015b). We performed a regression analysis, based on a wider set of data from the 2013 survey, in order to investigate a profile of the companies that indicate frequent usage of the informal practices described in Table 6.2b. We used the PLUM (polytomous universal model) procedure in SPSS based on McCullagh's (1980) methodology. The PLUM procedure has been designed specifically to account for a polytomous (multinomial) dependent variable in regression analysis. In our case, the dependent variable is the firms' answer to the block of questions from Table 6.2b on the frequency of usage of specific informal practices by their peers, with a scale ranging from 1 (never) to 5 (systematically). Although a firm's perception of corruption and informal practices is not a clear and direct indication of that firm's experience with and/or involvement in corrupt practices, we assume here that a firm's high perception of corruption indicates the degree of that firm's involvement in business corruption. Indeed, the spread of the perception of corruption among firms may cause a spread of corruption via a self-fulfilling prophesy mechanism. For example, based on data from 30 West and East European countries, Frey and Torgler (2007) show that the spread of corruption in terms of tax evasion increases if taxpayers perceive that tax evasion is widespread. Our independent variables are a firm's size estimated as a log of the number of employees; the log of the firm's age;[4] the percentage of the firm's products/services that are sold and bought domestically; the ownership structure dummy (domestic = 1, foreign or joint venture = 0); the firm's business model (we distinguish between the Business-to-Business (B2B) only model and a combined Business-to-Business and Business-to-Customer (B2B&B2C) model, with the Business-to-Customer (B2C) only model as a reference group); the size of the city where the firm operates (regional (oblast) capital,[5] provincial city with more than 50 000 inhabitants, and a reference group – provincial city with less than 50 000 inhabitants); the firm's income for the last year reported (categorical variable with seven levels) and regional dummies[6] with Donbas as the reference region. Table 6.3 outlines the descriptive statistics of the data we use and Table 6.4 outlines the regression estimation results.

The results from our ordinal regression analysis suggest that a firm's age is irrelevant to the specific informal practices used by firms in Ukraine, but the firm size does matter. We find a significant positive relationship between the number of employees and a firm's frequency of usage of such practices as receiving kickbacks from job candidates, using company funds, facilities or staff for personal gain, and using unethical informal tools such as *kompromat* (compromising information) (Ledeneva, 2006) against competitors. The percentage of products and services sold domestically relates negatively and is statistically significant for the frequencies of usage of almost all informal practices. It seems that firms oriented significantly toward export operations are more exposed to informal corrupt practices in Ukraine. The same conclusion can be applied to domestically owned firms – they are more frequent users of all informal practices, except receiving kickbacks from job candidates, where they are indistinguishable from foreign-owned firms or joint ventures. There are mixed relationships between the firms' business model and the informal practices they use; however, we find a strong positive relationship between the firms' use of

Table 6.3   Firms' average characteristics, year 2013 survey

Variable	N	Min.	Max.	Mean	St. dev.
Number of employees	625	20	8100	251	595
Year of firm establishment	624	1930	2013	1995	17
% products/services sold domestically	625	0	100	91.1	20.3
% products/services bought domestically	625	0	100	88.2	25.2
Domestic ownership (domestic = 1, foreign or joint venture = 0)	625	0	1	0.92	0.27
Business-to-Business only business model (B2B = 1)	625	0	1	0.21	0.41
Combined Business-to-Business and Business-to-Customer business model (B2B&B2C = 1)	625	0	1	0.07	0.26
Business-to-Customer only business model (B2C = 1)	625	0	1	0.72	0.45
Regional capital city	625	0	1	0.6	0.5
Provincial city with more than 50 000 inhabitants	625	0	1	0.2	0.4
Provincial city with less than 50 000 inhabitants	625	0	1	0.2	0.4

the B2B business model and their exposure to such corrupt practices as selecting contractors of open tenders on the basis of informal relationships, receiving kickbacks or other rewards from suppliers, and paying salaries and bonuses to staff in cash without paying taxes and social fees. We also find, other things being equal, that the firms operating in large regional capital cities are more inclined to select contractors on the basis of informal relationships and receive kickbacks from suppliers. Interestingly, we find regional differences in the application of the two most frequent informal practices in Ukraine. It turns out that all regions of Ukraine differ from the Donbas region in their less frequent usage of selecting contractors of open tenders on the basis of informal relationships and paying salaries and bonuses to staff in cash without paying taxes and social fees. This result is in line with Denisova-Schmidt and Huber (2014), where they found that corruption is perceived to be less prevalent in the south and in the west compared to the east.

Overall, many firms in Ukraine do not consider the aforementioned practices to be corruption. Moreover, most firms do not consider corruption to be an obstacle. Only 7 percent of the respondents saw corruption as a systematical obstacle for their business in 2013; others replied often (18 percent), sometimes (35 percent), seldom (23 percent) and never (17 percent) to the question 'How often does corruption hinder the

Table 6.4 *Dependence of firm's perception of corruption and informal practices among peers on firm-specific characteristics in Ukraine*

Dependent variable	1 – Unfair tenders	2 – Kickbacks from suppliers	3 – Cash salaries and bonuses	4 – Kickbacks from job candidates	5 – Using company funds for personal gain	6 – Using *kompromat* against competitors
Log(Year of firm establishment)	0.045 (0.062)	0.029 (0.064)	0.002 (0.063)	0.053 (0.070)	-0.034 (0.061)	0.038 (0.071)
Log(Number of employees)	0.024 (0.052)	0.068 (0.056)	0.025 (0.055)	0.202*** (0.062)	0.141*** (0.054)	0.204*** (0.061)
% products/services sold domestically	-0.002 (0.003)	-0.008*** (0.003)	-0.006** (0.003)	-0.003 (0.003)	-0.009*** (0.003)	-0.009*** (0.003)
% products/services bought domestically	-0.001 (0.002)	-0.004* (0.002)	-0.002 (0.002)	-0.003 (0.002)	-0.004* (0.002)	-0.005** (0.002)
Domestic ownership dummy	0.517*** (0.190)	0.704*** (0.221)	0.350* (0.199)	0.349 (0.228)	0.412** (0.192)	0.907*** (0.256)
B2B business model dummy	0.212* (0.121)	0.320*** (0.125)	0.281** (0.122)	0.155 (0.137)	0.168 (0.121)	0.184 (0.135)
Both B2B and B2C business model dummy	-0.138 (0.184)	-0.270 (0.213)	-0.274 (0.199)	-0.685*** (0.264)	-0.275 (0.189)	-0.355 (0.232)
City, a regional capital, dummy	0.387*** (0.122)	0.478*** (0.133)	0.128 (0.125)	0.264* (0.146)	0.072 (0.121)	-0.026 (0.138)
Provincial city, more than 50000 inhabitants, dummy	0.131 (0.144)	0.303* (0.159)	0.009 (0.150)	0.310* (0.172)	0.145 (0.145)	0.109 (0.164)
West	-0.546*** (0.207)	-0.250 (0.216)	-0.348** (0.204)	0.127 (0.238)	-0.304 (0.197)	-0.337 (0.228)
North	-0.622*** (0.218)	0.006 (0.225)	-0.472** (0.216)	0.101 (0.248)	-0.150 (0.206)	-0.097 (0.234)

Center	−0.490**	−0.007	−0.361*	0.139	−0.267	−0.206
	(0.213)	(0.222)	(0.209)	(0.244)	(0.205)	(0.230)
South	−0.768***	−0.341	−0.596***	−0.133	−0.560***	−0.444*
	(0.220)	(0.230)	(0.218)	(0.252)	(0.209)	(0.239)
East	−0.352	−0.106	−0.427*	−0.649**	−0.501**	−0.292
	(0.226)	(0.239)	(0.228)	(0.286)	(0.222)	(0.255)
Firm's income dummies	Yes	Yes	Yes	Yes	Yes	Yes
Constant	Yes	Yes	Yes	Yes	Yes	Yes
Link function	Compl. Log-log	Probit	Probit	Probit	Compl. Log-log	Probit
Goodness of fit, Pearson test p-value	0.631	0.804	0.288	0.000	0.988	0.870
Cox and Snell pseudo R^2	0.080	0.105	0.075	0.115	0.086	0.108
Test of parallel lines, p-value	0.066	0.062	0.504	0.000	0.924	0.777

Notes:
Dependent variable is firm's opinion concerning widespread use of specific informal practices in doing business among peers: see Table 6.2b for details.
Ordinal regression using PLUM procedure in SPSS. ***, **, * indicate significance at 1, 5 and 10 percent level, respectively.

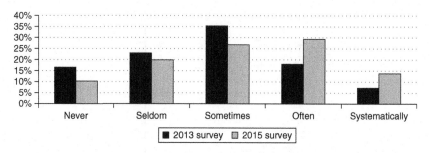

Figure 6.1   Differences in the answers to the question 'How often does corruption hinder the development of your business?' in 2013 and 2015

development of your business?' Interestingly, and perhaps optimistically, the answers to this question in the 2015 survey differ considerably from the previous survey. In 2015, many more firms see corruption as an obstacle to doing business (see Figure 6.1). On the one hand, businesses are still using or even increasing their usage of certain corrupt practices; on the other hand, they indicate a significantly more negative attitude to corruption as the usual way of doing business in Ukraine. The number of businesses that view corruption as an obstacle to their development has almost doubled since 2013, from 23 percent to 43 percent, showing that perceptions have changed more than the objective levels of business corruption in Ukraine.

These attitudes may explain the relatively infrequent use of anti-corruption strategies within the interviewed firms. However, the change in attitudes and perceptions between 2013 and 2015 may be tracked in Table 6.5, which shows the firms' average responses to the question 'To what extent do firms comparable to yours use the following strategies to manage and counter the informal practices of public authorities?' Interestingly, the results indicate that fewer firms allocate budgets for developing informal relationships with and making proactive proposals to representatives of regional authorities and regulatory agencies. At the same time, a significantly higher percentage of firms create and dissemi-nate Codes of Corporate Behavior, or create alliances with other compa-nies in the region to counter unscrupulous actions taken by representatives of the authorities or the regulatory agencies.

We again apply ordinary regression for the 2013 dataset in order to establish a firm profile, that is the firms' characteristics related to their intensity of using various strategies to deal with the informal (corrupt) strategies employed by the authorities, as described in Table 6.6. We use the same explanatory variables as for the previous regression analysis shown in Table 6.4. The results are shown in Table 6.7. It turns out that

Table 6.5 Anti-corruption strategies

	Survey 2013*			Survey 2015		
	Never or to small extent	To middle extent or widely	Missing	Never or to small extent	To middle extent or widely	Hard to say/no answer
'Buffer' strategy – the use of subcontractors, agents and third parties to work with regional authorities and regulatory agencies	84.3% n = 527	15.4% n = 96	0.3% n = 2	68.3% n = 82	15.8% n = 19	15.8% n = 19
Allocation of annual budget for developing informal relationships with representatives of regional authorities and regulatory agencies	88.3% n = 552	11.3% n = 71	0.3% n = 2	75.8% n = 91	7.5% n = 9	16.7% n = 20
Proactive proposals to regional authorities and regulatory agencies on cooperation programs and methods	88.3% n = 552	11.4% n = 71	0.3% n = 2	79.2% n = 95	6.6% n = 8	14.2% n = 17
Creation and dissemination of Codes of Corporate Behavior	78.1% n = 488	21.6% n = 135	0.3% n = 2	60% n = 72	30% n = 34	10% n = 12
Active briefing of partners on the company's rules and standards on working with government and regulatory agencies	78.6% n = 491	21.1% n = 132	0.3% n = 2	68.3% n = 82	20% n = 24	11.7% n = 14

Table 6.5 (continued)

	Survey 2013*			Survey 2015		
	Never or to small extent	To middle extent or widely	Missing	Never or to small extent	To middle extent or widely	Hard to say/ no answer
Training of managers and regional staff in the internal rules of interaction with counterparties	74.4% n = 465	25.2% n = 158	0.3% n = 2	59.1% n = 71	19.2% n = 35	11.7% n = 14
Creation of alliances with other companies in the region to counter unscrupulous actions by representatives of the authorities or the regulatory agencies	86.5% n = 541	13.1% n = 82	0.3% n = 2	63.3% n = 76	21.7% n = 26	15% n = 18
Use of the media to counter unscrupulous actions by authorities or regulatory agencies	87.7% n = 548	12% n = 75	0.3% n = 2	70.8% n = 85	15% n = 26	14.2% n = 17
Use of the courts to counter uns crupulous actions by authorities or regulatory agencies	87.2% n = 545	12.5% n = 78	0.3% n = 2	70% n = 84	15.8% n = 19	14.2% n = 17
Formal approaches to state officials to counter unscrupulous actions by regional and community authorities or regulatory agencies	89.4% n = 559	10.3% n = 64	0.3% n = 2	76.7% n = 92	8.3% n = 10	15% n = 18

Note: * The 2013 survey did not have an option 'Hard to say/no answer' for this question.

162

Table 6.6 Firms' usage of specific strategies to manage and counter the informal practices of public authorities in Ukraine, 2013 survey

Question: To what extent do firms comparable to yours use the following strategies to manage and counter the informal practices of public authorities? (Scale from 1 – never to 4 – widely)

Strategy	Mean	St. dev.	No. of answers
1. 'Buffer' strategy – the use of subcontractors, agents and third parties to work with regional authorities and regulatory agencies	1.69	0.79	623
2. Allocation of annual budget for developing informal relationships with representatives of regional authorities and regulatory agencies	1.58	0.74	623
3. Proactive proposals to regional authorities and regulatory agencies on cooperation programs and methods	1.53	0.72	623
4. Creation and dissemination of Codes of Corporate Behavior	1.80	0.90	623
5. Active briefing of partners on the company's rules and standards on working with government and regulatory agencies	1.75	0.87	623
6. Training of managers and regional staff in the internal rules of interaction with counterparties	1.84	0.93	623
7. Creation of alliances with other companies in the region to counter unscrupulous actions by representatives of the authorities or the regulatory agencies	1.56	0.77	623
8. Use of the media to counter unscrupulous actions by authorities or regulatory agencies	1.52	0.75	623
9. Use of the courts to counter unscrupulous actions by authorities or regulatory agencies	1.54	0.76	623
10. Formal approaches to state officials to counter unscrupulous actions by regional and community authorities or regulatory agencies	1.48	0.75	623

Table 6.7   Dependence of firms' perception of strategies that their peers use to manage and counter informal practices of public authorities on firm-specific characteristics

Dependent variable	1	2	3	4	5	6	7	8	9	10
Log(Year of firm establishment)	0.020	0.069	0.053	0.033	0.071	−0.001	0.020	0.013	0.024	0.145
	(0.060)	(0.062)	(0.063)	(0.059)	(0.060)	(0.060)	(0.063)	(0.064)	(0.063)	(0.112)
Log(Number of employees)	0.032	0.000	0.144***	0.098*	0.105**	0.141***	0.177***	0.189***	0.145***	0.286***
	(0.053)	(0.054)	(0.055)	(0.052)	(0.052)	(0.052)	(0.055)	(0.056)	(0.055)	(0.097)
% products/services sold domestically	−0.002	−0.004*	−0.004	0.000	−0.004*	0.000	−0.003	0.000	−0.003	−0.011**
	(0.003)	(0.003)	(0.003)	(0.003)	(0.002)	(0.002)	(0.003)	(0.003)	(0.003)	(0.004)
% products/services bought domestically	−0.003	−0.002	−0.002	−0.002	−0.003	−0.003*	−0.003*	−0.004*	−0.003	−0.002
	(0.002)	(0.002)	(0.002)	(0.002)	(0.002)	(0.002)	(0.002)	(0.002)	(0.002)	(0.004)
Domestic ownership dummy	0.061	0.196	0.334*	−0.042	0.040	0.068	0.108	0.032	0.258	0.244
	(0.185)	(0.192)	(0.201)	(0.180)	(0.183)	(0.182)	(0.189)	(0.193)	(0.199)	(0.344)
B2B business model dummy	−0.015	0.073	−0.069	−0.309***	−0.203*	−0.114	−0.342***	−0.216*	−0.289**	−0.540**
	(0.118)	(0.120)	(0.125)	(0.120)	(0.120)	(0.117)	(0.130)	(0.129)	(0.127)	(0.232)
Both B2B and B2C business model dummy	−0.049	−0.220	−0.013	−0.051	−0.158	−0.087	−0.055	−0.103	−0.163	0.078
	(0.183)	(0.193)	(0.189)	(0.179)	(0.183)	(0.180)	(0.190)	(0.193)	(0.193)	(0.325)
City, a regional capital, dummy	0.225*	0.343***	0.182	0.387***	0.163	0.190	−0.040	0.090	0.238*	0.176
	(0.122)	(0.127)	(0.128)	(0.123)	(0.121)	(0.119)	(0.125)	(0.128)	(0.129)	(0.226)
Provincial city, more than 50 000 inhabitants, dummy	0.036	0.128	0.052	0.400***	0.143	−0.090	−0.364**	−0.183	0.000	−0.243
	(0.149)	(0.154)	(0.157)	(0.148)	(0.147)	(0.147)	(0.159)	(0.161)	(0.159)	(0.285)
West	0.301	0.469**	0.468**	0.238	0.202	−0.112	0.207	0.440**	0.150	0.533
	(0.193)	(0.203)	(0.207)	(0.187)	(0.189)	(0.183)	(0.194)	(0.201)	(0.201)	(0.358)
North	0.324	0.589***	0.662***	0.179	0.116	−0.047	0.165	0.364*	0.503**	0.853**
	(0.205)	(0.215)	(0.219)	(0.200)	(0.203)	(0.196)	(0.209)	(0.215)	(0.211)	(0.377)

	(1)	(2)	(3)	(4)	(5)	(6)	(7)	(8)	(9)	(10)
Center	0.523***	0.360*	0.487**	0.128	0.380*	0.058	0.064	0.191	0.167	0.388
	(0.199)	(0.212)	(0.214)	(0.194)	(0.196)	(0.190)	(0.203)	(0.210)	(0.208)	(0.372)
South	0.124	0.336	−0.142	0.076	0.042	−0.218	−0.453**	−0.285	−0.102	−0.512
	(0.209)	(0.218)	(0.231)	(0.202)	(0.205)	(0.199)	(0.220)	(0.228)	(0.220)	(0.414)
East	0.322	0.481**	0.469**	0.159	0.168	−0.023	−0.182	−0.028	0.211	0.101
	(0.215)	(0.226)	(0.231)	(0.210)	(0.213)	(0.206)	(0.226)	(0.233)	(0.226)	(0.413)
Firm's income dummies	Yes	Yes	Yes	Yes	Yes	Yes	Yes	Yes	Yes	Yes
Constant	Yes	Yes	Yes	Yes	Yes	Yes	Yes	Yes	Yes	Yes
Link function	Probit	Probit	Probit	Probit	Probit	Probit	Probit	Probit	Probit	Logit
Goodness of fit, Pearson test p-value	0.042	0.004	0.08	0.41	0.102	0.067	0.057	0.003	0.801	0.000
Cox and Snell pseudo R^2	0.048	0.045	0.082	0.058	0.057	0.056	0.098	0.094	0.076	0.096
Test of parallel lines, p-value	0.051	0.825	0.666	0.002	0.999	0.044	0.743	0.942	1.000	0.451

Notes:
Dependent variable is firm's opinion concerning widespread use among peers of specific strategies to manage and counter informal practices used by public authorities; see Table 6.6 for details.
Ordinal regression using PLUM procedure in SPSS. ***, **, * indicate significance at 1, 5 and 10 percent level, respectively.

large companies are more systematic and strategic in managing informal relationships with authorities; the analysis reveals a significant positive relationship between firm size measured by the (log of the) number of employees and most of the strategies outlined. The exceptions are the first two strategies of using middlemen and the allocation of budget to work with authorities, where the small firms are indistinguishable from the large firms. Firms using the B2B business model are less inclined to use six out of ten of the strategies to manage/counter informal practices when dealing with authorities compared to firms using the B2C business model. Also, a firm's location in a regional capital city shows a positive and statistically significant relationship to the intensity of counter-corruption strategies used in half of the cases. Again, interestingly, we find significant regional differences in firms' usage of two strategies: firms in all regions except the South show significantly higher use of the strategies of allocation of annual budget for developing informal relationships with representatives of regional authorities, and proactive proposals to regional authorities and regulatory agencies on cooperation programs and methods compared to Donbas. In our opinion, this might be explained by the regional distortion of governance in Ukraine in 2013. According to the estimates of the *Weekly Mirror* newspaper,[7] in 2013, more than 75 percent of all positions in the Ukrainian government were held by people from the Donbas region, pushing firms from all the other regions to initiate proactive moves to secure their businesses.

What should Ukrainian business leaders do in such a corrupt environment? To mitigate corruption at the firm level, it is more efficient to look at specific informal practices and target them instead of fighting corruption in general (Shekshnia et al., 2013, 2014). But the willingness of the leaders is not enough; the institutional framework should also be adjusted.

NOTES

1. The Public Administration sector was excluded from this survey.
2. During the survey we found that many mid-sized and large businesses reported a lower number of employees. This is because they are trying to evade high taxes by employing people as independent contractors, which reduces their tax burden considerably.
3. The same approach to the assessment of business corruption is used in Denisova-Schmidt and Huber (2014), Denisova-Schmidt (2014) and Denisova-Schmidt et al. (2016), which investigate regional differences in business corruption in Ukraine based on the same survey data we use in this study.
4. We use logs for the number of employees and the firm's age to reduce heteroskedasticity in our data.
5. The smallest regional capital population is 117 000; the largest is 2 814 000.
6. We use a six-region division of Ukraine following Prytula and Pohorila (2016). Such a division is a compromise between the small sample issues and the eight-region division of

Ukraine that was well defined in Barrington and Herron (2004). The proposed division also accounts for the population density in Ukraine, so each region represents a relatively equal population. The composition of the six regions is as follows: Western region: Lviv, Ternopil, Ivano-Frankivsk Volyn, Rivne, Chernivtsi and Zakarpattia oblasts; Northern region: Zhytomyr, Chernihiv, Kiev and Sumy oblasts; Central region: Khmelnitskiy, Vinnytsa, Cherkassy, Poltava and Kirovohrad oblasts; Southern region: Odessa, Kherson and Mykolaiv oblasts and Crimea; Eastern oblasts: Dnipropetrovsk, Zaporizhzhia, Kharkiv oblasts; Donbas: Donetsk and Luhansk oblasts.

7. http://dt.ua/POLITICS/u-klyuchovih-ministerstvah-do-75-kerivnih-posad-zaymayut-vih idci-z-donbasu-128837_.html.

REFERENCES

Apressyan, R.G. (1997), 'Business ethics in Russia', *Journal of Business Ethics*, **16** (14), 1561–70.

Åslund, A. (2001), 'Ukraine's return to economic growth', *Post-Soviet Geography and Economics*, **42** (5), 313–28.

Åslund, A. (2005), 'The economic policy of Ukraine after the Orange Revolution', *Eurasian Geography and Economics*, **46** (5), 327–53.

Åslund, A. (2014), 'Why Ukraine is so poor, and what could be done to make it richer', *Eurasian Geography and Economics*, **55** (3), 236–46.

Barrington, L.W. and E.S. Herron (2004), 'One Ukraine or many? Regionalism in Ukraine and its political consequences', *Nationalities Papers*, **32** (1), 53–86.

Bilotkach, V. (2006), 'A tax evasion-bribery game: experimental evidence from the Ukraine', *European Journal of Comparative Economics*, **3** (1), 31–49.

Denisova-Schmidt, E. (2014), 'Korruption und informelle Praktiken im ukrainischen Geschäftsleben', *Ukraine-Analysen*, **130**, 16–19.

Denisova-Schmidt, E. and M. Huber (2014), 'Regional differences in perceived corruption among Ukrainian firms', *Eurasian Geography and Economics*, **55** (1), 10–36.

Denisova-Schmidt, E. and O. Kryzhko (2015), 'Managing informal business practices in Russia: the experience of foreign companies', *Mir Rossii*, **24** (4), 149–74.

Denisova-Schmidt, E. and Y. Prytula (2015a), 'The business environment in Ukraine: new country, old problems, more hope', 29 April, Edmond J. Safra Center for Ethics, Harvard University, available at: http://ethics.harvard.edu/blog/business-environment-ukraine-new-country-old-problems-more-hope.

Denisova-Schmidt, E. and Y. Prytula (2015b), 'To pay or not to pay taxes, that is the question', VoxUkraine, 12 June, available at: http://voxukraine.org/2015/06/12/to-pay-or-not-to-pay-taxes-that-is-the-question/.

Denisova-Schmidt, E., M. Huber and Y. Prytula (2016), 'Corruption among Ukrainian businesses: do firm size, industry and region matter?', in J. Leither and H. Meissner (eds), *State Capture, Political Risks and International Business Cases from the Black Sea Region*, Ashgate, forthcoming.

Frey, B. and B. Torgler (2007), 'Tax morale and conditional cooperation', *Journal of Comparative Economics*, **35**, 136–59.

Fuxman, L. (1997), 'Ethical dilemmas of doing business in post-Soviet Ukraine', *Journal of Business Ethics*, **16** (12/13), 1273–82.

Grossman, G. (1977), 'The "second economy" of the USSR', *Problems of Communism*, **26**, 25–40.

Hart, K. (2008), 'Informal economy', in Steven N. Durlauf and Lawrence E. Blume (eds), *The New Palgrave Dictionary of Economics*, 2nd edn, Basingstoke: Palgrave Macmillan, The New Palgrave Dictionary of Economics Online, doi:10.1057/9780230226203.0796, available at: http://www.dictionaryofeconomics.com/article?id=pde2008_I000102 (accessed 19 April 2015).

Karklins, R. (2005), *The System Made Me Do It: Corruption in Post-Communist Societies*, Ithaca, NY: M.E. Sharpe.

Kay, J. (2011), *Obliquity: Why Our Goals Are Best Achieved Indirectly*, London: Profile Books.

Knack, S. (2006), 'Measuring corruption in Eastern Europe and Central Asia: a critique of cross-country indicators', World Bank Policy Research Working Paper No. 3936, World Bank, Washington, DC.

Kuzio, T. (2014), 'Crime, politics and business in 1990s Ukraine', *Communist & Post-Communist Studies*, **47** (2), 195–210.

Ledeneva, A. (2006), *How Russia Really Works: The Informal Practices that Shaped Post-Soviet Politics and Business*, Ithaca, NY: Cornell University Press.

Ledeneva, A. (2009a), 'Corruption in post-Communist societies in Europe: a re-examination', *Perspectives on European Politics and Society*, **10** (1), 69-86.

Ledeneva, A. (2009b), 'From Russia with *blat*: can informal networks help modernize Russia?', *Social Research*, **76** (1), 257-88.

Ledeneva, A. (2013), *Can Russia Modernise? Sistema, Power Networks and Informal Governance*, Cambridge: Cambridge University Press.

Leipnik, O. and S. Kyrychenko (2013), 'The public utilities war and corruption in Ukraine', *Post-Communist Economies*, **25** (2), 159–74.

McCullagh, P. (1980), 'Regression models for ordinal data', *Journal of the Royal Statistical Society. Series B (Methodological)*, **42** (2), 109–42.

Markovskaya, A., W.A. Pridemore and C. Nakajima (2003), 'Laws without teeth: an overview of the problems associated with corruption in Ukraine', *Crime, Law and Social Change*, **39**, 193–213.

Onoshchenko, O. and C. Williams (2014), 'Evaluating the role of blat in finding graduate employment in post-Soviet Ukraine: the dark side of job recruitment?', *Employment Relations*, **36** (3), 254–65.

Prytula, Y. and N. Pohorila (2016), 'Recent regional economic development in Ukraine: does history help to explain the differences?', in U. Schmid (ed.), *Unity in Diversity*, forthcoming.

Rodgers, P., C.C. Williams and J. Round (2008), 'Workplace crime and the informal economy in Ukraine', *International Journal of Social Economics*, **35** (9), 666–78.

Rojansky, M.A. (2014), 'Corporate raiding in Ukraine: causes, methods and consequences', *Demokratizatsiya*, **22** (3), 411–44.

Shekshnia, S., A. Ledeneva and E. Denisova-Schmidt (2013), 'Reflective leadership vs. endemic corruption in emerging markets', INSEAD Working Paper 2013/121/EFE, INSEAD, Fontainebleau.

Shekshnia, S., A. Ledeneva and E. Denisova-Schmidt (2014), 'How to mitigate corruption in emerging markets: the case of Russia', Edmond J. Safra Working Papers No. 36, Edmond J. Safra Center for Ethics, Harvard University, Cambridge, MA.

Tanzi, V. (1998), 'Corruption around the world: causes, consequences, scope, and cures', IMF Staff Papers No. 45, IMF, Washington, DC.

7. A normative analysis of the measures to prevent the shadow economy in Finland

Markku Virtanen

INTRODUCTION

During the downturn of the economy, all sources of funds and a wide tax base are necessary for society. Thus, measures which erode the tax base should be prevented. The shadow economy is one such instrument that does so and is a large burden for economies[1] and does not follow the legal norms and manners of society. An important goal in many societies is to prevent the shadow economy and to give incentives to people in order to change their behaviour towards transparent legitimate transactions.

In Finland, the Government Platform (GP) of the former Prime Minister Jyrki Katainen paid quite a lot of attention to the shadow economy. Essentially, curtailing the grey economy has been one of the key measures in the growth policy and restructuring of the economy. In the GP, a specific chapter was devoted to 'intensified action to combat the shadow economy'. The instruments which have been introduced to do so include the establishment of the Grey Economy Information Unit (GEIU) under the organization of the tax authorities. This Unit contributes to tackling the shadow economy by producing and distributing information about the grey economy and action that can be taken against it. The campaign Black Economy – Black Future has been running in order to reduce the externalities caused by such shadow work (www.mustatulevaisuus.fi/).

Putniņš and Sauka (2011) have estimated the size of shadow market in Baltic States using a survey methodology. Their results show that the share of the shadow economy is decreasing in all the Baltic countries. However, the level of the shadow economy in Baltic States is relatively much higher than in Finland and other Nordic countries. This is shown in Table 7.1, which includes estimates of the shadow economy as a share of Gross Domestic Product in the Baltic States and Nordic countries in the period from 2003 to 2012. The share of the shadow economy in Finland has decreased more than four percentage points in these ten years. According to Schneider (2014a), the other Nordic countries have larger shadow economies than Finland. The relative size of the shadow economy in all the Baltic States is double the size of the shadow economy in Finland.

As a result of the tight fiscal situation of the Finnish economy, the public administration in this country has seen an opportunity to collect public funds by pursuing intensive efforts to prevent the grey economy. According to the Programme for Jyrki Katainen's government, the aim with the programme of action against the grey economy is to achieve a total of €300–400 million a year in increased tax receipts and social insurance contributions as well as to recover the proceeds of crime (Finnish Tax Administration, 2014).

This chapter poses the following research questions: What is the estimated share of different informal activities in the Finnish economy? What kinds of forms of shadow economy exist in Finland? What kinds of measures have been taken in order to reduce the size of the shadow economy in Finland? What is the outcome of the measures that have been introduced? The analysis will mainly concentrate on the domestic market. Thus, actions such as the use of tax havens and other forms of international tax evasion are excluded from the analysis.

WHAT IS THE ESTIMATED SHARE OF INFORMAL ACTIVITIES IN THE ECONOMY?

As Takala and Viren (2010) and Schneider and Enste (2000) state, there is no generally accepted methodology for measuring the shadow economy. Schneider and Enste (2000) use currency demand, the physical input (electricity consumption) method, and the model approach. They conclude: 'One should be very careful when interpreting the size of the shadow economy in a country using only one method.' For example, Schneider (2000) calculates the size of the shadow economy using the currency demand approach, which assumes that shadow transactions are undertaken in the form of cash payments. Viren (2015) criticizes this approach and suggests that it leads to blatantly too high estimates of the share of the shadow economy.

In 2012, GDP in market prices was about 200 billion euros. In Figure 7.1, the estimate of Schneider (2014a) in Table 7.1 has been used to describe the size of the shadow economy. It is interesting to notice that the size of the shadow economy remains quite stable, varying between 26–27 billion euros (market prices) even if the relative size varies between 13.3 per cent in 2012 and 17.6 per cent in 2003 and the absolute size

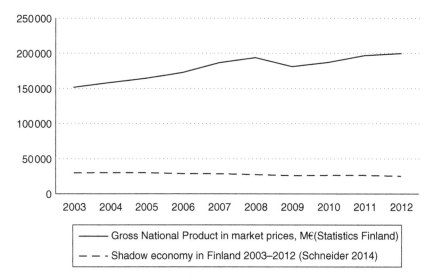

Figure 7.1   Gross domestic product at market prices and the estimated size of the shadow economy in Finland in 2003–14

is almost the same in both years (26.7 billion in 2003 and 26.6 billion in 2012).

The Grey Economy Information Unit (GEIU) notes that the definition of the size of the grey economy is a tricky issue:

> The central result of the reports commissioned by the European Commission over the past 20 years is that a single feasible and reliable method for measuring the grey economy has not been found. Research on the size of the grey economy in both Sweden and Finland are based on dividing the target area into parts and on the use of several different methods to supplement each other. Although the entire truth about the size of the grey economy cannot be determined, the selected approach appears to produce results that seem logical in international comparison. (Grey Economy Information Unit, 2014)

Tanzi (1999) suggests that reliable estimates of the size of the underground economy would be useful to policymakers. However, he continues: 'Unfortunately, as long as the estimates remain as divergent as they have been, they cannot provide much of a guidance for policy.' Even if the number of studies has increased substantially since the publication of his article, the estimates of its size seem to remain divergent.

According to Figure 7.1, the size of the shadow economy in Finland would have been more than 26 billion euros in 2012. This would most probably include all voluntary work and neighbour help, which could be taxable if acquired from the market. What is the share of different informal activities in the Finnish economy calculated by the Finnish researchers? Hirvonen et al. (2010) have estimated that the size of the grey economy in Finland is approximately 10–14 billion euros/year (20 per cent of the Finnish state budget, about 7 per cent of GDP). In different branches where the greatest efforts have been allocated, the losses are, however, quite small as a share of this totality. In the construction industry, 20 000 employees work without a legal position, which means losses of about 0.3 billion euros (Hirvonen et al., 2010). In addition, it is estimated that in value added taxation, there is a computational deficit of about 0.3 billion euros (Hirvonen et al., 2010). In the hospitality industry, the share of the grey economy is estimated to be 8–10 per cent of turnover (loss of 0.5 billion euros). Thus, these two focus areas would form less than 8 per cent of the size of the total grey economy and as much as 7 per cent of GDP.

Some Finnish researchers suggest that Hirvonen et al. (2010) overestimate the potential size of the informal economy (Viren, 2015; Takala and Viren, 2010). Takala and Viren (2010) criticize the outcome of these estimations and conclude that the estimates made by Statistics Finland (Nurminen, 2008, cited in Viren, 2015), where the size of the grey economy is estimated to be 1.5 per cent of GDP, could be more accurate. This means that the volume of the grey economy could be about 3 billion euros annually. Based on the figures of National Accounts and Tax Authority I would suggest that the truth lies between these estimates, and the size of the grey economy is 6–8 billion euros, which corresponds quite well to the size proposed by Lith (1997). However, most obviously only less than half of this amount could be available for taxable income since the total control of the behaviour and usage of money of private individuals in Western economies is impossible.

It should be noticed that the efforts to control 'negative' externalities lead to changes in behaviour and these dynamic effects are almost impossible to estimate; for example, how small firms tolerate the risk of being responsible for the statutory payments of their subcontractors. If they evaluate that the risk is too high, this may lead to business closures, which finally decreases the total volume of collected taxes. In Finland in the construction industry, closures have increased by more than 21 per cent and openings decreased by almost 10 per cent from the third quarter of 2013 to the third quarter of 2014. Tight economic conditions are of course one reason for the poor development of the industry but one explanation could be the heavy administrative burden which has been imposed. This may overburden especially the self-employed and small businesses, which act as main contractors.

The major drivers towards the shadow economy include a heavy tax burden and social security contributions together with labour market

Table 7.1   *Shadow economy in Nordic and Baltic countries in 2003–12 (% of GDP)*

	2003	2004	2005	2006	2007	2008	2009	2010	2011	2012
Denmark	17.4	17.1	16.5	15.4	14.8	13.9	14.3	14.0	13.8	13.4
Estonia	30.7	30.8	30.2	29.6	29.5	29.0	29.6	29.3	28.6	28.2
Finland	**17.6**	**17.2**	**16.6**	**15.3**	**14.5**	**13.8**	**14.2**	**14.0**	**13.7**	**13.3**
Latvia	30.4	30.1	29.1	29.0	27.5	26.5	27.1	27.3	26.5	26.1
Lithuania	32.0	31.7	31.1	30.6	29.7	29.1	29.6	29.7	29.0	28.5
Norway	18.6	18.2	17.6	16.1	15.4	14.7	15.3	15.1	14.8	14.2
Sweden	18.6	18.1	17.5	16.2	15.6	14.9	15.4	15.0	14.7	14.3

Source: Schneider (2014a).

regulations and rigidity (Schneider, 2005). However, the argumentation about the causes and consequences is not very straightforward. If high taxes per GDP cause an increase in the size of the grey economy, does this mean that the increase in the size of the public sector inevitably leads to an increase in the size of the shadow economy (Viren, 2015)? Comparing the size of the public sector in the Nordic and Baltic countries reveals that in the Nordic countries the share of public sector is more than 50 per cent of GNP whereas in the Baltic States this share is substantially under 40 per cent. Table 7.1 shows that in all Nordic countries, the estimated share of the shadow economy was less than 15 per cent in 2012, whereas in the Baltic States the share was more than 25 per cent.

One of the problems in estimating the size of the shadow economy is the difficulty in defining the unit of analysis. The majority of the measures introduced in GEIU reports focus on businesses, but if we take a wider definition of underground economic activities similar to Schneider (2002), consumers make a large number of decisions on tax evasion and avoidance. This definition includes, for example, barter trade (tax evasion) and all do-it-yourself work and neighbour help. Since we do not have any direct observations from the shadow economy other than the inspections of tax authorities in business organizations, it is difficult or maybe even impossible to estimate the size of the grey economy using some proxy variable like energy consumption.

FORMS AND MEASURES TO PREVENT THE SHADOW ECONOMY IN FINLAND

In this section, the focus is upon reviewing tax evasion and tax avoidance mainly from the business perspective and excludes illegal activities like smuggling and drug dealing. This means that forms of the grey economy include such tax evasion as unreported income from entrepreneurial activity, unreported and unregistered wages, salaries and assets. On the tax avoidance side, employee discounts and fringe benefits could be included, if the measures are mainly directed to decision makers of businesses.

In Finland Jyrki Katainen's government took measures to prevent the shadow economy by establishing a cross-administrative Minister Group and Grey Economy Information Unit (GEIU) to focus on the issue. The government allocated a significant increase in the resources to the tax authorities, 20 million euros per annum, in order to foster prevention of the shadow economy.

The Grey Economy Information Unit, which started its activity in 2011, defines the grey economy as follows:

> The grey economy means such activities of an organisation in which the organisation fails to meet the statutory obligations arising from its operations so that the payment of taxes, statutory pension, accident or unemployment insurance contributions or the fees charged by the Finnish Customs can be avoided or unjustified refunds received.

Similarly, in this chapter, the shadow or grey economy is defined as such activities where statutory obligations are defaulted on in order to avoid payment of statutory taxes, accident or employment insurances, pension insurance premiums or customs duties, or to receive refunds from actions which are not justified. The concept also includes measures taken to obtain unjust financial advantage through avoidance of taxes or payments.

The Action Program of the Prevention of the Grey Economy and White-collar Crime (APPGE) listed 35 recommended measures to tackle this realm. These included, for example, the following measures:

- the Act on the Contractor's Obligations and Liability when Work is Contracted Out;
- the Tax Debt Register;
- Public Procurements Act – Public Procurement Procedures;
- the building sector tax number;
- the monthly notification procedure for the building sector;
- the notification obligation on small building clients;
- an authorized contractor system;
- the obligation to provide a receipt;
- Public Transport Act and the Goods Transport Act;

- special distraint collection;
- using administrative sanctions rather than criminal proceedings in cases of minor crimes;
- establishment of the Grey Economy Information Unit.

Having a look at these forms of shadow economy in Finland, it can be concluded that the focus has been in order of appearance on the following activities:

- building trade;
- hospitality services;
- transportation;
- real estate services;
- scrap;
- working life.

Of course, the Grey Economy Information Unit and other authorities pay attention to such illegal activities as organized crime, money laundering, product forgeries, smuggling and desecration of the environment too, but they are outside the focus of this analysis.

What kinds of measures have been taken in order to reduce the size of the shadow economy in Finland? To answer this, the focus here is upon the measures mainly introduced by the Action Programme of the Prevention of the Grey Economy and White-collar Crime (APPGE). The APPGE includes 22 projects, which mostly concentrate on legislation. The objective of the Action Programme is to reduce the grey economy and white-collar crime. Other objectives include the support of legitimate business activity and healthy competition, safeguarding the accumulation of taxes and other charges, maintaining and ensuring the financial base of public services. The changes in the following acts, activities and fields were proposed:

1. the Act on the Contractor's Obligations and Liability, and Procurement Act;
2. building trade: changes in the Act, tax number and reverse charge in value added taxation;
3. payment of salaries and employer obligations;
4. hospitality services – hotel and catering;
5. foreign labour and businesses;
6. international investment activities;
7. provision and exchange of information between authorities;
8. criminal processes.

Since points 5 to 8 are excluded from the focus of this chapter, they are not dealt with here. Under the Act on the Contractor's Obligations and Liability when Work is Contracted Out (1233/2006), it is a contractor's responsibility to check that their contracting partner has discharged their statutory obligations since 2007. The information required in this Act includes registration of the contracting partner in the tax register, extract from the trade register, a certificate of tax payments and pension insurance, accident insurance, and the applicable collective agreement. On December 2014, the Tax Debt Register was established to publish information on whether a business has tax debts or reporting deficiencies.

The building trade has been the target of the measures of the abovementioned Act. Special amendments of the Act on the Contractor's Obligations and Liability when Work is Contracted Out in the building trade entered into force on 1 September 2012. These amendments included regulations that in the construction industry firms are required to give their workers on a specific construction site a Tax Number. Thus, the workers on a construction site must have a name tag where this Tax Number is displayed. The Tax Administration takes care of the Tax Number Register, from which foreign employees may also get their Finnish identity code and Tax Number. In the building trade, reverse value added taxation was introduced in 2012. According to this system, the buyer is responsible for paying value added taxes when the buyer is a businessperson who sells construction services or rents employees for construction services.

Amendments to the Act (1233/2006), which came into force in July 2013, also include the requirement to pay all salaries to employees' bank accounts. Cash payment is accepted only when there is a compelling reason, for example if the worker does not have a bank account. From the beginning of the year 2014, businesses have been obliged to offer a receipt for cash transactions to all customers. In usual outdoor market trade, the sellers are not under this obligation if the sold article is not alcohol. It was proposed that type-approved cash registers should be required in the hotel and catering industry, but this proposal was not accepted.

THE RESULTS OF SPECIAL MEASURES IN PREVENTING SHADOW ECONOMY

The outcome of the proposed and implemented measures is of course one cornerstone in prevention of the shadow economy. How many resources have been allocated to these tasks and what are the benefits of this activity to society? The financial objective of the APPGE is to generate a 300–400 million euro increase in tax and social security payments and

Table 7.2   Tax audits, tax audits of grey businesses in 2008–14 and monitoring measures

	2008	2009	2010	2011	2012	2013	2014
The number of tax audits			3553	3427	3151	3362	4666
The number of audited grey businesses	821	802	719	732	725	688	713
Revealed grey economy M€							
Black wages	56	51	47	42	48	51	89
Missing sales	49	52	51	65	55	64	68
Veiled distribution of profits, company	5	11	13	14	7	8	5
Veiled distribution of profits, shareholders	24	37	32	29	28	27	36
Total	**134**	**151**	**143**	**150**	**138**	**150**	**198**
Proposals for debiting, M€							
Withholding tax	21	19	17	13	17	17	12
Value-added tax	22	20	24	15	14	20	13
Direct tax	24	30	29	29	26	29	31
Total	**67**	**69**	**70**	**57**	**57**	**66**	**56**
Receipts with incorrect content							
Number of receipts	5260	6522	3687	7002	5902	11486	4052
Value of receipts, M€	44	38	64	50	40	81	38
The number of monitoring measures							
Tax audits (all companies)			3553	3427	3151	3362	4666
Monitoring visits					538	491	2021
Reviews of comparative data					267	444	7093
					3956	**4297**	**7093**

Source: http://www.vero.fi.

repayment of criminal profit. The estimated figure also includes the prevention of losses of taxes and criminal profit (Verohallinto, n.d.a).

According to the reports of GEIU, the total number of different monitoring activities has increased in 2014 compared with the previous year. The number of all the monitoring measures has increased substantially in 2014. The increase is largely due to the increase in monitoring visits and tax audits of all companies (Table 7.2).

However, if only the tax audits of grey businesses are analysed, it seems that the number of tax audits seems to be slightly decreasing in spite of the allocation of additional funds to these activities (Figure 7.2).

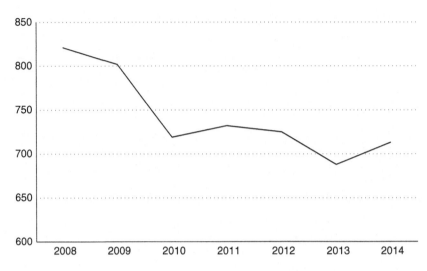

Figure 7.2   The number of audited grey businesses in 2008–14

We find two exceptions in these numbers. The revealed black wages have increased almost 75 per cent in 2014 and the amount and value of receipts with incorrect content has doubled from 2012 to 2013. This seems to be a result of some special effort, since in 2014, the amount and value of the receipts with incorrect content has dropped even to a lower level than in previous years.

The volume of the revealed grey economy seems to be quite stable over the years from 2008 to 2013 and varying between 130–150 million euros, but as was already stated, the year 2014 is an exception when the volume increases to almost 200 million euros (Figure 7.3). Similarly, the variance of proposals for debiting different taxes does not include any sudden changes but varies between 57–70 million euros (Table 7.2).

During the parliamentary term, the authorities have received 20 million euros additional funding for each year in order to combat the shadow economy. According to the GEIU, about 2000 person-years have been allocated and will be allocated to prevent the shadow economy. This includes the measures of all the authorities. If we calculate that the average salary of an employee varies between 2300 and 2800 euros per month and add other personnel expenses, we may conclude that the allocation of funds for combating the shadow economy varies between 80 and 100 million euros.

When the proposals for debiting (Table 7.2) and the collected amount (Viren, 2015) are compared, it will be obvious that the allocation of funds

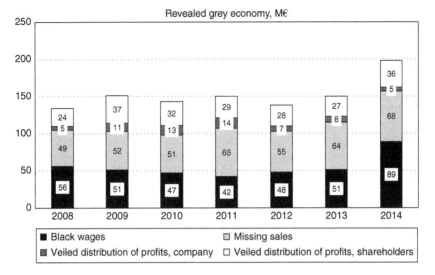

Source: Harmaan talouden valvontatilastoja, www.vero.fi.

Figure 7.3   The volume of revealed grey economy in 2008–14, M€

for prevention of the shadow economy is as large as the received outcome through taxation. It may be that in fiscal terms the government invests more in preventing the shadow economy than it receives as income from different debiting activities.

DISCUSSION AND CONCLUSIONS

In this analysis, I have investigated the normative measures of prevention of the shadow economy in Finland. Significant programmes and efforts have been introduced during the previous parliamentary period in order to prevent the grey economy in different fields of society. The first set of visible measures came after the Government Platform and included the establishment of the cross-administrative Minister Group and Grey Economy Information Unit, which coordinated the actions for reducing the shadow economy. The campaign Black Economy – Black Future was also introduced. The authorities received annually 20 million euros in additional funds for the work during the parliamentary term. The prevention of the shadow economy is also mentioned in the Government Platform of the new Sipilä government, which was appointed at the end of May 2015. Nevertheless, the shadow economy seems to be a much bigger problem in the Baltic States than in the Nordic countries. According to Schneider (2014a), in the Nordic countries, the share of the shadow economy is lowest in Finland. In the Baltic States, the size of the shadow economy is twice as big as it is in Finland.

Several changes in legislation have been introduced and enforced in Finland to prevent the shadow economy. In particular, the Act on the Contractor's Obligations and Liability when Work is Contracted Out has been changed to curb malpractice in the construction industry and other fields where subcontracting is used extensively. The construction business has been also the focus area for the introduction of a tax number and reverse charge in value added taxation. The amount of cash used in transactions has been reduced by the fact that all salaries must now be paid into an employee's bank account. Some proposals, such as the requirement of type-approved cash registers, were cancelled.

Schneider (2014a) proposes first that the higher the tax burden in a country, the larger the shadow economy, and second, that the more electronic payments in a country, the smaller the shadow economy. Finland and the other Nordic countries have both a high tax burden and large share of electronic payments. According to the calculations of Schneider, the size of the shadow economy of these countries cannot be considered very low either. The message of the study by Schneider (2014a) that payment systems help to combat the shadow economy is somehow distorted because the analysis is sponsored by Visa, which quite evidently supports the decrease in the usage of cash and increase of debt in the economy. It should also be remembered that in National Accounts, savings are equal to investment and usually households are the surplus units whose savings are transferred to business for investments.

The memorandum of the GEIU states: 'Scarce resources should not be allocated for actions from which no real results are to be expected'. This statement should be kept in mind when evaluating the efforts of the prevention of the grey economy. Various authorities have invested more than 2000 person-years in preventing the grey economy in recent years (GEIU, 2014). This means that the costs of the programme have been 80–100 million euros. When we take into account that collected taxes in 2002–12 have varied between 60–70 million euros annually, it could be asked, are we using scarce resources effectively? From society's point of view, obeying the laws is important and gives a solid background for the functioning of the market economy. However, for self-employed and micro-businesses, some regulations may cause such costs and risks that their alternatives are either the closing of operations or switching to the informal economy. For example, it seems that in the construction industry, the stock of enterprises has been decreasing in the first three quarters of the year 2014 compared with the same quarters in 2013 (OSF, 2015). Thus, it may be that new regulations and measures cause the number of businesses to decrease and the dynamic effects of the prevention of the grey economy are essentially smaller than estimated. On the other hand, the volume of the proposals for debiting does not mean that this amount could be collected. Most probably, those who hide their actions purposefully have a low propensity to pay their taxes and penalties. The payments are collected through distraint and there is a risk that the costs of collection are high compared to the compensation received.

If high taxes and government regulations are the main causes of the existence of the shadow economy (Ahumada et al., 2008), why have most of the introduced preventive measures increased the regulations? The majority of the proposed actions and measures in preventing the grey economy are some kind of norms, restrictions or requirements of tighter control, whereas positive incentives for affecting behaviour are totally missing. From the perspective of an economy, the grey market could be seen as an externality since it may lead to market disturbances. The efforts, activities and cooperation between different authorities are emphasized but the major problem is behaviour and decisions in businesses. Instead of proposing the remedy for negative externalities, for example by introducing more restrictive legislation and measures, which affect the cost competitiveness of businesses, more emphasis could be allocated to positive externalities.

In Jyrki Katainen's GP, the tax credit for domestic help or household expenses was introduced as a way to reduce the grey economy. Deduction of household expenses gives the households an incentive to make payments transparent. Education and training are typical examples of positive externalities. In some branches of industry, the pressure of competition and the need to be socially acceptable lead to activity in the shadow economy. In Finland we have some ethnic restaurants in the capital area where the annual turnover in the four-year period varies between 17 000 and 36 000 euros, which can hardly cover the rent costs. Instead of punishing these entrepreneurs directly, it should be investigated whether they could they get assistance from education and training in business knowledge and usual Finnish practices.

For policy makers, this analysis suggests that more attention should be paid to the relationship between the input and outcome of the measures introduced to prevent the grey economy. For society, prevention of immoral activity most probably has more value than money. However, it could be asked if it is better to avoid social exclusion instead of purist moral action. Entrepreneurs benefit from the analysis since it increases their consciousness and knowledge of activities of the GEIU and the contents of the programme and the campaign as well as their potential impact on their businesses. For the research community the chapter raises new research questions and gives some background and framework for more in-depth studies about the phenomenon. In particular we need more research on the dynamic effects of the launched actions as well as the positive externalities, that is, incentives for desired behaviour. It is to be hoped that this chapter will thus encourage greater evaluation of the potential effects of policy measures, something which has so far been sadly lacking despite the supposed shift towards evidence-based policy making.

NOTE

1. In this study, grey economy, black economy, informal economy and shadow economy are used as synonyms of each other.

REFERENCES

Ahumada, H., F. Alverdo and A. Canavese (2008), 'The monetary method to measure the shadow economy: the forgotten problem of initial conditions', *Economics Letters*, **101** (2), 97–9.

Black Economy – Black Future, available at: http://www.mustatulevaisuus.fi/?gclid=CPLE7PS0pbgCFUrJtAodtyIAVw (accessed 22 May 2015).

Finnish Tax Administration (2014), 'The grey economy 2014', available at: https://www.vero.fi/en-US/Tax_Administration/News/The_Grey_Economy_2014_annual_published(35333) (accessed 22 May 2015).

Grey Economy Information Unit (GEIU) (2014), 'Harmaa talous: valvonta-tilastoja 2014' ('The grey economy: supervision statistics 2014', in Finnish), available at: https://www.vero.fi/download/Harmaa_talous_valvontatilastoja_2014/%7BBC7D4076-50A7-4037-B7A7-AB3C86595B3B%7D/10681 (accessed 25 May 2015).

Hirvonen, Markku, P. Litha and R. Walden (2010), 'Suomen kansain-välistyvä harmaa talous. Eduskunnan tarkastusvaliokunnan julkaisu 1/2010' ('Globalizing grey economy in Finland. An investigation of the Finnish shadow economy commissioned by the Finnish Parliament 1/2010').

Lith, P. (1997), 'A report on the Finnish shadow economy' (in Finnish with English abstract), VATT Discussion Papers 142, available at: http://www.vatt.fi/file/vatt_publication_pdf/k142.pdf.

Official Statistics of Finland (OSF) (2015), 'Enterprise openings and closures' (e-publication), Helsinki: Statistics Finland, available at: http://www.stat.fi/til/aly/index_en.html (accessed 3 June 2015).

Putniņš, T.J. and A. Sauka, A. (2011), 'Size and determinants of shadow econo-mies in the Baltic States', *Baltic Journal of Economics*, **11** (2), 5–25.

Schneider, F. (2000), 'Dimensions of the shadow economy', *The Independent Review*, **V** (1), 81–91.

Schneider, F. (2002), 'Size and measurement of the informal economy in 110 countries around the world', paper presented at a Workshop of Australian National Tax Centre, ANU, Canberra, Australia, 17 July.

Schneider, F. (2005), 'Shadow economies around the world: what do we know?', *European Journal of Political Economy*, **21**, 598–642.

Schneider, F. (2014a), 'Size and development of the shadow economy of 31 European and 5 other OECD countries from 2003 to 2012: some new facts', available at: http://www.economics.uni-linz.ac.at/members/Schneider/files/publi cations/2012/ShadEcEurope31.pdf.

Schneider, F. (2014b), 'The shadow economy in Europe, 2013', VISA & AT Kearney, available at: http://www.visa-europe.fr/media/images/shadow%20economy%20 white%20paper-58-8752.pdf.

Schneider, F. and D.H. Enste (2000), 'Shadow economies: sizes, causes, and consequences', *Journal of Economic Literature*, **38** (March), 77–114.

Takala, K. and M. Viren (2010), 'Is cash used only in the shadow economy?', *International Economic Journal*, **24** (4), 525–40.

Tanzi, V. (1999), 'Uses and abuses of estimates of the underground economy', *The Economic Journal*, **109**, F338–F347.

Verohallinto (Finnish Tax Administration) (n.d.a), available at: http://www.vero.fi/, http://www.vero.fi/en-US.

Verohallinto (Finnish Tax Administration) (n.d.b), available at: https://www.vero. fi/fi-FI/Tietoa_Verohallinnosta/Tilastoja_ja_tutkimuksia/Tilastoja_Verohal linnon_toiminnasta/Verohallinnon_tilastoja_Verovalvonnan_to(32671) (in Finnish) (accessed 24 May 2015).

Viren, M. (2015), 'Why so little revenues are obtained from a presumed large shadow economy?', *Economics of Governance*, **16** (2), 101–23.

8. The informal economy in the Caucasus and Central Asia: size and determinants*

Yasser Abdih and Leandro Medina

1 INTRODUCTION

The characterization of the informal economy has been debated both in policy and academic circles. There is no unique definition of the informal economy in the literature, and terms such as shadow economy, black economy and unreported economy have been used to define it.

According to Feige (2005), the informal economy 'has been used so frequently, and inconsistently'; he argued that the informal economy comprises those economic activities that circumvent the costs and are excluded from the benefits and rights incorporated in the laws and administrative rules covering property relationships, commercial licensing, labor contracts, torts, financial credit, and social systems.

Measuring informality is important given that workers in informal conditions have little or no social protection or employment benefits, and these conditions undermine inclusiveness in the labor market. According to the World Bank *World Development Indicators*, 65 percent of the labor force in Kazakhstan and 64 percent in Azerbaijan do not contribute to a retirement pension scheme. In Armenia and the Kyrgyz Republic, more than 58 percent of the labor force lack pension coverage. Economic activity largely goes underground to avoid the burden of administrative regulation and taxation.[1]

Different methods have been proposed to estimate the size of the informal economy. Direct approaches, mostly based on surveys and samples, rely on voluntary replies or tax auditing and other compliance methods to measure the informal economy; the results are sensitive to how the questionnaire is formulated and therefore unlikely to capture all informal activities.

Indirect approaches, also called indicator approaches, use indirect information to estimate the size of the informal economy. For example, the discrepancy between the official and actual labor force approach states that a decline in labor force participation in the official economy can be seen as an indication of an increase in the size of the informal economy, if total labor force participation is assumed to be constant.[2] Most direct and indirect methods consider just one indicator of all effects of the informal economy.

This study has three related objectives. First, it attempts to provide macroeconomic estimates of the size of the informal economy for countries in the Caucasus and Central Asia (CCA). Second, it aims to give insights into the key underlying determinants of informality in these countries. And third, it seeks to present decision makers with policy advice to address informality and its adverse implications.

In achieving these objectives, the study makes three key contributions. First, it fills a gap in the literature by shedding light on a group of countries – the CCA countries – that appear to have large informal economies, but have not received much attention. Second, it utilizes a Multiple Indicator–Multiple Cause (MIMIC) empirical model, thereby allowing analysis of various aspects and dimensions of informality. And third, the study looks at a more comprehensive set of causal variables of informality than many existing empirical studies.

Our key results are as follows. Our estimates indicate that the size of the informal economy in CCA countries is large, ranging from 26 percent of GDP in the Kyrgyz Republic to around 35 percent of GDP in Armenia. We also find that a burdensome tax system, rigid labor markets, low institutional quality, and excessive regulation in financial and product markets are the key determinants of informality in these countries – findings that render themselves to clear policy recommendations to address informality and foster inclusion.

The rest of the chapter is organized as follows: the next section provides conceptual considerations. Section 3 reviews the empirical methodology. Section 4 presents the variables of interest used in this analysis. Section 5 presents the econometric estimation results and the calculation of the size of the informal economy. Section 6 concludes and offers policy recommendations.

2   CONCEPTUAL FRAMEWORK

The size of the informal economy depends on a variety of factors. The specialized literature highlights the tax burden, labor market rigidities, lack of institutional quality, and product and financial market rigidities (see, for example, Schneider et al., 2010; Feldmann, 2009; and Schneider and Enste, 2000).

- *Tax burden*: The tax and social security burdens are among the main causes of the informal economy. The larger the difference between the total cost of labor in the official economy and after-tax earnings, the greater the incentive to avoid this difference by joining the informal economy.
- *Labor rigidity*: The intensity of labor market regulations is another important factor that reduces the freedom of choice for actors engaged in the official economy. Furthermore, tight labor regulations help increase unemployment. These regulations, which decrease the freedom of both the employer and the employee, reduce the likelihood of formal economy employment, thus generating opportunities in the informal sector.
- *Institutional quality*: Institutional quality has a strong bearing on competitiveness and growth. A weak judiciary system, excessive bureaucracy, lack of transparency, and directed credit to connected borrowers and strategic enterprises exacerbate the incentives to informality. Furthermore, the stronger the enforcement capability and quality of government are, the lower is the expected size of the informal economy.
- *Regulatory burden in financial and product markets*: Burdensome regulations in product markets, in the form of procedures for starting a business, registering property, and dealing with construction permits, as well as difficulties in the credit market (such as availability and affordability of financial services), on the one hand, increase the size of the informal economy. On the other hand, any legislation aimed at increasing local competition and reducing monopolies and the extent of market dominance would contribute to reducing the size of the informal economy.

3   EMPIRICAL METHODOLOGY

Most methods exploited in the literature – and surveyed in Schneider and Enste (2000) and Vuletin (2008) – consider only one indicator of the informal economy, such as electricity consumption or money demand. However, more than one manifestation or symptom of the informal economy may show up simultaneously. The MIMIC approach used in this chapter explicitly considers various causes, as well as several effects of the informal economy. The model exploits the associations between observables causes and observable effects of the unobserved informal economy to estimate the size of the informal economy itself.[3] The model can be described as:

$$y = \lambda IE + \varepsilon \tag{8.1}$$

$$IE = \gamma'x + \upsilon \qquad (8.2)$$

Where IE is the unobservable latent variable, $y' = (y_1, \ldots, y_p)$ is a vector of indicators for IE, $x' = (x_1, \ldots, x_q)$ is a vector of causes of IE, λ and γ are the $(p \times 1)$ and $(q \times 1)$ vectors of the parameters, and ε and υ are the $(p \times 1)$ and scalar errors. Equation (8.1) relates the informal economy to its indicators, while equation (8.2) associates the informal economy with a set of observable causes. Assuming that the errors are normally distributed and mutually uncorrelated with $\text{var}(\upsilon) = \sigma_\upsilon^2$ and $\text{cov}(\varepsilon) = \Theta_\varepsilon$, the model can be solved for the reduced form as a function of observable variables by combining equations (8.1) and (8.2):

$$y = \pi x + \mu \qquad (8.3)$$

where $\pi = \lambda\gamma'$, $\mu = \lambda\upsilon + \varepsilon$ and $\text{cov}(\mu) = \lambda\lambda'\sigma_\upsilon^2 + \Theta_\varepsilon$.

As y and x are data vectors, equation (8.3) can be estimated by maximum likelihood using the restrictions implied in both the coefficient matrix π and the covariance matrix of the errors μ. Since the reduced form parameters of equation (8.3) remain unaltered when λ is multiplied by a scalar and γ and σ_υ^2 are divided by the same scalar, the estimation of equations (8.1) and (8.2) requires a normalization of the parameters in equation (8.1), and a convenient way to achieve this is to constrain one element of λ to some pre-assigned value.

Since the estimation of λ and γ is obtained by constraining one element of λ to an arbitrary value, it is useful to standardize the regression coefficients $\hat{\lambda}$ and $\hat{\gamma}$ as $\hat{\lambda}^s = \hat{\lambda}(\frac{\hat{\sigma}_{IE}}{\hat{\sigma}_y})$ and $\hat{\gamma}^s = \hat{\gamma}(\frac{\hat{\sigma}_x}{\hat{\sigma}_{IE}})$.

The standardized coefficient measures the expected change (in standard-deviation units) of the dependent variable due to a one standard-deviation change of a given explanatory variable, when all other explanatory variables are held constant. Using the estimates of the γ^s vector and setting the error term υ to its mean value of zero, the predicted values for the informal economy can be estimated using equation (8.2). Then, by using information for one country from various independent studies regarding the specific size of the informal economy measured as a percentage of GDP, the ordinal within-sample predictions for the informal economy can be converted into percentages of GDP.

4 DATA

Even though this study focuses on the CCA countries, the estimation takes into account data from a sample of 26 countries. The sample is restricted to the year 2008, a year where most of the data were available for all countries. The countries included in this study are: Albania, Armenia, Azerbaijan, Belarus, Bosnia and Herzegovina, Bulgaria, Croatia, Estonia, Georgia, Hungary, Kazakhstan, Kyrgyz Republic, Latvia, Lithuania, Macedonia, Moldova, Mongolia, Montenegro, Poland, Romania, Serbia, Slovak Republic, Slovenia, Tajikistan, Turkey and Ukraine.

As discussed in section 2, there are four main causal variables that affect the size of the informal economy. These are: the tax burden, labor rigidity, institutional quality and regulatory burden in financial and product markets.

Tax Burden

We measure this effect by exploiting the World Bank's *Doing Business* Paying Taxes ranking. *Doing Business* records the taxes and mandatory contributions that a medium-size company must pay in a given year, as well as measures of the administrative burden of paying taxes and contributions.[4] It exploits three indicators: payments, time and the total tax rate borne by a case study firm in a given year. The number of payments indicates the frequency with which the company has to file and pay different types of taxes and contributions, adjusted for the manner in which those payments are made. The time indicator captures the number of hours it takes to prepare, file and pay three major types of taxes: profit taxes, consumption taxes, and labor taxes and mandatory contributions. The total tax rate measures the tax cost borne by the standard firm.

Labor Rigidity

We capture this by the Fraser Index, which includes the following sub-components:

1. Hiring regulations and minimum wage. The index measures (a) whether fixed-term contracts are prohibited for permanent tasks; (b) the maximum cumulative duration of fixed-term contracts; and (c) the ratio of the minimum wage for a trainee or first-time employee to the average value added per worker.
2. Hiring and firing regulations. This sub-component is based on the World Economic Forum's *Global Competitiveness Report* question: 'The hiring and firing of workers is impeded by regulations or flexibly determined by employers'.
3. Centralized collective bargaining. This sub-component is based on the World Economic Forum's *Global Competitiveness Report* question:

'Wages in your country are set by a centralized bargaining process or up to each individual company'.

4. Hours regulations. The rigidity of hours index has five components: (a) whether there are restrictions on night work; (b) whether there are restrictions on weekly holiday work; (c) whether the work week can consist of 5.5 days; (d) whether the work week can extend to 50 hours or more (including overtime) for 2 months a year to respond to a seasonal increase in production; and (e) whether paid annual vacation is 21 working days or fewer.

5. Mandated cost of worker dismissal. This sub-component is based on the World Bank's *Doing Business* data on the cost of advance notice requirements, severance payments, and penalties due when dismissing a redundant worker.

6. Conscription. Data on the use and duration of military conscription were used to construct rating intervals. Countries with longer conscription periods received lower ratings (source: International Institute for Strategic Studies, *The Military Balance* (various issues); War Resisters International, *World Survey of Conscription and Conscientious Objection to Military Service*.

Institutional Quality

To measure the quality of institutions, we use the World Bank's *Governance Indicators*, specifically, the average of four sub-components:

1. Control of corruption. This sub-component captures perceptions of the extent to which public power is exercised for private gain, including both petty and grand forms of corruption, as well as 'capture' of the state by elites and private interests.

2. Rule of law. Captures perceptions of the extent to which agents have confidence in and abide by the rules of society, and in particular the quality of contract enforcement, property rights, the police, and the courts, as well as the likelihood of crime and violence.

3. Regulatory quality. Captures perceptions of the ability of the government to formulate and implement sound policies and regulations that permit and promote private sector development.

4. Government effectiveness. This sub-component captures perceptions of the quality of public services, the quality of the civil service and the degree of its independence from political pressures, the quality of policy formulation and implementation, and the credibility of the government's commitment to such policies.

Regulatory Burden in Financial and Product Markets

To capture this aspect, we use an indicator that takes into account both financial and product market restrictions. The financial market sub-component includes the World Economic Forum *Global Competitiveness Report's* financial market development indicators; particularly, availability of financial services, affordability of financial services, and the ease of access to loans. The product market sub-component takes into account the World Economic Forum *Global Competitiveness Report's* goods market efficiency indicators; in particular, the intensity of local competition, extent of market dominance, and effectiveness of anti-monopoly policy.

Since the informal economy cannot be directly measured, indicators that capture and reflect its characteristics must be used. The indicator variables used in this study are: self-employment as percentage of total employment from the International Labour Organization, and currency held outside depository corporations (as a percentage of broad money).

The intuition is that the informal economy typically avoids any formal transactions in the financial system, and hence needs cash in order to function. Therefore, a large amount of money held outside depository corporations (as a percentage of broad money) would signal a large informal economy. In the same vein, a large proportion of self-employment in total employment would also signal a large informal economy.

5   MAIN RESULTS AND DISCUSSION

In this section, we present the model estimation results, the calculation of the size of the informal economy, and the relative contribution of each causal variable to the size of the informal economy.

Multiple Indicator–Multiple Cause Model Estimation

The MIMIC model is represented in Figure 8.1. The tax burden, labor rigidity, institutional quality, and regulatory burden in financial and product markets are the cause variables of the informal economy, while self-employment (as a percentage of total employment) and currency held outside depository corporations (as a percentage of broad money) are the indicator variables.

The coefficients on the causal and indicators variables have the expected signs, and are statistically significant. In particular, a one standard deviation increase in the tax burden, labor rigidity, institutional quality and

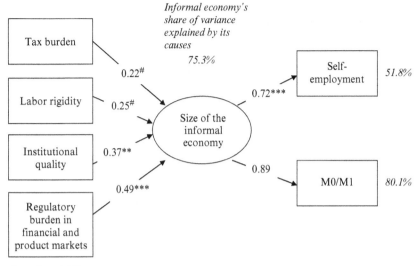

Overall model fit:
Discrepancy function (CMIN)(*p*-value): 0.852
Root mean square error of approximation (RMSEA): 0

Notes:
The panel estimation takes into account data from a sample of 26 countries for the year
2008. The countries included in this estimation are: Albania, Armenia, Azerbaijan, Belarus,
Bosnia and Herzegovina, Bulgaria, Croatia, Estonia, Georgia, Hungary, Kazakhstan,
Kyrgyz Republic, Latvia, Lithuania, Macedonia, Moldova, Mongolia, Montenegro,
Poland, Romania, Serbia, Slovak Republic, Slovenia, Tajikistan, Turkey and Ukraine. The
standardized regression coefficients and their respective significance levels are displayed by
the arrow pointing in the direction of influence.
Significant at 15 percent level; * at the 10 percent level; ** at the 5 percent level; *** at the
1 percent level.

In order to remove the structural indeterminacy of the coefficients, the non-standardized
coefficient associated with M0/M1 was set to 1. For this reason the *t*-test cannot be
performed on this coefficient.

Source: Authors' calculations.

Figure 8.1   Multiple Indicator–Multiple Cause estimation results

regulatory burden in financial and product markets increases the size of
the informal economy by 0.22, 0.25, 0.37 and 0.49 standard deviations
respectively. Furthermore, the joint influence of the casual variables
explains over 75 percent of the informal economy variance.

In addition, increases in the informal economy raise self-employment
(as a percentage of total employment) and currency outside depository

corporations (as a percentage of broad money), and explain 52 and 80 percent of their respective variances.

Different goodness-of-fit statistics are constructed to evaluate the MIMIC model. These measures are based on fitting the model to sample moments, which involves comparing the observed covariance matrix to the one estimated under the assumption that the model being tested is true. The discrepancy function (CMIN) is one of the most common fit tests, and is the minimum value of discrepancy function between the sample covariance matrix and the estimated covariance matrix. The chi-square value should not be significant as there is a good model fit, while a significant chi-square indicates lack of a satisfactory model. The root mean square error of approximation (RMSEA) is another test known to be less sensitive to the sample size. By convention, there is good model fit if the RMSEA is less than 0.05. The CMIN and RMSEA values are 0.852 and 0, respectively (Table 8.1).

Table 8.1   Multiple Indicator–Multiple Cause estimation non-standardized results, 2008

	Coefficient	S.E.
Cause		
Tax burden	4.918#	3.364
Labor rigidity	4.993#	3.245
Institutional quality	3.369**	1.766
Regulatory burden in financial and product markets	7.032***	2.638
Indicator		
Self employment	0.603***	0.170
M0/M1	1.000	
Overall model fit		
Discrepancy function (CMIN) (p-value):	0.852	
Root mean square error of approximation (RMSEA):	0	

Notes:
The panel estimation takes into account data from a sample of 26 countries for the year 2008. The countries included in this estimation are: Albania, Armenia, Azerbaijan, Belarus, Bosnia and Herzegovina, Bulgaria, Croatia, Estonia, Georgia, Hungary, Kazakhstan, Kyrgyz Republic, Latvia, Lithuania, Macedonia, Moldova, Mongolia, Montenegro, Poland, Romania, Serbia, Slovak Republic, Slovenia, Tajikistan, Turkey and Ukraine.
Significant at 15 percent level; * at the 10 percent level; ** at the 5 percent level; *** at the 1 percent level.

In order to remove the structural indeterminacy of the coefficients, the non-standardized coefficient associated with M0/M1 was set to 1. For this reason the *t*-test cannot be performed on this coefficient.

Source: Authors' calculations.

The Size of the Informal Economy

The standardized values of the informal economy are obtained from the estimated benchmark model (Figure 8.1). To transform these values into absolute informal economy sizes (measured as a percentage of GDP), we first normalize the ordinal values by the estimated value for Armenia. This gives the size of the informal economy for all countries relative to Armenia. Then, we multiply the latter by the size of the informal economy in Armenia (measured as a percentage of GDP) as estimated by detailed independent studies, to recover the size of the informal economy for all other countries measured as a percentage of GDP.[5]

Table 8.2 and Figure 8.2 show the ordinal values relative to Armenia, as well as the absolute values of the size of the informal economy, for the sample countries. Associated with lower levels of informality is Kyrgyz Republic, and with higher levels of informality are Armenia and Kazakhstan, with an informal economy size of around 35 and 33 percent of GDP respectively, with other CCA countries located in between.[6]

The relative contributions of the alternative causes of the informal economy are depicted in Figure 8.3. On average, the tax burden, labor rigidity, institutional quality, and regulatory burden in financial and product markets contribute around 10, 12, 31 and 46 percent, respectively, to the size of the informal economy. However, the contributions by country appear to be somewhat heterogeneous (see also Table 8.3).

Our results are in line with prior research. Specifically, our estimate of the size of the informal economy in the average CCA country of 31.5 percent of GDP is close to the transition countries' average of about 34 percent of GDP reported in Buehn and Schneider (2012). Our estimates

Table 8.2   Size of the informal economy, 2008

Country	Relative value	Absolute value (% of GDP)
Kyrgyz Republic	0.750	26.3
Georgia	0.859	30.1
Azerbaijan	0.899	31.5
Tajikistan	0.938	32.8
Kazakhstan	0.944	33.0
Armenia	1.000	35.0
Mean	0.898	31.5
Standard Deviation	0.087	3.0

Source: Authors' calculations.

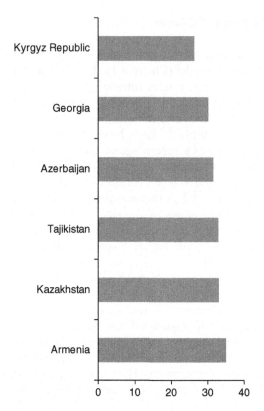

Source: Authors' calculations.

Figure 8.2   Estimated size of the informal economy (as a percentage of GDP), 2008

are also consistent with those of Schneider et al. (2010) – a study that covers a sample of 162 countries for the years from 1999 to 2007. For the 18 common countries in both studies, there is a positive correlation of 0.53 between the absolute sizes of the informal economy, and the Spearman rank correlation test has a value of 0.68, which rejects at the 1 percent significance level the null hypothesis that the rankings have zero correlation. Also, Vuletin (2008), utilizing a sample of mainly Latin American and Caribbean countries, finds that the size of the informal economy rises by about 0.29 standard deviations as a result of a one standard deviation increase in his index of labor market rigidity, by 0.24 standard deviations as a result of a one standard deviation increase in his index of the tax burden, and by about 0.5 standard deviations as a result of a one standard

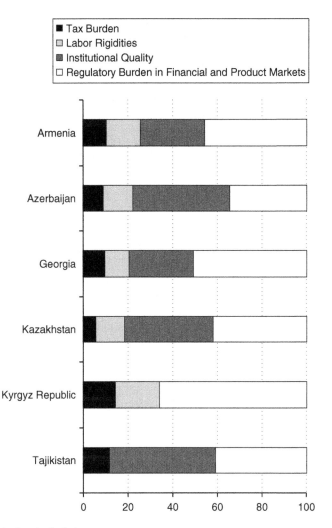

Source: Authors' calculations.

Figure 8.3 *Contribution of each cause variable to the size of the informal economy (in percent), 2008*

deviation increase in his index of regulatory burden. These are very close to our estimates of 0.25, 0.22 and 0.49, respectively.

Our findings are robust. Inspection of the data revealed no presence of outliers that could potentially drive or distort the results. Intuitively, this makes sense since the countries in the sample are not widely heterogeneous

Table 8.3   Relative contribution of cause variables to the size of the
informal economy, 2008

Country	Tax Burden	Labor Rigidities	Institutional Quality	Regulatory Burden in Financial and Product Markets
Armenia	10.6	15.0	28.8	45.7
Azerbaijan	9.1	13.4	43.0	34.5
Georgia	9.9	10.6	29.0	50.6
Kazakhstan	5.8	12.8	39.7	41.7
Kyrgyz Republic	14.5	19.6	0.0	65.9
Tajikistan	11.7	0.0	47.6	40.7
Mean Percentage	10.3	11.9	31.3	46.5

Source: Authors' calculations.

in their characteristics, and face broadly similar issues regarding informality. Also, we experimented with alternative measures of the causal variables used in the literature, and found that our results still hold. This is not surprising given that many of these alternative measures are highly correlated with ours. For example, the correlation coefficient between our measure of labor market institutions and the Heritage Foundation Index of Labor Freedom is about 0.8, and the correlation with the Labor Flexibility Index of the World Economic Forum's Global Competitiveness Indicators is about 0.6.[7]

6   CONCLUSION AND POLICY IMPLICATIONS

In this study, we empirically quantify the size of the informal economy in CCA countries. Utilizing a Multiple Indicator–Multiple Cause model, we find informality in these countries to be prevalent and large, in the range of 26 to 35 percent of GDP. Our results indicate that high levels of informality tend to be associated with high levels of self-employment and money held outside the banking system. Most importantly, our results shed light on the key factors underlying informality in the CCA – we find that excessive regulation in financial and product markets, low quality of institutions, rigid labor markets, and burdensome tax systems have conspired to drive people and firms into the informal economy.

These results have important implications for policymakers in the Caucasus and Central Asia. To reduce the barriers to business and labor formality, which are also barriers to more inclusive growth, policymakers should tackle the main causes of informality. Specifically, policymakers should:

- *Improve the regulatory framework for business.* They should simplify entry regulations and reduce compliance costs, and at the same time create an environment that fosters a fairer enforcement of regulation. Furthermore, measures to promote the availability and affordability of financial services, as well as measures that would aim at increasing local competition, easing trade barriers, and reducing monopolies and the extent of market dominance, would contribute to reducing the size of the informal economy. This approach is conducive to investment and growth, and is inclusive as it allows all firms and workers to compete on a level playing field.
- *Reform labor market institutions.* Overly restrictive labor market regulations can impede job creation in the formal sector, contribute to driving firms and workers into the informal economy, and reinforce segmentation in the labor market. As a result, workers in the formal sector enjoy protection while informal workers have little or no protection at all. Policy should aim to relax such rigid regulations to achieve more compliance and improved employment outcomes, while preserving the right to collective bargaining and developing effective social protection systems.
- *Reduce the tax burden.* Lowering corporate tax rates (where these are excessive) and simplifying tax regulations would increase formality, and could raise tax revenues, as evidence from Brazil and Egypt suggests (Gatti et al., 2011).[8] Such reforms will provide incentives for existing informal firms to formalize and, hence, pay taxes; existing formal firms will have greater incentive to invest; and new firms will have greater incentive to operate in the formal economy.

NOTES

*   The views expressed in this chapter are those of the authors and do not necessarily represent those of the IMF or IMF policy.
1.   In Kazakhstan, people that move from rural areas to the cities often choose not to work in the formal sector due to the strict internal migration regulations.
2.   For a comprehensive review, see Schneider and Enste (2000).
3.   See Loayza (1997).
4.   The taxes and contributions measure includes: the profit or corporate income tax, social contributions and labor taxes paid by the employer, property taxes, property transfer taxes, dividend tax, capital gains tax, financial transactions tax, waste collection taxes, vehicle and road taxes, and any other small taxes or fees.
5.   See Tunyan (2005); Davoodi and Grigorian (2007).

6. It is worth noting that Armenia has a sizable share of self-employed people in the agriculture sector, mainly poor subsistence farmers. This fact could play an important role in the results, assuming that the self-employment ratio differs in its composition by country. This study takes into the account the aggregate measure.

7. Our results regarding the impact of labor market institutions on the size of the informal economy are consistent with prior research, and do not derive from the specific labor measure used in this chapter. First, using an exact empirical methodology such as ours, as well as a labor measure that is different from the measure used in this chapter and one that does not derive from any of the sources used to construct our measure, Vuletin (2008) finds a virtually identical impact to ours on informality of labor market rigidity. Second, the estimates reported in this chapter are consistent with those reported in Schneider et al. (2010) – including on the ranking of countries common to both studies. This, together with the fact that Schneider et al. (2010) do not use labor market regulations as an explanatory variable in their study, provides evidence that our results are not driven by the specific labor measure used. Indeed, the results of our chapter suggest that the contribution of labor rigidities to the size of the informal economy is small relative to the other determinants such as institution quality and the regulatory burden in financial and product markets. Finally, and as mentioned in the text, our labor measure is highly correlated with well-known and widely used alternative measures of labor market institutions.

8. In the successful country cases, the lowering of tax rates was usually accompanied by important reductions in loopholes, to avoid eroding the tax base.

REFERENCES

Buehn, A. and F. Schneider (2012), 'Shadow economies around the world: novel insights, accepted knowledge, and new estimates', *International Tax and Public Finance*, **19** (1), 139–71.

Davoodi, H. and D. Grigorian (2007), 'Tax potential versus tax effort: a cross-country analysis of Armenia's stubbornly low tax collection', IMF Working Paper 07/106, Washington, DC: International Monetary Fund.

Feige, E. (2005), 'Overseas holdings of US currency and the underground economy', Macroeconomics 0501022, EconWPA.

Feldmann, H. (2009), 'The unemployment effects of labor regulation around the world', *Journal of Comparative Economics*, **37** (1), 76–90.

Gatti, R., D. Angel-Urdinola, J. Silva and A. Bodor (2011), 'Striving for better jobs: the challenge of informality in the Middle East and North Africa', Washington, DC: World Bank.

Loayza, N. (1997), 'The economics of the informal sector: a simple model and some empirical evidence from Latin America', World Bank Policy Research Working Paper, WPS 1727, Washington, DC: World Bank.

Schneider, F. and D. Enste (2000), 'Shadow economies: size, causes, and consequences', *Journal of Economic Literature*, **38**, 77–114.

Schneider, F., A. Buehn and C. Montenegro (2010), 'Shadow economies all over the world: new estimates for 164 countries from 1999 to 2007', World Bank Policy Research Working Paper No. 5356, Washington, DC: World Bank.

Tunyan, B. (2005), 'The shadow economy of Armenia: size, causes and consequences', Working Paper No. 05/02, Armenian International Policy Research Group.

Vuletin, G. (2008), 'What is the size of the pie? Measuring the informal economy in Latin America and the Caribbean', *Money Affairs*, **21**, 161–91.

PART III

Policy Perspectives and Strategies on
Decreasing Shadow Economies

9. What is to be done about entrepreneurship in the shadow economy?[1]

Colin C. Williams

INTRODUCTION

The chapters in this edited volume have revealed how the growing body of literature on shadow entrepreneurship is improving understanding of the magnitude, characteristics and rationales underpinning this form of entrepreneurial endeavour. In this chapter, attention turns to the policy implications. Given this growing understanding, what is to be done about entrepreneurship in the shadow economy?

To answer this question, this chapter first evaluates the array of potential hypothetical policy choices available for tackling entrepreneurship in the shadow economy. Identifying that the overwhelming consensus is that shadow entrepreneurship needs to be brought into the legitimate economy, the second section of this chapter then provides a conceptual framework for understanding the range of potential policy approaches and measures available for achieving this objective. This is followed in the third section by a brief review of the direct controls that might be employed to move shadow entrepreneurship into the declared economy, followed in the fourth section by the indirect controls that might be used to do so. Rather than view these direct and indirect controls as either/or choices, the fifth and final section then demonstrates the various policy approaches that can be adopted which combine direct and indirect controls when tackling shadow entrepreneurship. The outcome will be a comprehensive review of the policy options, approaches and measures available to policy-makers along with some suggestions regarding how they can be combined.

HYPOTHETICAL POLICY CHOICES

Logically, there are four hypothetical policy choices available to policy-makers with regard to entrepreneurship in the shadow economy. Policy-makers can choose either: to take no action; to pursue the eradication of shadow entrepreneurship; to move legitimate entrepreneurship into the shadow economy; or finally, to transform shadow entrepreneurship into legitimate entrepreneurship. Even if some of these hypothetical policy choices may appear to be a little far-fetched at first glance, commentators have advocated each and every one of these policy choices over recent decades. In consequence, one cannot reject any of these policy choices without evaluating their implications.

Take No Action

A first hypothetical policy choice is for governments to take no action whatsoever regarding shadow entrepreneurship. Rationales for doing nothing about shadow entrepreneurship might be that it is a seed-bed for new venture creation, a breeding ground for the micro-enterprise system and a test-bed for fledgling enterprises and therefore no action should be taken. Indeed, a 2012 survey of 595 small business owners in the UK reveals that 20 per cent report that they traded in the shadow economy when starting up their business venture, with 64 per cent stating that the main reason for doing so was to test the viability of their business venture (Williams and Martinez, 2014a, 2014b).

The problem with taking no action regarding shadow entrepreneurship, however, and as Table 9.1 summarizes, is that entrepreneurship in the shadow economy has significant deleterious implications for legitimate businesses, shadow economy businesses, customers and governments. Until now, no known rigorous evaluations have been conducted of the extent to which any of these supposed deleterious and beneficial impacts are in fact valid in practice. This is a significant gap that needs to be filled in future studies. Despite this lack of an evidence-base, however, the strong consensus of both scholars and policy-makers is that on balance, the deleterious impacts outweigh the beneficial impacts of shadow entre-preneurship. As such, the overwhelming consensus is that taking no action about shadow entrepreneurship is not a feasible option. Interventions are thus seen to be required to tackle shadow entrepreneurship. What form of intervention, therefore, is needed?

Table 9.1 Deleterious and beneficial impacts of shadow entrepreneurship

Deleterious impacts	Beneficial impacts
For shadow entrepreneurs:	
Lack of access to credit and financial services, partly due to limited credit history.	Source of income to stay out of poverty.
Difficult to expand business which cannot be openly advertised.	Flexibility in when, where and how work
Raises barriers of entry to the formal market due to inability to provide employment history to support their skills and experience.	Reduces barriers to entry into employment because shadow work often starts with work for close social relations
For legitimate entrepreneurs:	
Produces unfair competitive advantage for shadow over legitimate entrepreneurs	Provides entrepreneurs with escape route from corrupt public sector officials
Results in deregulatory cultures pushing legitimate entrepreneurs into a 'race to the bottom' away from regulatory compliance	Provides exit strategy in contexts where the regulatory burden stifles business development
Results in 'hyper-casualization' as more legitimate entrepreneurs shift into the shadow economy	Enables outsourcing and sub-contracting to reduce production costs
For customers:	
Lack of legal recourse if poor job is done, insurance cover, guarantees in relation to the quality of the work conducted, and certainty that health and safety regulations are followed.	More affordable goods or service can be provided to customers if payment is made in cash without receipts
For governments:	
Loss of public revenue in terms of non-payment of taxes owed	Income from shadow entrepreneurship spent in the formal economy boosts demand for formal goods and services and contributes to 'official' economic growth.
Reduces ability of the government to achieve social cohesion by reducing the public revenue available to pursue social integration and mobility	'On the job' training in shadow businesses reduces pressure on state and its agencies during times of reduced public spending.
Loss of regulatory control over work conditions and service provision in the economy	Breeding ground for the micro-enterprise system
Encourages a more casual attitude towards the law more widely	Test-bed for fledgling business ventures

Sources: Derived from Barbour and Llanes (2013), Williams (2006) and Williams and Nadin (2012b).

Move Legitimate Entrepreneurship into the Shadow Economy

A second hypothetical policy choice is to shift legitimate entrepreneurship into the shadow economy. Although this has not been argued by any commentators since it is difficult to see what overall benefits would result, there have been policy proposals which in some respects speak to some of the tenets of this approach. Some commentators, that is, have advocated a deregulation of the legitimate economy as the way forward with regard to tackling shadow entrepreneurship. This is based on the belief that shadow entrepreneurship arises due to the over-regulation of the market (Sauvy, 1984; De Soto, 1989, 2001), and the objective is therefore to deregulate the legitimate economy in order that all activities are performed in a manner akin to what is currently the shadow economy, although they would not be engaged in shadow entrepreneurship because they would be conforming to the regulations that remain.

However, there are some intransigent problems with this policy approach. The view is that deregulation reduces the shadow economy. However, there is growing evidence that decreasing the level of state intervention in the economy does not result in a formalization of shadow entrepreneurs but quite the opposite, that is, to a greater level of shadow entrepreneurship (Kus, 2010, 2014; Williams, 2013b, 2014a, 2014d). Indeed, even if deregulation were to lead to higher levels of legitimate entrepreneurship, the outcome would appear to be a levelling down rather than up of working conditions (Williams, 2006, 2014a). In sum, even if deregulation were to reduce the magnitude of shadow entrepreneurship which, by definition, is a product of the regulations imposed on legitimate entrepreneurship, the impact would be probably to widen inequalities and a deterioration of working conditions compared with more regulated states.

Eradicate Shadow Entrepreneurship

Another interventionist option is to seek to eradicate shadow entrepreneurship. If shadow entrepreneurs are viewed as 'rational economic actors' who will evade tax so long as the pay-off is greater than the expected cost of being caught and punished (Allingham and Sandmo, 1972), their eradication can be achieved by changing the cost/benefit ratio confronting those engaged or thinking about participating in shadow entrepreneurship (for example, Grabiner, 2000; Hasseldine and Li, 1999; Richardson and Sawyer, 2001). This can be achieved by raising the costs of operating as a shadow entrepreneur, first by increasing the perceived or actual likelihood of detection and second by increasing the penalties and sanctions for doing so. In this 'negative reinforcement' approach therefore, the eradication of shadow entrepreneurship is pursued through the use of 'sticks' to punish 'bad' (non-compliant) behaviour.

However, whether this is, first, practical, and second, desirable, is open to question. On the practicality side, the issue is whether this is effective. Although some studies reveal that improving detection and/or penalties reduces shadow work (De Juan et al., 1994; Slemrod et al., 2001), others identify that the shadow economy grows (Bergman and Nevarez, 2006; Murphy, 2005) and thus that 'it is not sensible to penalize illicit work with intensified controls and higher fines' (Schneider and Enste, 2002: 192). This is because such a penalizing approach can alienate shadow entrepreneurs, reducing their willingness to comply and increasing the extensiveness of the shadow economy by reducing their belief in the fairness of the system (Murphy, 2005).

It can also be questioned whether the eradication of shadow entrepreneurship is desirable. If shadow entrepreneurship is recognized as a breeding ground for the micro-enterprise system and a seedbed for enterprise culture, this sphere is a potential asset that needs to be harnessed and a driver of economic development (for example, Williams, 2006). Seeking its eradication will therefore eliminate precisely the entrepreneurship and enterprise culture that governments are seeking to nurture. The consequent challenge for policy-makers is to 'join up' their policy approach towards shadow entrepreneurship with their agendas to nurture enterprise culture and entrepreneurship. Indeed, unless this is achieved, then governments with each new initiative to eradicate shadow entrepreneurship will destroy precisely the entrepreneurship and enterprise culture that they wish to foster.

Transform Shadow Entrepreneurship into Legitimate Entrepreneurship

Rather than take no action, transfer legitimate entrepreneurship to the shadow economy or stamp out shadow entrepreneurship, a final potential choice is to transform shadow entrepreneurship into legitimate entrepreneurship (Dekker et al., 2010; European Commission, 2007, Renooy et al., 2004; Small Business Council, 2004, Williams, 2006; Williams and Nadin, 2012a, 2012b, 2013, 2014; Williams and Renooy, 2013). The positive impacts of legitimizing shadow entrepreneurship vary according to whether legitimate and shadow businesses, customers or the government are considered.

So far as legitimate enterprises are concerned, transforming shadow entrepreneurship into legitimate entrepreneurship would stop the unfair competitive advantage of shadow businesses over those playing by the rules (Evans et al., 2006; Renooy et al., 2004). It would also enable the business community to pursue a 'high road' rather than a 'low road' approach by shifting towards greater regulatory standards on working conditions such as health and safety and labour standards (Grabiner, 2000; Renooy et al., 2004; Williams and Windebank, 1998). For shadow entrepreneurs, meanwhile, the key benefits of legitimizing are manifold. They can escape the pressure to enter exploitative relationships with the legitimate realm (Gallin, 2001; Williams and Windebank, 1998) and achieve the same levels of legal protection as legitimate entrepreneurs (ILO, 2014; Morris and Polese, 2014). They are also able to secure formal intellectual property rights for their products and processes (De Beer et al., 2013) and overcome the structural impediments which prevent them from expanding, such as their lack of access to advice and support as well as capital (ILO, 2014).

For customers, the advantages of legitimizing shadow entrepreneurship are that such customers benefit from legal recourse if a poor job is done, have access to insurance cover, enjoy guarantees with regard to the work conducted, and have more certainty that health and safety regulations are being followed (Williams and Martinez, 2014c).

Finally, for governments, the benefits of transforming shadow entrepreneurship into legitimate entrepreneurship are that it improves the level of public revenue, thus enabling governments to pursue higher expenditure on social integration and mobility projects (Williams and Windebank, 1998). It also enables the creation of more formal jobs and thus improves employment participation rates, and facilitates a joining-up of the policy approach towards shadow entrepreneurship with the policy approaches towards entrepreneurship and social inclusion (Dekker et al., 2010; European Commission, 2007, Small Business Council, 2004). It also results in a more positive attitude towards the law more widely (Polese, 2014; Renooy et al., 2004; Sasunkevich, 2014).

Summary of Hypothetical Policy Choices

This review of the four hypothetical policy choices available regarding shadow entrepreneurship reveals that the first option of taking no action is unacceptable. This would leave intact the current negative impacts on legitimate entrepreneurs (for example, unfair competition), shadow entrepreneurs (for example, the inability to gain access to credit to expand), customers (for example, no guarantee of health and safety standards) and governments (for example, taxes owed are not collected). Second, transforming legitimate entrepreneurship into shadow entrepreneurship is unacceptable because it levels working conditions down rather than up, and third and finally, eradicating shadow entrepreneurship is unacceptable since it results in governments repressing and eradicating precisely the entrepreneurial endeavour and enterprise culture that they otherwise wish to foster. Transforming shadow entrepreneurship into legitimate entrepreneurship thus appears to be the most viable policy choice. How, therefore, can this be achieved?

POLICY APPROACHES AND MEASURES

To provide a way of understanding the diverse array of policy approaches and measures available for transforming shadow entrepreneurship into legitimate entrepreneurship, Figure 9.1 sets out a heuristic conceptual framework. This distinguishes between direct and indirect controls. Direct controls seek to transform shadow entrepreneurship into legitimate entrepreneurship by ensuring that the benefits of operating in the legitimate economy outweigh the costs of working in the shadow economy. This is accomplished either by using deterrence measures to increase the costs of non-compliance ('sticks') and/or by making the conduct of legitimate entrepreneurship more beneficial and easier ('carrots'). Indirect controls, meanwhile, shift away from using 'sticks' and 'carrots', and instead focus on developing the psychological contract (or what might also be called the social contract) between the state and its citizens by fostering a high trust, high commitment culture among those engaged in entrepreneurship.

Here, we consider each policy approach in turn in order to highlight the range of policy approaches and array of measures available for transforming shadow entrepreneurship into legitimate entrepreneurship.

DIRECT CONTROLS APPROACH

The conventional policy approach for tackling the shadow economy is to use direct controls. As the OECD (2008: 82) summarize, 'Combating shadow employment requires a comprehensive approach to reduce the costs and increase the benefits to business and workers of operating formally'. To evaluate this direct controls approach therefore, first, the use of deterrence measures to detect and punish non-compliant ('bad') behaviour (that is, shadow entrepreneurship) is reviewed, followed secondly by the use of incentives (or what might be better called 'bribes') that make it easier to undertake and reward compliant ('good') behaviour (that is, legitimate entrepreneurship).

Deterrence Measures

During the early 1970s, Allingham and Sandmo (1972) argued that the non-compliant, such as shadow entrepreneurs, are rational economic

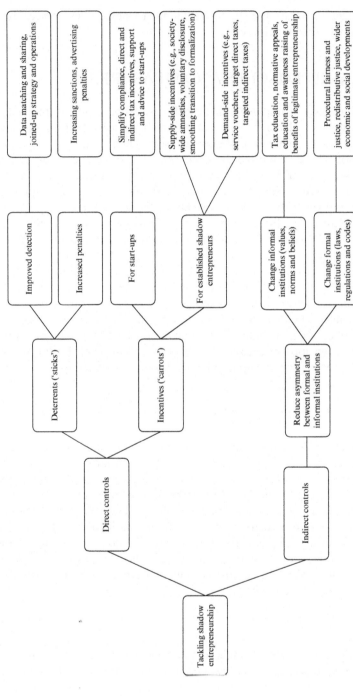

Figure 9.1 A typology of policy approaches and measures for tackling shadow entrepreneurship

actors who will evade tax when the pay-off is greater than the expected cost of detection and punishment. To deter them from doing so therefore, the objective is to change the cost/benefit ratio facing those participating or considering participation in shadow entrepreneurship (for example, Grabiner, 2000; Hasseldine and Li, 1999; Job et al., 2007; Richardson and Sawyer, 2001). When using deterrence measures, this is to be achieved by focusing on the cost side of the equation and increasing the actual and perceived risks and costs associated with participation in shadow entre-preneurship. This is pursued first by raising the perceived or actual likeli-hood of detection and/or second by increasing the penalties and sanctions for those caught. This is therefore a 'negative reinforcement' approach; it seeks behaviour change by using 'sticks' that punish non-compliant ('bad') behaviour.

A large and expanding body of literature nevertheless reveals that raising the penalties or the probability of detection does not lead to greater compliance (Feld and Frey, 2002; Murphy, 2005; Varma and Doob, 1998; Shaw et al., 2008; Webley and Halstead, 1986). Instead, it increases non-compliance, not least due to a breakdown of trust between the state and its citizens (Ayres and Braithwaite, 1992; Murphy and Harris, 2007; Tyler et al., 2007; Williams, 2001). Indeed, the most telling rebuttal of the use of deterrents is the finding that many voluntarily comply even when the level of penalties and risks of detection would suggest that they should act in a non-compliant manner if they were truly rational economic actors (Murphy, 2008). Obviously therefore, other factors must be at work engen-dering this commitment to compliant behaviour that lie beyond the level of deterrents.

Another reason for adopting a cautionary approach to the use of deter-rence measures is that they have a range of unintended and unwanted broader impacts. As already mentioned, they lead to one hand of govern-ment deterring precisely the entrepreneurial endeavour and enterprise culture that other hands of government wish to nurture. When this is com-bined with the recognition that punishing non-compliant ('bad') actions is not necessarily the most effective means of changing the behaviour of shadow entrepreneurs, the result has been that many have begun to ques-tion the value of such measures. New measures have thus emerged.

Incentive Measures

With the growing recognition across governments that the goal is to trans-form shadow entrepreneurship into legitimate entrepreneurship, rather than simply seeking to eradicate it, a shift has begun to take place in the policy approaches away from deterrence measures and towards providing incentives to encourage shadow entrepreneurs to legitimize their endeavours (Small Business Council, 2004; Williams, 2006). Put another way, rather than punish 'bad' (non-compliant) behaviour, measures have been sought that reward 'good' (compliant) behaviour, rather than taking it as given. When tackling shadow entrepreneurship, and as displayed in Figure 9.1 above, these measures take two forms.

On the one hand, a range of measures can be introduced that provide incentives for entrepreneurs at the business start-up stage to establish their ventures on a legitimate basis. These measures can include the simplification of compliance so as to make it easy to do so, the use of direct and indirect tax incentives that make it beneficial to start up legitimately, and the provision of support and advice to entrepreneurs about how to start up on a legitimate basis. An example is the initiative in Portugal entitled 'On the Spot' (*empresa na hora*) which makes it easy for nascent entrepreneurs to establish a business venture. This 'one-stop shop' makes it possible to create a company in a single office in a single day. Upon completion, the definitive legal person identification card is provided, the social security number given and the company immediately receives its memorandum and articles of association and an extract of the entry in the Commercial Register. Compliance is ensured by having all the details sent to the tax authorities. Between 2005, when the initiative started, and September 2008, 59 068 new enterprises were created. The average time taken is 1 hour 14 minutes and the average cost of setting up a company is €360.

On the other hand, a range of measures can be introduced that provide incentives for established shadow entrepreneurs to make the transition to legitimate entrepreneurship. Such measures can take the form of either supply-side measures targeting shadow entrepreneurs or demand-side measures targeting their customers and providing them with incentives to use legitimate rather than shadow enterprises. First, therefore, supply-side measures that in effect seek to 'bribe' shadow entrepreneurs to make the transition to legitimate entrepreneurship include the use of society-wide amnesties, voluntary disclosure schemes and the introduction of schemes that facilitate them to undergo a smooth transition to legitimacy.

Second, demand-side measures that again effectively 'bribe' customers to use legitimate rather than shadow enterprises when sourcing goods and services include the use of, for example, service vouchers and targeted direct and indirect tax incentives. An example is the Home-Job Plan in Denmark. This provides a 15 per cent tax deduction to people having work undertaken in their household so as to prevent them from using shadow enterprises. The types of household work covered by the tax deduction scheme includes: house cleaning, including windows; indoor and outdoor maintenance, including new installations; gardening; and babysitting, including bringing and picking up children from school. The measure is targeted especially at work undertaken by micro and small enterprises in the home repair, maintenance and improvement sector, such as plumbing and heating, electricity and construction work. The estimated tax value of these deductions is €134 million (DKK 1 billion) in 2011 and around €234 million (DKK 1.75 billion) in 2012 and 2013. In 2011, 270 000 people used the tax deduction and most of the work involved home improvement, maintenance and repair. They have on average reported deductions of DKK 9800 (€1315) per person. In total, the deductions reported amount to DKK 2.7 billion (€362 million). The tax value of those deductions is around DKK 900 million (€121 million) (see Williams, 2015b).

INDIRECT CONTROLS APPROACH

The problem with using direct controls to alter the cost/benefit ratio confronting shadow entrepreneurs is that they are not always rational economic actors with perfect information available. They are limited in their ability to compute the costs and benefits, often misperceive or do not perceive the real costs of their actions and are influenced by social context. Most importantly, they are not just motivated by self-interest and what is most profitable for them but by additional motives, including redistribution, fairness, reciprocity, social customs, norms and morality (Alm, 2011). Given this, a move has taken place away from the use of 'sticks' and 'carrots' to change behaviour. Instead, indirect controls seek to improve the psychological contract between the state and entrepreneurs in order to nurture a high trust, high commitment culture (Alm et al., 1995; Torgler, 2003; Weigel et al., 1987; Wenzel, 2002). The intention is to engender willing or voluntary commitment to compliant behaviour rather than force entrepreneurs to comply using threats, harassment and/or bribes (Kirchler, 2007; Torgler, 2007, 2011).

To understand the tools used in this approach, it is first necessary to recognize that there exists an institutional incongruity between the laws, codes and regulations of formal institutions and the norms, beliefs and values of informal institutions. Shadow entrepreneurship occurs where the norms, values and beliefs differ from the laws and regulations, resulting in what formal institutions deem to be illegal activities being seen as socially legitimate in terms of the norms, values and beliefs of entrepreneurs. To tackle shadow entrepreneurship therefore, there is a need to reduce this institutional incongruence. This can be achieved by changing either the informal institutions and/or the formal institutions.

Changing the Informal Institutions

To change this institutional incongruence, one approach is to change the norms, values and beliefs of potential and existing entrepreneurs regarding the acceptability of working in the shadow economy so that these are in symmetry with the laws, regulations and codes of formal institutions. This can be achieved by improving tax knowledge using awareness-raising campaigns about the costs of shadow entrepreneurship and benefits of legitimate entrepreneurship work, and normative appeals.

Improving tax knowledge
Educating entrepreneurs about taxation is important if the norms, values and beliefs are to be in symmetry with the codified laws and regulations of formal institutions. To do this, entrepreneurs require two types of education. First, there is the need to educate entrepreneurs about what the current tax system requires them to do by providing easily consumable information regarding their responsibilities. A significant portion of tax evasion is unintentional, resulting from a lack of knowledge, misunderstandings and a false interpretation of tax law (Hasseldine and Li, 1999; Natrah, 2013). A way forward, in consequence, is to provide greater information to taxpayers (Internal Revenue Service, 2007; Vossler et al., 2011).

Second, and more broadly, entrepreneurs also need to be educated about the value and benefits of paying taxes in order to prevent intentional evasion by developing an intrinsic motivation to comply. In many countries, for example, entrepreneurs make substantial voluntary donations to private charities but at the same time are reticent about paying their taxes, despite these private charities having parallel missions to government. This is doubtless because they know what happens to voluntary charity donations but do not know or understand what happens to their taxes (Li et al., 2011). A solution to reduce intentional evasion in consequence is to educate entrepreneurs about where their taxes are spent. This can be done by informing them of the current and potential public goods and services received (Bird et al., 2006; Saeed and Shah, 2011). Signs such as 'your taxes are paying for this' on civil construction schemes (for example, new roads) are one way of doing so by conveying a clear message of where taxes are being spent. Signs in hospitals, schools, medical centres and on ambulances can also be used in this regard.

Awareness-raising campaigns
A further way of changing attitudes towards compliance is to use awareness-raising campaigns. These can either inform: entrepreneurs of the costs and risks of operating in the shadow economy; potential customers

of the risks and costs; entrepreneurs of the benefits of being legitimate; and/or potential customers of the benefits of using the legitimate economy. Indeed, the evidence shows that such advertising campaigns are effective and cost efficient. In the UK, an evaluation of the advertising campaigns run by the tax office reveals that as a result, some 8300 additional people registered to pay tax who would not otherwise have done so, paying tax of £38 million over three years, providing a return of 19:1 on the expenditure of £2 million. This compares with an overall return of 4.5:1 on the £41 million a year spent on all its compliance work in 2006–2007 (National Audit Office, 2008).

Using normative appeals
Normative appeals to entrepreneurs to declare their activities are another potential way forward. Their effectiveness, however, depends in part on the nature of the appeal made. Chung and Trivedi (2003) examine the impact of normative appeals on a friendly persuasion group who were required to both generate and read a list of reasons why they should comply fully, compared with a control group not asked to do so. The participants in the friendly persuasion groups report higher earnings than the control group.

Changing the Formal Institutions

Besides changing the norms, values and beliefs of entrepreneurs in relation to compliance in order to align these with the codes and regulations of formal institutions, policy can also seek to change the formal institutions to align with the norms, values and beliefs of society. This is particularly important in societies in which there is a lack of trust in government, which may arise as a result of public sector corruption (European Commission, 2014), or in societies where entrepreneurs do not believe that they receive back from government what they expect. Two types of change are required so far as formal institutions are concerned. First, there is often a need to change internal *processes* in the formal institutions to improve the perception amongst entrepreneurs that there is tax fairness, procedural justice and redistributive justice. Second, there is often a need to change the *products* of formal institutions by pursuing wider economic and social developments. Here, each is considered in turn, starting with the changes required in internal processes in the formal institutions.

Enhancing procedural justice
Procedural justice refers to the extent to which entrepreneurs perceive the government to have treated them in a respectful, impartial and responsible manner (Braithwaite and Reinhart, 2000; Murphy, 2005; Taylor, 2005;

Tyler, 1997; Wenzel, 2002). This has a significant effect on compliance. If entrepreneurs view the tax administration as treating them in such a manner, then entrepreneurs will be more likely to engage in compliant behaviour (Hartner et al., 2008; Murphy, 2003; Murphy et al., 2009; Torgler and Schneider, 2007; Wenzel, 2002). As Wenzel (2006) finds, the compliance rate was significantly higher among taxpayers who perceived there to be interactional fairness. Being treated politely, with dignity and respect, being given a say, and having genuine respect shown for one rights and social status all enhance compliant behaviour (Alm et al., 1993; Feld and Frey, 2002; Gangl et al., 2013; Hartner et al., 2008; Murphy 2005; Tyler, 1997, 2006; Wenzel, 2002).

Improving procedural fairness

Procedural fairness refers to the extent to which entrepreneurs believe that they are paying their fair share compared with others (Kinsey and Gramsick, 1993; Wenzel, 2004a, 2004b). Entrepreneurs receiving procedurally fair treatment are more likely to trust the authorities and to be more inclined to accept its decisions and follow its directions (Murphy, 2005). The fairness of the tax system is one of the most important determinants as to whether they do so (Bobeck and Hatfield, 2003; Hartner et al., 2008, 2011; Kirchgässner, 2010, 2011; McGee, 2005, 2008; McGee et al., 2008; Molero and Pujol, 2012). Conversely, where there are grievances among entrepreneurs that they are not receiving fair treatment, non-compliance increases (Bird et al., 2006).

Developing redistributive justice

Redistributive justice refers to whether entrepreneurs believe they are receiving the goods and services they deserve given the taxes that they pay (Kinsey and Gramsick, 1993; Kinsey et al., 1991; Richardson and Sawyer, 2001; Thurman et al., 1984). Taxes are prices paid for the goods and services that governments provide. The question for the moral evaluation of taxes is whether the price corresponds to the value of these goods and services (that is, whether it is seen as 'just'), namely whether there is a 'just price' (Kirchgässner, 2010). Entrepreneurs see themselves as more justified in being non-compliant and breaking the psychological contract with the state, the less they perceive the tax system as fair. To achieve a high rate of tax compliance, therefore, the tax system must be seen as fair. If entrepreneurs do not receive the goods and services that they believe they deserve given the taxes that they pay, then non-compliance increases (McGee, 2005). The result is that governments need to educate entrepreneurs about where their taxes are spent. In situations where entrepreneurs do not know, or do not fully understand, what public goods and services are provided with their taxes, then compliance is lower than in situations where citizens are more fully aware of what public goods and services are received and they agree with how their taxes are spent (Lillemets, 2009). There is a need, therefore, for government to explain how taxes are spent and to elicit agreement regarding the public goods and services that are provided by government.

Changing the Products of Formal Institutions: Wider Economic and Social Developments

To achieve a high-commitment culture and self-regulation amongst entrepreneurs, it is also necessary to change the products of formal institutions in terms of the wider economic and social developments pursued (Vanderseypen et al., 2013; Williams and Renooy, 2013, 2014). Until now, and as discussed above, there have been three contrasting theoretical standpoints regarding what broader economic and social developments are required to reduce shadow entrepreneurship.

First, the 'modernization' thesis purports that shadow entrepreneurship decreases as economies modernize and develop and therefore that economic development and growth is required to reduce the level of shadow entrepreneurship (ILO, 2012). Second, the 'neo-liberal' thesis asserts that the prevalence of shadow entrepreneurship is a direct result of high taxes, public sector corruption and state interference in the free market and therefore that tax reductions, resolving public sector corruption and reducing the regulatory burden are required (De Soto, 1989, 2001; London and Hart, 2004; Nwabuzor, 2005; Sauvy, 1984; Schneider and Williams, 2013). Third and finally, the 'structuralist' thesis argues that the pervasiveness of shadow entrepreneurship is the outcome of inadequate levels of state intervention in work and welfare. The focus therefore should be less upon transforming shadow entrepreneurship into legitimate entrepreneurship and more upon introducing social protection, reducing inequality and pursuing labour market interventions to help vulnerable groups (Castells and Portes, 1989; Davis, 2006; Gallin, 2001; Slavnic, 2010; Taiwo, 2013).

Recent years have witnessed evaluations of these competing perspectives regarding which economic and social developments are associated with smaller shadow economies (Vanderseypen et al., 2013; Williams, 2013a, 2014a, 2014b, 2014c, 2015c; Williams and Renooy, 2013, 2014; Williams et al., 2013) and lower levels of shadow entrepreneurship (Williams, 2013a). Analysing the relationship between cross-national variations in the level of shadow entrepreneurship and cross-national variations in the various aspects of the broader economic and social environment deemed important by each of the above perspectives, Williams (2013a) calls for a synthesis of various tenets of all three theses. He finds that shadow entrepreneurship is lower in wealthier economies with stable high quality government bureaucracies and those with lower poverty levels, more equality, greater levels of social protection, more effective redistribution via social transfers and greater state intervention in the labour market to protect vulnerable groups.

JOINING UP DIRECT AND INDIRECT CONTROLS

To tackle shadow entrepreneurship, it is not solely an either/or choice between the use of either direct or indirect controls. Although the focus of most national governments until now has been upon the use of direct controls, especially the use of punitive measures that seek to increase the costs of participating in shadow entrepreneurship by increasing the risks of detection and levels of punishment (see OECD, 2015; Williams, 2015b), this does not mean that the solution is therefore to shift towards the use of either 'bribes' or indirect controls as the solution. These approaches and measures are not mutually exclusive.

Indeed, there has been growing recognition that even if indirect controls are a useful and innovative new means of transforming shadow entrepreneurship into legitimate entrepreneurship which could be usefully adopted (Williams, 2014a; Williams and Renooy, 2013), they might be necessary but on their own they are an insufficient means of doing so. Direct controls are also required. For example, governments may seek to change the culture of government departments, such as tax offices, towards a more customer-oriented approach and introduce public campaigns to elicit greater commitment to compliance, whilst simplifying regulatory compliance for business start-ups and introducing incentives for established shadow entrepreneurs (for example, amnesties, tax deductions). However, at the same time, and in relation to those who fail to comply, they may also need to pursue improvements in the probability of detection and tougher sanctions for those subsequently caught.

The current debate, therefore, is not so much over whether to use direct or indirect controls. There is an emergent consensus that both are required. Rather, the major issue is determining which specific policy measures in each approach are most effective and what is the most effective way of putting these measures together in various combinations and sequences to engender effective compliance. For example, measures to improve detection through inspections are currently often combined with campaigns to raise awareness. Tougher sanctions, furthermore, often follow amnesties and voluntary disclosure schemes. However, whether these are the most effective combinations and sequences that can be used needs to be evaluated. Nevertheless, two particular approaches have come to the fore in recent years in the literature that provide ways of combining these policy approaches in particular sequences, namely the responsive regulation approach and the slippery slope framework.

Responsive Regulation

Responsive regulation encourages entrepreneurs to think openly about their obligations and accept responsibility for regulating themselves in a way that is consistent with the law. This is an approach that seeks to win their 'hearts and minds' in order to engender a culture of commitment to compliance so that they regulate themselves rather than needing to be regulated by external rules. Nevertheless, although this approach gives primacy to the use of indirect controls, it does not exclusively limit itself to such measures (see Braithwaite, 2009).

The Australian Tax Office, for example, has gone some way towards adopting this responsive regulation approach. As Figure 9.2 displays, in the first instance indirect controls are used to facilitate voluntary self-regulated compliance, followed by persuasion and only as a last resort

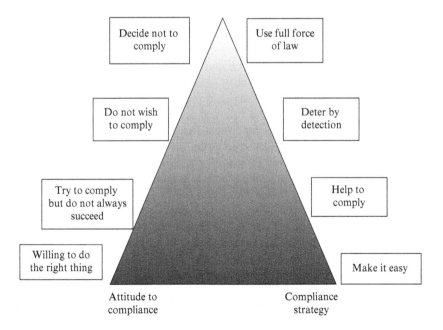

Figure 9.2   Responsive regulation approach

for the small minority who refuse to be compliant does it use punitive measures (Braithwaite, 2009; Job et al., 2007). In other words, the responsive regulation approach is based on a regulatory pyramid as graphically depicted. This sequences the measures used from the least intrusive at the bottom, which are used first, to the most intrusive at the top, which are employed as a last resort. This approach is founded upon the belief that tax authorities do not need in the majority of cases to pursue the coercion option at the top of the pyramid to engender compliance. Instead, it commences with the indirect control measures at the bottom of the pyramid, and only if these do not work with some groups does the level of intrusiveness then escalate up the pyramid until it reaches the policy intervention that elicits the desired response of compliance. This is founded upon the recognition that there exists a continuum of attitudes towards compliance, and different policy responses can therefore be temporally sequenced starting with commitment measures and moving through to sanctions.

Of course, whether this ordering is the appropriate combination and temporal sequence is debatable. Until now, there has been no evaluation of whether this sequencing is the most appropriate and/or effective means of engendering compliance. Although it seems logically to be the most appropriate and effective, no evidence-base currently exists of whether this is the case.

Slippery Slope Framework

Another way of combining direct and indirect controls is to adopt the 'slippery slope framework' (Kirchler et al., 2008). This distinguishes two types of compliance approach, namely voluntary compliance (akin to an indirect controls approach) and enforced compliance (akin to a direct controls approach). Voluntary compliance is viewed as occurring where there is trust in the authorities. Enforced compliance, meanwhile, is viewed as requiring the authorities to have power (that is, the ability to get citizens to do what they were not going to do before, in the way in which the authorities wish them to do it). When there is no trust in authorities and authorities have no power, then shadow entrepreneurship will be prevalent.

To tackle shadow entrepreneurship, therefore, one can increase either the power of authorities and/or trust in the authorities. The direct controls approach, as shown above, puts the emphasis on increasing the power of authorities, whilst the indirect controls approach puts more emphasis on increasing the trust of authorities. In practice, however, these are not mutually exclusive approaches. Both can be used together to engender compliance. The slippery slope framework accepts that this is the case and seeks to combine both in order to elicit legitimate entrepreneurship.

Wahl et al. (2010) randomly presented participants with one of four different descriptions of a fictitious country, in which the authorities were depicted on the one hand as either trustworthy or untrustworthy, and on the other hand as either powerful or powerless. Their results reveal that participants paid significantly more taxes when both power and trust were high. They additionally revealed that voluntary compliance was highest when the authorities were both trustful and powerful, while enforced compliance was highest when authorities were portrayed as powerful, but not trustworthy. This is further reinforced by two additional surveys of real-world taxpayers (Muehlbacher et al., 2011a, 2011b). The outcome is that a combination of both greater trust in authorities and the greater power of authorities is seen to be a potent combination. Grounded in this finding, the suggestion is that pursuing both is the most effective means of tackling shadow entrepreneurship (Kogler et al., 2015).

CONCLUSIONS

This chapter has reviewed what might be done to tackle shadow entrepreneurship. To do this, it has reviewed four hypothetical policy choices, namely: taking no action; pursuing the eradication of shadow entrepreneurship; moving legitimate entrepreneurship into the shadow economy; and transforming shadow entrepreneurship into legitimate entrepreneurship. This has revealed that doing nothing would leave intact the current negative impacts on legitimate entrepreneurs (for example, unfair competition), shadow entrepreneurs (for example, the inability to gain access to credit to expand), customers (for example, no guarantee of health and safety standards) and governments (for example, taxes owed are not collected). Transforming legitimate entrepreneurship into shadow entrepreneurship would level working conditions down rather than up, whilst eradicating shadow entrepreneurship would result in governments repressing and eradicating precisely the entrepreneurial endeavour and enterprise culture that they otherwise wish to foster. Transforming shadow entrepreneurship into legitimate entrepreneurship is thus revealed to be the most viable policy choice. How, therefore, can this be achieved?

The chapter has then shown that this can be achieved using either direct controls or indirect controls and the various direct control measures have been reviewed along with the various indirect controls that might be employed. What this reveals is that the currently dominant approach of using a particular set of direct controls that seek to improve detection and increase the punishment for 'bad' behaviour is a rather limited approach and that there is a much larger toolkit available for tackling shadow entrepreneurship. These various tools, moreover, are not mutually exclusive. To show this, the final section of this chapter has outlined various policy approaches that can be adopted which combine direct and indirect controls when tackling shadow entrepreneurship, namely a responsive regulation approach and a slippery slope framework. The outcome is that a comprehensive review has been provided of the various policy choices, approaches and measures available to policy-makers along with some suggestions regarding how they can be combined.

NOTE

1. This chapter is a derived version of Williams (2015a).

REFERENCES

Allingham, M. and A. Sandmo (1972), 'Income tax evasion: a theoretical analysis', *Journal of Public Economics*, **1** (2), 323–38.

Alm, J. (2011), 'Designing alternative strategies to reduce tax evasion', in M. Pickhardt and A. Prinz (eds), *Tax Evasion and the Shadow Economy*, Cheltenham, UK and Northampton, MA, USA: Edward Elgar Publishing, pp. 13–32.

Alm, J., B. Jackson and M. McKee (1993), 'Fiscal exchange, collective decision institutions and tax compliance', *Journal of Economic Behaviour and Organization*, **22** (2), 285–303.

Alm, J., I. Sanchez and A. de Juan (1995), 'Economic and non-economic factors in tax compliance', *Kyklos*, **48** (1), 3–18.

Ayres, I. and J. Braithwaite (1992), *Responsive Regulation: Transcending the Deregulation Debate*, New York: Oxford University Press.

Barbour, A. and M. Llanes (2013), *Supporting People to Legitimise their Informal Businesses*, York: Joseph Rowntree Foundation.

Bergman, M. and A. Nevarez (2006), 'Do audits enhance compliance? An empirical assessment of VAT enforcement', *National Tax Journal*, **59** (4), 817–32.

Bird, R., J. Martinez-Vazquez and B. Torgler (2006), 'Societal institutions and tax effort in developing countries', in J. Alm, J. Martinez-Vazquez and M. Rider (eds), *The Challenges of Tax Reform in the Global Economy*, New York: Springer, pp. 283–338.

Bobeck, D.D. and R.C. Hatfield (2003), 'An investigation of the theory of planned behaviour and the role of moral obligation in tax compliance', *Behavioural Research in Accounting*, **52** (1), 13–38.

Braithwaite V. (2009), *Defiance in Taxation and Governance: Resisting and Dismissing Authority in a Democracy*, Cheltenham, UK and Northampton, MA, USA: Edward Elgar Publishing.

Braithwaite, V. and M. Reinhart (2000), 'The Taxpayers' Charter: does the Australian Tax Office comply and who benefits?', Centre for Tax System Integrity Working Paper No. 1, Australian National University, Canberra.

Castells, M. and A. Portes (1989), 'World underneath: the origins, dynamics and effects of the informal economy', in A. Portes, M. Castells and L. Benton (eds), *The Informal Economy: Studies in Advanced and Less Developing Countries*, Baltimore, MD: Johns Hopkins University Press, pp. 1–19.

Chung, J. and V.U. Trivedi (2003), 'The effect of friendly persuasion and gender on tax compliance behaviour', *Journal of Business Ethics*, **47** (2), 133–45.

Davis, M. (2006), *Planet of Slums*, London: Verso.

De Beer, J., K. Fu and S. Wunsch-Vincent (2013), 'The informal economy, innovation and intellectual property: concepts, metrics and policy considerations', Economic Research Working Paper No. 10, World Intellectual Property Organization, Geneva.

De Juan, A., M.A. Lasheras and R. Mayo (1994), 'Voluntary tax compliant behavior of Spanish income taxpayers', *Public Finance*, **49**, 90–105.

De Soto, H. (1989), *The Other Path: The Economic Answer to Terrorism*, London: Harper and Row.

De Soto, H. (2001), *The Mystery of Capital: Why Capitalism Triumphs in the West and Fails Everywhere Else*, London: Black Swan.

Dekker, H., E. Oranje, P. Renooy, F. Rosing and C.C. Williams (2010), *Joining up the Fight against Undeclared Work in the European Union*, Brussels: DG Employment, Social Affairs and Equal Opportunities.

European Commission (2007), *Stepping Up the Fight Against Undeclared Work*, Brussels: European Commission.

European Commission (2014), *Special Eurobarometer 397: Corruption*, Brussels: European Commission.

Evans, M., S. Syrett and C.C. Williams (2006), *Informal Economic Activities and Deprived Neighbourhoods*, London: Department of Communities and Local Government.

Feld, L.P. and B. Frey (2002), 'Trust breeds trust: how taxpayers are treated', *Economics of Government*, **3** (2), 87–99.

Gallin, D. (2001), 'Propositions on trade unions and informal employment in time of globalisation', *Antipode*, **19** (4), 531–49.

Gangl, K., S. Muehlbacher, M. de Groot, S. Goslinga, E. Hofmann, C. Kogler, G. Antonides and E. Kirchler (2013), 'How can I help you? Perceived service orientation of tax authorities and tax compliance', *Public Finance Analysis*, **69** (4), 487–510.

Grabiner, Lord (2000), *The Informal Economy*, London: HM Treasury.

Hartner, M., S. Rechberger, E. Kirchler and A. Schabmann (2008), 'Procedural justice and tax compliance', *Economic Analysis and Policy*, **38** (1), 137–52.

Hartner, M., S. Rechberger, E. Kirchler and M. Wenzel (2011), 'Perceived distributive fairness of EU transfer payments, outcome favourability, identity and EU-tax compliance', *Law and Policy*, **33** (1), 22–31.

Hasseldine, J. and Z. Li (1999), 'More tax evasion research required in new millennium', *Crime, Law and Social Change*, **31** (1), 91–104.

ILO (2012), *Statistical Update on Employment in the Informal Economy*, Geneva: International Labour Organisation.

ILO (2014), 'Transitioning from the informal to the formal economy', Report V (1), International Labour Conference, 103rd Session, Geneva: ILO.

Internal Revenue Service (2007), 'Understanding taxes', available at http://www.irs.gov/app/understandingTaxes/jsp/ (accessed 14 May 2014).

Job, J., A. Stout and R. Smith (2007), 'Culture change in three taxation administrations: from command and control to responsive regulation', *Law and Policy*, **29** (1), 84–101.

Kinsey, K. and H. Gramsick (1993), 'Did the tax reform act of 1986 improve compliance? Three studies of pre- and post-TRA compliance attitudes', *Law and Policy*, **15**, 239–325.

Kinsey, K., H. Gramsick and K. Smith (1991), 'Framing justice: taxpayer evaluations of personal tax burdens', *Law and Society Review*, **25**, 845–73.

Kirchgässner, G. (2010), 'Tax morale, tax evasion and the shadow economy', Discussion Paper No. 2010-17, Department of Economics, University of St Gallen, St Gallen, Switzerland.

Kirchgässner, G. (2011), 'Tax morale, tax evasion and the shadow economy', in F. Schneider (ed.), *Handbook of the Shadow Economy*, Cheltenham, UK and Northampton, MA, USA: Edward Elgar Publishing, pp. 347–74.

Kirchler, E. (2007), *The Economic Psychology of Tax Behaviour*, Cambridge: Cambridge University Press.

Kirchler, E., E. Hoelzl and I. Wahl (2008), 'Enforced versus voluntary tax compliance: the "slippery slope" framework', *Journal of Economic Psychology*, **29**, 210–25.

Kogler, C., S. Muehlbacher and E. Kirchler (2015), 'Testing the "slippery slope framework" among self-employed taxpayers', *Economics of Governance*, **16** (2), 125–42.

Kus, B. (2010), 'Regulatory governance and the informal economy: cross-national comparisons', *Socio-Economic Review*, **8** (3), 487–510.

Kus, B. (2014), 'The informal road to markets: neoliberal reforms, private entrepreneurship and the informal economy in Turkey', *International Journal of Social Economics*, **41** (4), 278–93.

Li, S.X., C.C. Eckel, P.J. Grossman and T.L. Brown (2011), 'Giving to government: voluntary taxation in the lab', *Journal of Public Economics*, **95**, 1190–201.

Lillemets, K. (2009), 'Maksumoraal maksukäitumise kujundajana ja selle peamised isikupõhised mõjutegurid', available at: http://www.riigikogu.ee/rito/index.php?id=14002&op=archive2 (accessed 11 May 2014).

Llanes, M. and A. Barbour (2007), *Self-Employed and Micro-Entrepreneurs: Informal Trading and the Journey towards Formalization*, London: Community Links.

London, T. and S.L. Hart (2004), 'Reinventing strategies for emerging markets: beyond the transnational model', *Journal of International Business Studies*, **35** (5), 350–70.

McGee, R.W. (2005), 'The ethics of tax evasion: a survey of international business academics', paper presented at the 60th International Atlantic Economic Conference, New York, 6–9 October.

McGee, R.W. (2008), *Taxation and Public Finance in Transition and Developing Countries*, New York: Springer.

McGee, R.W., J. Alver and L. Alver (2008), 'The ethics of tax evasion: a survey of Estonian Opinion', in R.W. McGee (ed.), *Taxation and Public Finance in Transition and Developing Countries*, Berlin: Springer, pp. 119–36.

Molero, J.C. and F. Pujol (2012), 'Walking inside the potential tax evader's mind: tax morale does matter', *Journal of Business Ethics*, **105**, 151–62.

Morris, J. and A. Polese (2014), 'Introduction: informality – enduring practices, entwined livelihoods', in J. Morris and A. Polese (eds), *The Informal Post-Socialist Economy: Embedded Practices and Livelihoods*, London: Routledge, pp. 1–18.

Muehlbacher, S., E. Kirchler and H. Schwarzenberger (2011a), 'Voluntary versus enforced tax compliance: empirical evidence for the "slippery slope" framework', *European Journal of Law and Economics*, **32**, 89–97.

Muehlbacher, S., C. Kogler and E. Kirchler (2011b), 'An empirical testing of the slippery slope framework: the role of trust and power in explaining tax compliance', University of Vienna Department of Economics Working Paper, Vienna.

Murphy, K. (2003), 'Procedural fairness and tax compliance', *Australian Journal of Social Issues*, **38** (3), 379–408.

Murphy, K. (2005), 'Regulating more effectively: the relationship between procedural justice, legitimacy and tax non-compliance', *Journal of Law and Society*, **32** (4), 562–89.

Murphy, K. (2008), 'Enforcing tax compliance: to punish or persuade?', *Economic Analysis and Policy*, **38** (1), 113–35.

Murphy, K. and N. Harris (2007), 'Shaming, shame and recidivism: a test of re-integrative shaming theory in the white-collar crime context', *British Journal of Criminology*, **47**, 900–917.

Murphy, K., T. Tyler and A. Curtis (2009), 'Nurturing regulatory compliance: is procedural fairness effective when people question the legitimacy of the law?', *Regulation and Governance*, **3**, 1–26.

National Audit Office (2003), *Tackling Fraud against the Inland Revenue*, London: The Stationery Office.

National Audit Office (2008), *Tackling the Hidden Economy*, London: The Stationery Office.

Natrah, S. (2013), 'Tax knowledge, tax complexity and tax compliance: taxpayers' view', *Procedia: Social and Behavioural Sciences*, **109**, 1069–76.

Nwabuzor, A. (2005), 'Corruption and development: new initiatives in economic openness and strengthened rule of law', *Journal of Business Ethics*, **59** (1/2), 121–38.

OECD (2008), *OECD Employment Outlook*, Paris: OECD.

OECD (2015), *Informal Entrepreneurship*, Paris: OECD.

Polese, A. (2014), 'Drinking with Vova: an individual entrepreneur between illegality and informality', in J. Morris and A. Polese (eds), *The Informal Post-Socialist Economy: Embedded Practices and Livelihoods*, London: Routledge, pp. 85–101.

Renooy, P., S. Ivarsson, O. van der Wusten-Gritsai and R. Meijer (2004), *Undeclared Work in an Enlarged Union: An Analysis of Shadow Work – An In-depth Study of Specific Items*, Brussels: European Commission.

Richardson, M. and A. Sawyer (2001), 'A taxonomy of the tax compliance literature: further findings, problems and prospects', *Australian Tax Forum*, **16** (2), 137–320.

Saeed, A. and A. Shah (2011), 'Enhancing tax morale with marketing tactics: a review of the literature', *African Journal of Business Management*, **5** (35), 13659–65.

Sasunkevich, O. (2014), 'Business as casual: shuttle trade on the Belarus–Lithuania border', in J. Morris and A. Polese (eds), *The Informal Post-Socialist Economy: Embedded Practices and Livelihoods*, London: Routledge, pp. 135–51.

Sauvy, A. (1984), *Le travail noir et l'économie de demain*, Paris: Calmann-Levy.

Schneider, F. and D. Enste (2002), *The Shadow Economy: An International Survey*, Cambridge: Cambridge University Press.

Schneider, F. and C.C. Williams (2013), *The Shadow Economy*, London: Institute of Economic Affairs.

Shaw, J., J. Slemrod and J. Whiting (2008), *Administration and Compliance*, London; Institute for Fiscal Studies.

Slavnic, Z. (2010), 'Political economy of informalization', *European Societies*, **12** (1), 3–23.

Slemrod, J., M. Blumenthal and C.W. Christian (2001), 'Taxpayer response to an increased probability of audit: evidence from a controlled experiment in Minnesota', *Journal of Public Economics*, **79**, 455–83.

Small Business Council (2004), *Small Business in the Informal Economy: Making the Transition to the Formal Economy*, London: Small Business Council.

Taiwo, O. (2013), 'Employment choice and mobility in multi-sector labour markets: theoretical model and evidence from Ghana', *International Labour Review*, **152** (3–4), 469–92.

Taylor, N. (2005), 'Explaining taxpayer noncompliance through reference to tax-payer identities: a social identity perspective', in C. Bajada and F. Schneider (eds), *Size, Causes and Consequences of the Underground Economy: An International Perspective*, Aldershot: Ashgate, pp. 39–54.

Thurman, Q.C., C. St John and L. Riggs (1984), 'Neutralisation and tax evasion: how effective would a moral appeal be in improving compliance to tax laws?', *Law and Policy*, **6** (3), 309–27.

Torgler, B. (2003), 'To evade taxes or not: that is the question', *Journal of Socio-Economics*, **32**, 283–302.

Torgler, B. (2007), 'Tax morale in Central and Eastern European countries', in N. Hayoz and S. Hug (eds), *Tax Evasion, Trust and State Capacities: How Good is Tax Morale in Central and Eastern Europe?*, Bern: Peter Lang, pp. 155–86.

Torgler, B. (2011), 'Tax morale and compliance: review of evidence and case studies for Europe', World Bank Policy Research Working Paper No. 5922, World Bank, Washington, DC.

Torgler, B. and F. Schneider (2007), 'Shadow economy, tax morale, governance and institutional quality: a panel analysis', IZA Discussion Paper No. 2563, IZA, Bonn.

Tyler, T. (1997), 'The psychology of legitimacy: a relational perspective in voluntary deference to authorities', *Personality and Social Psychology Review*, **1** (4), 323–45.

Tyler, T.R. (2006), *Why People Obey the Law*, Princeton, NJ: Princeton University Press.

Tyler, T.R., L. Sherman, H. Strang, G. Barnes and D. Woods (2007), 'Reintegrative shaming, procedural justice and recidivism: the engagement of offenders' psychological mechanisms in the Canberra RISE drinking and driving experiment', *Law and Society Review*, **41**, 533–86.

Vanderseypen, G., T. Tchipeva, J. Peschner, P. Rennoy and C.C. Williams (2013), 'Undeclared work: recent developments', in European Commission (ed.), *Employment and Social Developments in Europe 2013*, Brussels: European Commission, pp. 231–74.

Varma, K. and A. Doob (1998), 'Deterring economic crimes: the case of tax evasion', *Canadian Journal of Criminology*, **40**, 165–84.

Vossler, C.A., M. McKee and M. Jones (2011), 'Some effects of tax information services reliability and availability on tax reporting behaviour', available at: http://mpra.ub.uni-muenchen.de/38870/ (accessed 11 May 2014).

Wahl, I., B. Kastlunger and E. Kirchler (2010), 'Trust in authorities and power to enforce tax compliance: an empirical analysis of the "slippery slope" framework', *Law and Policy*, **32**, 383–406.

Webley, P. and S. Halstead (1986), 'Tax evasion on the micro: significant stimulations per expedient experiments', *Journal of Interdisciplinary Economics*, **1**, 87–100.

Weigel, R., D. Hessin and H. Elffers (1987), 'Tax evasion research: a critical appraisal and theoretical model', *Journal of Economic Psychology*, **8** (2), 215–35.

Wenzel, M. (2002), 'The impact of outcome orientation and justice concerns on tax compliance: the role of taxpayers' identity', *Journal of Applied Psychology*, **87**, 639–45.

Wenzel, M. (2004a), 'An analysis of norm processes in tax compliance', *Journal of Economic Psychology*, **25** (2), 213–28.

Wenzel, M. (2004b), 'The social side of sanction: personal and social norms as moderators of deterrence', *Law and Human Behaviour*, **28**, 547–67.

Wenzel, M. (2006), 'A letter from the tax office: compliance effects of informational and interpersonal fairness', *Social Fairness Research*, **19**, 345–64.

Williams, C.C. (2001), 'Tackling the participation of the unemployed in paid informal work: a critical evaluation of the deterrence approach', *Environment and Planning C*, **19** (5), 729–49.

Williams, C.C. (2006), *The Hidden Enterprise Culture: Entrepreneurship in the Underground Economy*, Cheltenham, UK and Northampton, MA, USA: Edward Elgar Publishing.

Williams, C.C. (2013a), 'Evaluating cross-national variations in the extent and nature of informal employment in the European Union', *Industrial Relations Journal*, **44** (5–6), 479–94.

Williams, C.C. (2013b), 'Tackling Europe's informal economy: a critical evaluation of the neo-liberal de-regulatory perspective', *Journal of Contemporary European Research*, **9** (3), 261–79.

Williams, C.C. (2014a), *Confronting the Shadow Economy: Evaluating Tax Compliance Behaviour and Policies*, Cheltenham, UK and Northampton, MA, USA: Edward Elgar Publishing.

Williams, C.C. (2014b), 'Out of the shadows: a classification of economies by the size and character of their informal sector', *Work, Employment and Society*, **28** (5), 735–53.

Williams, C.C. (2014c), 'Tackling enterprises operating in the informal sector in developing and transition economies: a critical evaluation of the neo-liberal policy approach', *Journal of Global Entrepreneurship Research*, **2** (9).

Williams, C.C. (2015a), 'Tackling entrepreneurship in the informal sector: an overview of the policy options, approaches and measures', *Journal of Developmental Entrepreneurship*, **20** (1).

Williams, C.C. (2015b), *Informal Entrepreneurship: Policy Briefing*, Paris: OECD.

Williams, C.C. (2015c), 'Evaluating cross-national variations in envelope wage payments in East-Central Europe', *Economic and Industrial Democracy: An International Journal*, **36** (2), 283–303.

Williams, C.C. and A. Martinez (2014a), 'Do small business start-ups test-trade in the informal economy? Evidence from a UK small business survey', *International Journal of Entrepreneurship and Small Business*, **22** (1), 1–16.

Williams, C.C. and A. Martinez (2014b), 'Is the informal economy an incubator for new enterprise creation? A gender perspective', *International Journal of Entrepreneurial Behaviour and Research*, **20** (1), 4–19.

Williams, C.C. and A. Martinez (2014c), 'Why do consumers purchase goods and services in the informal economy?', *Journal of Business Research*, **67** (5), 802–6.

Williams, C.C. and S. Nadin (2012a), 'Tackling entrepreneurship in the informal economy: evaluating the policy options', *Journal of Entrepreneurship and Public Policy*, **1** (2), 111–24.

Williams, C.C. and S. Nadin (2012b), 'Tackling the hidden enterprise culture: government policies to support the formalization of informal entrepreneurship', *Entrepreneurship and Regional Development*, **24** (9–10), 895–915.

Williams, C.C. and S. Nadin (2013), 'Harnessing the hidden enterprise culture: supporting the formalization of off-the-books business start-ups', *Journal of Small Business and Enterprise Development*, **20** (2), 434–47.

Williams, C.C. and S. Nadin (2014), 'Facilitating the formalisation of entrepreneurs in the informal economy: towards a variegated policy approach', *Journal of Entrepreneurship and Public Policy*, **3** (1), 33–48.

Williams, C.C. and P. Renooy (2013), *Tackling Undeclared Work in 27 European Union Member States and Norway: Approaches and Measures since 2008*, Dublin: European Foundation for the Improvement of Living and Working Conditions.

Williams, C.C. and P. Renooy (2014), *Flexibility@Work 2014: Bringing the Undeclared Economy out of the Shadows – The Role of Temporary Work Agencies*, Amsterdam: Randstad.

Williams, C.C. and J. Windebank (1998), *Informal Employment in the Advanced Economies: Implications for Work and Welfare*, London: Routledge.

Williams, C.C., J. Round and P. Rodgers (2013), *The Role of Informal Economies in the Post-Soviet World: The End of Transition?*, London: Routledge.

Index

227